HARDPRESS

ISBN: 9781313886109

Published by:
HardPress Publishing
8345 NW 66TH ST #2561
MIAMI FL 33166-2626

Email: info@hardpress.net
Web: http://www.hardpress.net

HOMER:

AN INTRODUCTION TO THE ILIAD

AND THE ODYSSEY.

PUBLISHED BY

JAMES MACLEHOSE AND SONS, GLASGOW,

Publishers to the University.

MACMILLAN AND CO., LONDON.

London, . . . Simpkin, Hamilton and Co.
Cambridge, . . Macmillan and Bowes.
Edinburgh, . . Douglas and Foulis.

MDCCCXCVIII.

HOMER:

AN INTRODUCTION TO THE ILIAD

AND THE ODYSSEY

BY

R. C. JEBB, Litt.D.

REGIUS PROFESSOR OF GREEK AND FELLOW OF TRINITY COLLEGE,
CAMBRIDGE, AND M.P. FOR THE UNIVERSITY: HON. D.C.L.
OXON.: HON. LL.D. HARVARD, EDINBURGH, GLASGOW
AND DUBLIN: HON. DOCT. PHILOS. BOLOGNA.

Sixth Edition.

GLASGOW:
JAMES MACLEHOSE AND SONS,
Publishers to the University.
1898

PREFACE.

THE purpose of this book is to furnish, in a compact form, a general introduction to the study of Homer.

The four chapters into which it is divided deal respectively with four aspects of the subject :—(1) The general character of the Homeric poems, and their place in the history of literature: (2) their historical value, as illustrating an early period of Hellenic life : (3) their influence in the ancient world, and the criticism bestowed on them in antiquity: (4) the modern inquiry into their origin.

So far as I am aware, there is no one book, English or foreign, which collects the principal results of modern study in each of these departments.

Mr Monro, the Provost of Oriel, was kind enough to read a considerable part of these pages, while they were still in an unfinished state, and to give me the benefit of his opinion on several points. Professor

Seymour, of Yale, during a visit to England last summer, gave me a signal proof of friendship in the care with which he went through the book,—then nearly completed,—and the kindness with which he permitted me to profit by some suggestions.

My thanks are also due to Professor Butcher, the Rev. M. A. Bayfield, Mr Sidney Colvin, and Mr Walter Leaf, for various tokens of kind interest in this work.

R. C. JEBB.

THE COLLEGE, GLASGOW,
December, 1886.

Note to the Second Edition.

THE first edition, published in January, 1887, was exhausted in February. The present edition is substantially identical with the first, while on a few points of detail it has profited by some criticisms with which I have been favoured.

R. C. J.

March, 1887

CONTENTS.

CHAPTER I.

GENERAL LITERARY CHARACTERISTICS OF THE POEMS.

CHAPTER II.

THE HOMERIC WORLD.

CHAPTER III.

HOMER IN ANTIQUITY.

CHAPTER IV.

THE HOMERIC QUESTION.

HOMER.

CHAPTER I.

General Literary Characteristics of the Poems.

1. The literature of Greece, and of Europe, begins with Homer, whose name will be used here to denote 'the *Iliad* and the *Odyssey*,' without implying that one man composed the whole of both or of either. The interest of Homer is twofold, poetical and historical. He is the greatest epic poet of the world, and the only representative of the earliest artistic form which the Greek mind gave to its work. He is also the first author who presents any clear or vivid picture of Aryan civilisation. An entire period of early Hellenic life which, but for him, would be almost a blank, is seen to be connected by an unbroken course of development with the later Hellenic age.

Homeric poems —their twofold interest.

2. The Homeric poems themselves attest a pre-Homeric poetry. They are the creations of a matured art. But the earlier and ruder essays of that art have left few traces. The little that is known can be briefly summed up, so far as it directly concerns the study of Greek literature.

Pre-Homeric poetry.

(1) The Greeks had old folk-songs on the death of a beautiful youth,—Linus, Hylas, Ialemus, Hyacinthus, Adonis,—*i.e.* on the spring yielding to summer, the summer

(1) Songs of the seasons.

to autumn, or the like.   In the *Iliad* the 'Linos' is a solo
sung by a youth to the lyre at a vintage festival, among the
maidens and youths who carry the baskets of grapes, and
who dance in time to the song (*Il.* 18. 569)[1].   The origin
of such songs was Semitic.   But they suited that early
phase of the Aryan mind in which religion was chiefly
a sense of divinity in the forces of outward Nature, and
which, in India, is represented by the Vedic hymns.   A
distinctively Greek element began early to show itself in
the numerous local legends as to the personal relationships
of the youth who had perished.

(2) Le-
gendary
bards.

(a) Thra-
cian
group.

(b) South-
ern
group.

(c) Asia-
tic group.

(2) A later stage than that in which the Linus-song
originated is represented by the legends of the earliest
Greek bards.   (a) Some of these are called 'Thracian,' and
are associated with the worship of 'the Muses'—the god-
desses of memory, or record, a worship which can be traced
as spreading from the northern coasts of the Aegean to
the district Pieria at the N.E. corner of Thessaly, and
thence southwards to the Boeotian Helicon and the Phocian
Parnassus.   (b) Other prehistoric bards are specially associated with hymns to Apollo,—indicating a stream of
influence which passed from Asia, through Crete and other
Aegean islands, to Greece Proper.   (c) A third group
of early bards is connected with Asia Minor, especially

---

[1] These Nature-songs were brought from the East to Greece, and
then, in Greek fashion, were linked with local myths.   The song of
Linos probably came from Phrygia through Thrace, and was specially
localised at Argos.   Sappho used the form Οἰτόλινος, which, acc. to
Paus. 9. 29. 8, she derived from very ancient hymns, ascribed to
the Athenian Pamphos.   Herodotus (2. 79) identifies *Linos* with the
Egyptian prince *Maneros*, (=*ma-n-hra*, 'come to me', the refrain of a
song in which Isis was represented as mourning Osiris) : and says that
the song (ἄεισμα) 'Linos' was famous in Cyprus, Phoenicia, and elsewhere.   'Linos' came from αἴλινον, *ai lenu*, 'woe for us', the refrain
of the Phoenician mourners in Syria and Cyprus for *Thammuz* (Ezek.
viii. 14), the Greek *Adonis*.   Similar conceptions were the Lydian and
Phrygian *Attes* or *Atys*, the Bithynian *Bormos*, the Mysian *Hylas*, the
Lacedaemonian *Hyacinthos*, the Arcadian *Skephros* (σκέφρος=ξηρός),
the Thracian *Ialemos*.

Phrygia, and with Asiatic worship, such as that of Cybele[1]. Taken collectively, these sparse and vague traditions have a clear general meaning. They point to an age when the Hellenic tribes were still in passage from Asia to Europe. *General result.* They show that a cultivation of poetry,—partly Pre-Hellenic in its religious motive, but already Hellenic in its form,— had begun before the Hellenic populations had settled down in their European seats.

(3) Lastly, Homer himself mentions those heroic lays *(3)Forms of song mentioned by Homer.* (κλέα ἀνδρῶν) out of which Epic poetry grew; also the *hymenaeus*, or marriage-chant, and the *thrênus*, or dirge,— both, in Homer's time, already secular, and sung by the people,—no longer, as in ancient India, parts of a ritual, to be sung by priests.

3.   Down to about 700 B.C. the kind of poetry which *Epic poetry.* we call 'Epic'[2] was the only literature which the Greeks possessed. The idea of 'epic' poetry, as a species, could not exist until 'lyric' (or, as the Greeks said, 'melic') had taken a distinct form. Then, later still, came 'dramatic' poetry. 'Epic poetry,' as the Greeks of the fourth century B.C. understood it, was defined by its differences from 'lyric' and 'dramatic.' As distinguished from 'lyric,' it meant poetry which was recited, not sung to music. As

---

[1] (*a*) To the Thracian group belong, among others, Orpheus (=the Indian Ṛibhu,—the Ṛibhus figuring in the Indian hymns as great artificers, the first men who were made immortal),—Musaeus, Eumolpus, Thamyris ; (*b*) to the Southern group, *Olen* of Lycia, *Chrysothemis* of Crete, *Philammon* of Delphi, Pamphos of Attica,—makers of hymns to Apollo, Demeter, etc.; (*c*) to the Asiatic group, Olympus, the pupil of Marsyas, and Hyagnis, who made hymns to Cybele. These were merely so many names of ancient but vague prestige, to which later composers attached their own work,—being in the old hymn-literature what the Boeotian Bakis was in the traditional oracular lore.

[2] Aristotle never uses the word ἐπικός, which seems not to occur before the later Alexandrian age. He calls Epic Poetry ἡ ἐποποιΐα, or (as contrasted with drama), ἡ διηγηματικὴ καὶ ἐν μέτρῳ μιμητική (*Poet.* 23), *i.e.* narrative poetry which imitates by means of verse *only* (without help from τὸ πράττειν).

distinguished from 'dramatic,' it meant poetry which merely narrated. It is well to begin by observing the broad characteristics which Homer presents to the mind of Aristotle.

Aristotle
on Ho-
mer. 4. Aristotle's conception of an epic poem demands, first, that it should have a dignified theme; next, that it should form an organic whole,—*i.e.*, it must have unity; and, within this unity, there must be an ordered progress. The events must form a connected series, and must conduce to a common end. Thus the unity proper to an epic is not merely such unity as a history may owe to the fact that all the events which it relates are comprised in a certain period of time. The *Iliad* does not treat the whole Trojan War, but a part of it, diversifying this by episodes. The *Odyssey* does not attempt to relate everything that ever happened to Odysseus. The superiority of Homer's judgment in this respect, as compared with that of some other epic poets, may be illustrated (Aristotle remarks) by a dramatic test. The *Iliad* and the *Odyssey* would not furnish more than one tragedy apiece, or two at the most. But no fewer than eight dramas had been carved out of the '*Little Iliad*,'—an epic chronicle of the events from the death of Achilles to the fall of Troy. The special merits for which Aristotle praises Homer are chiefly the following :—(1) Homer combines unity with variety[1]: (2) he is excellent both in diction and in sentiment: (3) he keeps himself in the background,—telling his story as much as possible by the actions and words of the persons themselves, and marking their characters well: (4) he is artistic in fiction—boldly using the improbable or supernatural element,—for which epic poetry gives more scope than drama,—but

---

[1] It is an inherent defect of an epic, as compared with a tragedy, (Aristotle remarks,) that it must have less unity. If the epic poet's theme is *strictly* one, his poem will appear either curt or spun-out (μύουρος—ὑδαρής). Homer has overcome this difficulty as far as possible: ταῦτα τὰ ποιήματα συνέστηκεν ὡς ἐνδέχεται ἄριστα, καὶ ὅ τι μάλιστα μιᾶς πράξεως μίμησίς ἐστι (*Poet.* 26).

with a charm so skilful that the illusion is not broken[1]. Aristotle's remarks on Homer bring out the singularity in the history of Greek poetry, that it begins with master-pieces. He regards Homer as at once the earliest of poets and the most finished of epic artists[2]. This estimate is subject, indeed, to one qualification. Aristotle apparently regarded the length of the Homeric epics as somewhat too great for the ideal of epic symmetry[3].

At the outset it is necessary that the reader should have clearly before his mind the general type of structure exhibited by each of the two epics. The subjoined sketch will serve to show this, while in details it will be found convenient for subsequent reference.

5. The *Iliad* owes its unity, not to the person of Achilles, but to his wrath. His withdrawal from the Greek host leaves Greek heroism more nearly on a level with Trojan, and so admits of the battle-scenes which describe a doubtful war. Hence the framework of the poem is necessarily elastic. As a help to the memory, the story of the *Iliad* may be

Structure of the Iliad.

---

[1] *Poet.* 24 δεδίδαχε δὲ μάλιστα Ὅμηρος καὶ τοὺς ἄλλους ψεύδειν ('to feign') ὡς δεῖ. Aristotle instances τὰ ἐν Ὀδυσσείᾳ ἄλογα τὰ περὶ τὴν ἔκθεσιν,—the account of the landing of Odysseus in Ithaca,—where the Homeric charm disguises the improbability (τοῖς ἄλλοις ἀγαθοῖς ἀφανίζει ἡδύνων τὸ ἄτοπον).

[2] After mentioning the several requirements of epic poetry, he says— οἷς ἅπασιν Ὅμηρος κέχρηται καὶ πρῶτος καὶ ἱκανῶς (*Poet.* 24).

[3] *Poet.* c. 24, with Twining's note (vol. II. p. 331). The limit of due length for an epic is that it should be possible for us to 'comprehend the beginning and the end in one view.' This means, to read, or hear, the whole epic, without discomfort, in one day,—as is shown by the comparison with 'tragedies set for one hearing.' And, for this purpose, the epic should be 'shorter than the ancient' epics,—a phrase which must include Homer. (The *Iliad* contains 15,693 lines; the *Odyssey*, 12,110.) I do not know whether it has been pointed out how interesting is this indication of Aristotle's feeling, in relation to the modern view that the epics have grown by additions beyond their first design. Surmising nothing of the kind, and profoundly admiring Homer, the Greek critic yet cannot altogether disguise the offence to his sense of measure.

divided into three parts.   The first ends with book IX.,
when the Greeks sue to Achilles, and are repulsed.   The
second ends with book XVIII., the last in which he remains
aloof from the war.

The asterisks denote those books in which Achilles
himself appears.   The Greek titles of the books, given in
brackets, have come down from the Alexandrian age.

*I.   (A. Λοιμός. Μῆνις.) In the tenth year of the war, Apollo
plagues the Greeks, because the daughter of Chryses, his priest, has
been taken by Agamemnon ; who, being required to restore her,
wrongs Achilles by depriving him of his captive, the maiden Briseïs.
Thereupon Achilles retires from the war, and Zeus swears to Thetis,
the hero's mother, that the Greeks shall rue this wrong done to her son.

II.   (B. Ὄνειρος.   Βοιωτία ἢ κατάλογος τῶν νεῶν.) Zeus sends the
Dream-god to the sleeping Agamemnon, and beguiles him to marshal
all his host for battle.   An assembly of the Greek army shows that the
general voice is for going back to Greece—but at last the army is
rallied.—Catalogue of the Greek and Trojan forces (vv. 484—877).

III.   (Γ. Ὅρκοι.   Τειχοσκοπία.   Πάριδος καὶ Μενελάου μονομαχία.)
The Trojan Paris having challenged the Greek Menelaus to decide the
war by single combat, a truce is made between the armies.   Helen and
Priam survey the Greek host from the walls of Troy.   In the single
combat, Aphrodite saves Paris.

IV.   (Δ. Ὁρκίων σύγχυσις.   Ἀγαμέμνονος ἐπιπώλησις.)   The Trojan
Pandarus breaks the truce.   Agamemnon marshals the Greek host.
The armies join battle.

V.   (E. Διομήδους ἀριστεία.)   The prowess of the Greek Diomede;
who makes great slaughter of the Trojans, and, helped by Athene,
wounds even Aphrodite and Ares.

VI.   (Z. Ἕκτορος καὶ Ἀνδρομάχης ὁμιλία.)   Diomede and the Lycian
Glaucus (a Trojan ally) are about to fight, when they recognise each
other as hereditary guest-friends, and part in amity.—Hector goes from
the battle to Troy, and before sallying out again, bids farewell to his wife
Andromache.

VII.   (H. Ἕκτορος καὶ Αἴαντος μονομαχία.   Νεκρῶν ἀναίρεσις.) Single
combat of Hector and Ajax.   Burying of the dead.   The Greeks build
a wall to protect their camp by the Hellespont.

VIII.   (Θ. Κόλος μάχη—'the interrupted fight'—broken off by the
gods at v. 485.) Zeus, on Olympus, commands the gods to help neither
side; and then, going down to Ida, gives the Trojans the advantage
over the Greeks.   At Hector's instance the Trojans bivouac on the
battle-field.

*IX. (I. Πρεσβεία πρὸς Ἀχιλλέα. Λιταί.) Agamemnon sends envoys (Odysseus, Ajax, Phoenix) by night to Achilles, offering to restore Briseïs and to make amends; but Achilles rejects the offer.

X. (Κ. Δολώνεια.) Odysseus and Diomede, going by night towards the Trojan camp, slay Dolon, a Trojan spy; then they slay the sleeping Rhesus, chief of the Thracians, and take his horses.

*XI. (Λ. Ἀγαμέμνονος ἀριστεία.) Agamemnon does great deeds, but in vain; many of the leading Greek chiefs are disabled; and Patroclus, sent by Achilles to ask about the wounded physician Machaon, learns that the plight of the Greeks is desperate.

XII. (Μ. Τειχομαχία.) The Trojans, led by Hector, break through the wall of the Greek camp.

XIII. (Ν. Μάχη ἐπὶ ταῖς ναυσίν.) Zeus having turned his eyes for a while away from the Trojan plain, the sea-god Poseidon, watching from the peak of Samothrace, seizes the moment to encourage the Greeks. The Cretan Idomeneus does great deeds.

XIV. (Ξ. Διὸς ἀπάτη—i.e. the trick played on Zeus.) The Sleep-god, and Hera, lull Zeus to slumber on Ida. Poseidon urges on the Greeks, and the Trojan Hector is wounded.

XV. (Ο. Παλίωξις παρὰ τῶν νεῶν—not a correct title, for the Trojans are not routed.) Zeus awakens on Ida. At his bidding, Apollo puts new strength into Hector. The Trojan host presses again on the Greek ships : Ajax valorously defends them.

*XVI. (Π. Πατρόκλεια.) Patroclus intercedes for the Greeks with Achilles; who lends him his armour. In the guise of his friend, Patroclus takes the field, and drives the Trojans from the ships; and at last is slain by Hector.

XVII. (Ρ. Μενελάου ἀριστεία.) The Greeks and Trojans contend for the corpse of Patroclus. Menelaus does great deeds.

*XVIII. (Σ. Ὁπλοποιΐα.) Achilles learns the death of Patroclus, and makes moan for him; at the sound whereof, Thetis rises from the sea, and comes to her son. She persuades the god of fire, Hephaestus, to make new armour for Achilles. The shield wrought by Hephaestus is described.

*XIX. (Τ. Μήνιδος ἀπόρρησις.) Achilles renounces his wrath. He is reconciled to Agamemnon before the assembly of the Greek host. He makes ready to go forth to war with them; the horses are yoked to his chariot; when the horse Xanthus speaks with human voice, and foretells the doom of Achilles.

*XX. (Υ. Θεομαχία.) The gods come down from Olympus to join in the fight on the Trojan plain—some with the Greeks, some with the Trojans. Achilles fights with Aeneas, who is saved by Poseidon; and with Hector, who is saved by Apollo.

*XXI. (Φ. Μάχη παραποτάμιος.) The River-god Scamander fights with Achilles, who is saved by Hephaestus.

*XXII. (X. Ἕκτορος ἀναίρεσις.) Achilles fights with Hector, and chases him thrice round the walls of Troy. Zeus weighs in golden scales the lots of Achilles and Hector. Hector is doomed to die: Apollo deserts him, while Athene encourages Achilles. Achilles slays Hector.

*XXIII. (Ψ. Ἆθλα ἐπὶ Πατρόκλῳ.) The spirit of Patroclus appears to Achilles, and craves burial for the corpse: which is burned on a great pyre, with slaying of many victims : twelve Trojan captives are slain, and cast on the pyre. Games follow, in honour of the funeral.

*XXIV. (Ω. Ἕκτορος λύτρα.) As Achilles daily drags the corpse of Hector round the barrow of Patroclus, Apollo pleads with the gods, and Zeus stirs up Priam to go and ransom the body of his son. The god Hermes, in disguise, conducts the aged king across the plain; Achilles receives him courteously, and accepts the ransom; and Priam goes back to Troy with the corpse of Hector, to be mourned and buried.

Structure of the Odyssey.   6. The *Odyssey* owes its unity to the person of Odysseus, and this unity is necessarily of a closer kind than exists in the *Iliad*. The epic may conveniently be divided into groups of four books. (1) I.—IV. The adventures of Telemachus. (2) V.—VIII. The adventures of Odysseus, after leaving Calypso's isle, till he reaches Phaeacia. (3) IX.— XII. The previous adventures of Odysseus. (4) XIII.—XVI. Odysseus at the hut of Eumaeus in Ithaca. (5) XVII.— XX. The return of Odysseus to his house. (6) XXI.— XXIV. The vengeance on the suitors, and the re-establishment of Odysseus in his realm.

I. (a. Θεῶν ἀγορά. Ἀθηνᾶς παραίνεσις πρὸς Τηλέμαχον.) It is the tenth year since the fall of Troy. Odysseus is now detained by the nymph Calypso in Ogygia, an isle of the far west; while his wife, Penelope, in Ithaca, is beset by suitors, lawless men, who feast riotously in the house, as though it were their own. In the council of the gods, Athene urges that Poseidon, the sea-god, has vexed Odysseus long enough; and she herself goes to Ithaca, and stirs up Telemachus to go in search of his father.

II. (β. Ἰθακησίων ἀγορά. Τηλεμάχου ἀποδημία). Telemachus calls an assembly of the Ithacans, and appeals to them to protect his rights; but the suitors mock him, and nothing is done. Athene, however, disguised as a chief named Mentor, gets him a ship, wherein Telemachus, with the supposed Mentor, sails for Pylus in Elis.

III. (γ. Τὰ ἐν Πύλῳ.) Nestor, the old king of Pylus, receives them hospitably. At the banquet, 'Mentor' vanishes, and Nestor perceives that their guest has been the goddess Athene, to whom he pours a drink-offering. Then Telemachus sets out for Sparta, with Nestor's son, Peisistratus.

IV. (δ. Τὰ ἐν Λακεδαίμονι.) Menelaus, king of Sparta, receives them, and his wife Helen knows Telemachus by his likeness to his father. Having learned that his father is in Calypso's isle (Menelaus had been told this by the seer Proteus in Egypt), Telemachus prepares to return to Ithaca. Meanwhile Penelope hears of a plot by the suitors to slay her son; but Athene comforts her in a dream.

V. (ε. Καλυψοῦς ἄντρον. Ὀδυσσέως σχεδία.) The gods at last send Hermes, and tell Calypso to let Odysseus go; and she obeys. Odysseus builds himself a flat-bottomed vessel (not simply what we call 'a raft'), and puts to sea. On the 18th day his old enemy Poseidon espies him, and wrecks him; but the sea-goddess Ino (=Leucothea) gives him a veil which buoys him up, and at last he comes ashore at the mouth of a river in Scheria, the land of a great sea-faring folk, the Phaeacians.

VI. (ϛ. Ὀδυσσέως ἄφιξις εἰς Φαίακας.) Nausicaa, daughter of the Phaeacian king Alcinous, comes down to the river with her handmaids, to wash linen; and having done this, they play at ball. Their voices awake the sleeping Odysseus; he entreats their pity; and Nausicaa shows him the way to her father's city.

VII. (η. Ὀδυσσέως εἴσοδος πρὸς Ἀλκίνουν.) King Alcinous and his queen, Arētè, receive Odysseus in their splendid palace, and he tells his adventures since he left Calypso's isle.

VIII. (θ. Ὀδυσσέως σύστασις πρὸς Φαίακας.) Alcinous calls an assembly of the Phaeacians, and it is resolved that the stranger shall have a ship to take him home. Games are held. Then at a feast given by the king, the minstrel Demodocus sings of Troy: the stranger weeps; and the king presses him to tell his story.

[Books IX.—XII. were called collectively Ἀλκίνου ἀπόλογοι, the 'narratives to Alcinous'.]

IX. (ι. Κυκλώπεια.) Odysseus tells how, on leaving Troy, he came to the Cicones (in Thrace); afterwards to the Lotus-eaters; and then to the land of the Cyclopes, where he put out the one eye of Polyphemus.

X. (κ. Τὰ περὶ Αἰόλου καὶ Λαιστρυγόνων καὶ Κίρκης.) His adventures with the wind-god Aeolus; with the Laestrygonians; and with the enchantress Circe.

XI. (λ. Νέκυια.) How he went down to Hades, the place of the
dead, and spoke with many spirits of the departed.

XII. (μ. Σειρῆνες, Σκύλλα, Χάρυβδις, βόες Ἡλίου.) His adventures with the Seirens, and Scylla and Charybdis; and how his
comrades ate the sacred oxen of the sun in the isle Thrinacria; wherefore
they all perished at sea, and he came alone to Calypso's isle, Ogygia.

XIII. (ν. Ὀδυσσέως ἀνάπλους παρὰ Φαιάκων καὶ ἄφιξις εἰς Ἰθάκην.)
The Phaeacians take Odysseus back to Ithaca; and, as they are re-
turning, Poseidon turns their ship to stone. Athene appears to Odysseus
in Ithaca; changes him into the likeness of an old beggar-man; and
counsels him how he shall slay the suitors.

XIV. (ξ. Ὀδυσσέως πρὸς Εὔμαιον ὁμιλία.) Odysseus converses
with his old swine-herd Eumaeus, who knows him not.

XV. (ο. Τηλεμάχου πρὸς Εὔμαιον ἄφιξις.) Telemachus returns to
Ithaca, and seeks the dwelling of Eumaeus.

XVI. (π. Ἀναγνωρισμὸς Ὀδυσσέως ὑπὸ Τηλεμάχου.) Odysseus,
temporarily restored to his proper form by Athene (cp. XIII.), reveals
himself to his son. They concert a plan for slaying the suitors.

XVII. (ρ. Τηλεμάχου ἐπάνοδος εἰς Ἰθάκην—i.e. to the *town*: he
has been in the isle since xv.) Telemachus goes to the town. He
keeps his father's return a secret from his mother, telling her only what
he had heard abroad. Odysseus—once more the old beggar-man—
comes to the house with Eumaeus; the dog Argos knows his disguised
master, and welcomes him, and dies.

XVIII. (σ. Ὀδυσσέως καὶ Ἴρου πυγμή.) The disguised Odysseus
has a fight with Irus, a beggar living on the alms of the suitors;
who continue their revelry and insolence.

XIX. (τ. Ὀδυσσέως καὶ Πηνελόπης ὁμιλία. Τὰ νίπτρα.) Penelope
speaks with the poor stranger, whom she knows not for her lord,
and tells him how she has baffled the suitors by delay. She promised
to make her choice as soon as she should have woven a web, and every
night she undid the day's weaving. Eurycleia, the old nurse, washes
the stranger's feet; by a scar she knows Odysseus; who charges her to
be secret.

XX. (υ. Τὰ πρὸ τῆς μνηστηροφονίας.) Odysseus is troubled in
soul, as he lies awake in the porch of the house; Athene appears and
comforts him. While the suitors are revelling, the seer Theoclymenus,
who has second-sight, foresees their doom in a dread vision: but they
heed him not.

XXI. (φ. Τόξου θέσις.) Penelope proposes to the suitors that
they should try their skill with a bow which the hero Eurytus had once
given to Odysseus. Not one of them can even bend it; but the
stranger (Odysseus) strings it with ease, and sends an arrow through the
holes in twelve axe-heads, set up one behind another.

XXII. (χ. Μνηστηροφονία.) At that instant Odysseus casts off his disguise; with his son, and two trusty followers, he falls on the suitors in the palace-hall, and slays them: and the faithless serving-maids of the house are hanged.

XXIII. (ψ. Ὀδυσσέως ὑπὸ Πηνελόπης ἀναγνωρισμός.) The nurse Eurycleia (cp. XIX.) tells Penelope that Odysseus has come home; the wife recognises her lord, and hears from him the sum of his wanderings. Odysseus resolves to withdraw for a while to a farm some way from the town, to see his aged father, Laertes.

XXIV. (ω. Νέκυια δευτέρα. Σπονδαί.) The god Hermes leads the shades of the suitors down to Hades. Odysseus finds Laertes working in his garden, and reveals himself to his father. The Ithacans bury the suitors, and, after debate, resolve to avenge them; but are worsted by Odysseus and his following, and submit. Then the goddess Athene makes peace and a solemn covenant between the king Odysseus and his lieges in Ithaca.

Epics, like dramas, are classed by Aristotle as 'simple' or 'complex.' The *Iliad* is 'simple' (ἁπλῆ), because its action, like that of the *Prometheus Vinctus*, has a plain and direct course. The *Odyssey* is 'complex' (περιπεπλεγμένη), because the plot is complicated by the disguises of Odysseus, and the 'recognition,' like that in the *Oedipus Tyrannus*, is accompanied by a sudden reversal of the situation (περιπέτεια). Again, the *Iliad* is 'pathetic' (παθητική), because the mainspring of the hero's action throughout is passion,—wrath against Agamemnon, grief for Patroclus, and a fierce desire to avenge him. The *Odyssey* is 'ethic' (ἠθική), because the character of the patient and resourceful hero is displayed in action guided by reason[1].

[1] Arist. *Poet.* 24. This view—that Aristotle's παθητική and ἠθική refer to the dominant *motive of action* in the two epics respectively—has been lately developed by G. Günther, *Grundzüge der tragischen Kunst*, pp. 538—543 (Leipsic, 1885). It seems the most probable. If ἠθική meant merely, 'strong in portraiture of character,' it would apply to the *Iliad* no less than to the *Odyssey*. And if παθητική meant, as Twining and others take it, 'disastrous,'—*i.e.* 'containing tragic events,'—it would apply to the *Odyssey*—with its destruction of the hero's comrades, and its slaughter of the suitors—hardly less than to the *Iliad*.

Homeric
poetry—
its gene-
ral
stamp.

7. The capital distinction of Homeric poetry is that it has all the freshness and simplicity of a primitive age,—all the charm which we associate with the 'childhood of the world'; while on the other hand it has completely surmounted the rudeness of form, the struggle of thought with language, the tendency to grotesque or ignoble modes of speech, the incapacity for equable maintenance of a high level, which belong to the primitive stage in literature. This general character is that which Mr Matthew Arnold defines, in his excellent lectures on translating Homer, when he says that Homer's style has four principal qualities; it is rapid; plain in thought; plain in diction; and noble[1]. The English reader will perhaps see this most clearly if he compares Homer with our old ballads on the one hand, and, on the other, with a form of poetry which shares, indeed, the name and form of 'epic,' but is of an essentially different nature from the Homeric,—namely, the literary epic, such as the *Aeneid* or *Paradise Lost.*

Relation
to bal-
lad
poetry.

8. Before instituting any comparison between the ballads and Homer, we must guard ourselves by marking its limit. The old English and Scottish ballads, such as those in Percy's 'Reliques' and other collections, belong to a much ruder stage of poetical development than the *Iliad* and the *Odyssey*. In Greek there are no remains of the stage properly corresponding to our ballads; as in English, on the other hand, we have no Homer. The ballad' proper was a narrative poem, while the 'song' was the vehicle of personal feeling; and though the line was not rigidly drawn, still the balladist, by tradition and instinct, confined himself, as a rule, to simple narrative. The 'ballad' and the 'song' were contemporary products, whereas the Greek epic existed before Greece had any properly lyric poetry; and

---

[1] He remarks that, as a translator of Homer, Cowper fails to be rapid; Pope, to be plain in diction; and Chapman (imbued with the 'conceits' of the Elizabethan age) to be plain in thought,—Homeric though he is in so much,—'plain-spoken, fresh, vigorous, to a certain degree, rapid.'

the Homeric epic, while it is mainly a narrative, is also rich in the germs of the unborn lyric. Such are those utterances of thought and sentiment concerning human life,—utterances often so deeply suggestive and pathetic,— which fall from the lips of the Homeric persons, and which contribute to give the Homeric poems their profound and universal human interest,—a moral and philosophic significance, over and above their splendid pictures of action. As a medium of poetry, the relatively poor and narrow form in which the balladist worked cannot for an instant be compared with Homer's spacious and various epic. But we may illustrate certain Homeric qualities by inquiring how far they are, or are not, present in the ballads.

We find, then, that the ballads share with Homer the first three qualities named above; they are rapid in movement; plain in thought; and plain in diction. There are moments, further, when to these three qualities they add the fourth quality,—nobleness; and it is then that they become, in some degree, Homeric. Such moments usually occur under one of two conditions; viz., when the ballad describes a crisis of warlike action, or when it describes a vehement outburst of natural emotion. An example of the first kind is the part of *Chevy Chase* where 'a squire of Northumberland' warns the Percy's men that the Douglas is coming :

Homeric element in the ballads.

> 'Leave off the brittling of the deer !' he said,—
> 　'And to your bows look ye take good heed !
> 'For sith ye were o' your mothers born
> 　'Had ye never so mickle need.'
>
> The doughty Douglas on a steed
> 　He rode at his men beforne;
> His armour glitter'd as did a glede :
> 　A bolder baron never was born.
>
> 'Tell me what men ye are,' he says,—
> 　'Or whose men that ye be !
> 'Who gave you leave to hunt in this
> 　'Cheviot Chace in the spite of me?'

That is rapid; it is direct in thought and in language; further, it has a martial dignity of its own; and, uniting these qualities, it produces an effect on the mind somewhat analogous to that which is produced by the warlike scenes of the *Iliad*. Consider, again, the description in the *Iliad* of Achilles in his first passion of grief for the death of Patroclus,—Antilochus having just brought the news :—

'Thus spake he, and a black cloud of grief enwrapped Achilles, and with both hands he took dark dust, and poured it over his head, and defiled his comely face, and on his fragrant doublet black ashes fell, and himself in the dust lay mighty and mightily fallen, and with his own hands tore and marred his hair.'

In the ballad of 'Jamie Telfer,' Wat of Harden, a chieftain of Teviotside, sees his son Willie killed before his eyes in a Border foray. A chivalrous nature, in its first agony of grief and anger, is portrayed here also. The stanzas are ennobled by the intensity of natural pathos, and, despite all difference of form, are thus far Homeric in spirit :—

> But Willie was stricken ower the head,
>   And thro' the knapscap[1] the sword has gane;
> And Harden grat for very rage,
>   When Willie on the ground lay slane.
>
> But he's taen aff his gude steel cap,
>   And thrice he's waved it in the air;
> The Dinlay snaws were ne'er mair white
>   Nor the lyart locks of Harden's hair.
>
> 'Revenge! Revenge!' auld Wat 'gan cry;
>   'Fye, lads, lay on them cruellie,
> 'We'll ne'er see Teviotside again,
>   'Or Willie's death revenged sall be[2].'

The ordinary ballad tone.
But now take the ballad on its ordinary level of narrative, where it is not raised by any such glow of passion, and compare it with some analogous part of Homer. In the *Odyssey* King Alcinous suggests to his noble guest

[1] head-piece.—'Dinlay' (v. 7), a Liddesdale hill.—'lyart' (v. 8) = grey.

[2] Prof. Veitch's *History and Poetry of the Scottish Border* (Mac-Lehose, 1878), from which I take this (p. 397), would furnish many other fine examples: see esp. ch. XI.

(whom he does not yet know to be Odysseus) that he should stay in Phaeacia, and marry his daughter Nausicaa :—

'Would to father Zeus, and Athene, and Apollo, would that so goodly a man as thou art, and like-minded with me, thou wouldst wed my daughter, and be called my son, here abiding : so would I give thee home and wealth, if thou wouldst stay of thine own will : but against thy will shall none of the Phaeacians keep thee : never be this well-pleasing in the eyes of father Zeus.'

Absolutely simple and direct as that is, it is also perfect in refinement and in nobleness.

King Estmere, in the old ballad which bears his name, wishes to marry King Adland's daughter; and Adler, Estmere's brother, announces this to Adland :—

'You have a daughter,' said Adler young,—
 'Men call her bright and sheen;
'My brother would marry her to his wife,
 'Of England to be Queen.'

King Adland replies :—

'Yesterday was at my dear daughter
 'Sir Bremor, the King of Spain;
'And then she nicked him with Nay:
 'I fear she'll do you the same.'

I take this example, because the difference between the tone of King Adland and of King Alcinous seems a not unfair measure of the average difference between the ballad, when it is on its ordinary level, and Homer. It might be questioned whether Mr Matthew Arnold is quite just to the balladists in quoting as a typical verse,

When the tinker did dine, he had plenty of wine:

but, at any rate, the main point is indisputable; the balladist is altogether a ruder workman, and also stands on a much lower intellectual level, than the Homeric poet; whose style varies appropriately to his theme, but always and everywhere maintains its noble grace, maintains it, too, without the slightest stiffness, or visible effort; and whose thoughts on human life show a finer and deeper insight than that of the balladists. We have been glancing at our old ballads here as representing early folk-song, made by the people for the people. The result is to show that the Homeric poetry is something maturer and higher. Early folk-song has its moments of elevation, and in these comes nearer to Homer; but its general level is immeasurably lower.

Homer and the literary epic.

9. It is still more important, perhaps, to perceive the broad difference between the Homeric epic and the literary epic of later ages. The literary epic is composed, in an age of advanced civilisation, by a learned poet. His taste and style have been influenced by the writings of many poets before him. He commands the historical and anti-quarian literature suitable to his design. He composes with a view to cultivated readers, who will feel the more recondite charms of style, and will understand the literary allusions. The general character of the literary epic is well illustrated by the great passage of *Paradise Lost* where Milton is saying how far 'beyond compare of mortal prowess' were the legions of the fallen Archangel :—

And now his heart
Distends with pride, and, hardening in his strength,
Glories; for never, since created Man,
Met such embodied force, as named with these,
Could merit more than that small infantry
Warred on by cranes—though all the giant brood
Of Phlegra with the heroic race were joined
That fought at Thebes and Ilium, on each side
Mixed with auxiliar gods; and what resounds
In fable or romance of Uther's son,
Begirt with British and Armoric knights;
And all who since, baptized or infidel,
Jousted in Aspramont, or Montalban,
Damasco, or Morocco, or Trebisond,
Or whom Biserta sent from Afric shore
When Charlemain with all his peerage fell
By Fontarabia.

It is a single and a simple thought—the exceeding might of Satan's followers—that Milton here enforces by example after example. A large range of literature is laid under contribution,—the classical poets, the Arthurian cycle, the Italian romances of chivalry, the French legends of Charlemagne. The lost angels are measured against the Giants, the Greek heroes, the Knights of the Round Table, the champions of the Cross or the Crescent, and the paladins slain at Roncesvalles. Every name is a literary reminiscence. By the time that 'Aspramont' is reached, we begin to feel that the progress of the enumeration is no longer adding anything to our conception of prowess; we begin to be aware that, in these splendid verses, the poet is exhibiting his erudition. But this characteristic of the literary epic,—its proneness to employ the resources of learning for the production of a cumulative effect,—is only one of the traits which are exemplified by the passage. Homer would not have said, as Milton does, that, in comparison with the exiled Spirits, all the chivalry of human story was no better than '*that small infantry warred on by cranes;*' Homer would have said that it was no better than the Pygmies. Homer says plainly and directly what he means; the literary epic likes to say it allusively; and observe the turn of Milton's expression, —'*that* small infantry;' *i.e.*, 'the small infantry which, of course, you remember in the third book of the *Iliad.*' Lastly, remark Milton's phrase, 'since created Man,' meaning, 'since the creation of Man.' The idiom, so familiar in Greek and Latin, is not English, and so it gives a learned air to the style; the poet is at once felt to be a scholar, and the poem to be a work of the study. Homer's language is everywhere noble, but then it is also natural. So, within the compass of these few lines, three characteristics may be seen which broadly distinguish the literary epic from Homer. It is learnedly elaborate, while Homer is spontaneous; it is apt to be allusive, while Homer is direct; in language it is often artificially subtle, while Homer, though noble, is plain[1]. The Homeric quality

Summary.

[1] 'The unrivalled clearness and straightforwardness of his thinking' is a point in which Mr Matthew Arnold finds an affinity between Homer and Voltaire. Like Voltaire, Homer 'keeps to one thought at

which the literary epic best attains is nobleness; yet the
nobleness is of a different cast; it is a grave majesty,
of stately but somewhat monotonous strain; whereas the
noble manner of Homer lends itself with equal ease to
every mood of human life; it can render the vehemence of
dark passions, or reflect the splendour of battle, but it is
not less truly itself in shedding a sunny or tender grace
over the gentlest or homeliest scenes,—in short, it is everywhere the nobleness of nature.

Dryden and Addison on Homer. 10. It was once a commonplace of criticism to compare
Homer with the great literary epics as if they were works
of the same order. Dryden's lines are famous;—

> Three poets, in three distant ages born,
> Greece, Italy, and England did adorn:
> The first in loftiness of thought surpassed;
> The next in majesty; in both the last.
> The force of Nature could no further go;
> To make a third she joined the former two[1].

Here, classing the three poets together, Dryden is content with distinguishing Homer as sublime, Virgil as majestic,
and Milton as both. Addison, again, compares the *Iliad*,
the *Aeneid*, and *Paradise Lost* in respect of plot, characters,
sentiments, and language,—without indicating any sense of
the generic difference which separates the *Iliad* from the
other two. To ignore this difference, however, is even
more unjust to Virgil and to Milton than it is to Homer.
The epic poet in a literary age cannot escape from his age,
and the primary condition of justly estimating his poetry is
to recognise that it is *not* a voice from the primitive
world; but then he has a task of his own, such as was
not laid on the author of the *Iliad* and the *Odyssey*; he
has to deal with great masses of more or less intractable

a time, and puts that thought forth in its complete natural plainness,
instead of being led away from it by some fancy, striking him in connection with it.'

[1] They were first printed under White's portrait of Milton in the
edition of *Paradise Lost* published by Tonson in 1688. Masson's
edition of Milton, I. 20.

materials,—to select from them,—to organise the selected parts,—and to animate them with a vital breath; he has, in poetry, a constructive function analogous to that which, in prose, is performed by a Livy or a Gibbon; and who does not know with what marvellous power this task has been achieved—in different modes and in different degrees— by the genius of Virgil, of Dante, and of Milton? Then, towards the close of the last century, the origin of the Homeric poems began to be critically discussed,—and the new tendency was to make an assumption exactly opposite to that on which Addison's criticism rested. Wolf protested against comparing Homer with the literary epic poets, such as Milton. The fashion now was to compare Homer with the makers of primitive folk-songs or ballads. But, as we have seen, this was a mistake in the opposite direction. The first step towards appreciating Homer's place in literature has been gained if we clearly perceive wherein Homer mainly differs from *Chevy Chase* on the one hand, and from *Paradise Lost* on the other.

The Wolfians.

11. At this point we may refer, for illustration, to an analogy which our own literature offers,—one which, however imperfect, is in several respects suggestive,—the analogy of Walter Scott's poetry. The relation of Scott to Homer may be viewed from two different sides. If a direct literary comparison is made,—if the form of Scott's poetry is compared with that of Homer's,—the contrast is more evident than the likeness. If, on the other hand, we look for an analogy, and not for a direct resemblance,—if Scott's relation to our old balladists is compared with Homer's relation to a ruder age of song,—if the spirit in which Scott re-animates the age of chivalry is compared with the spirit in which Homer re-animates the age of Achaean heroism, —then a genuine kinship is discerned. For the English student of Homer, there could scarcely be a more interesting exercise than to estimate this unlikeness and this analogy; it is one which tests our appreciation of Homer in several ways; and, it may be added, it is one which

Homer and Walter Scott.

can be attempted with equal profit by those who entertain dissimilar views as to the precise poetical rank of Scott. To begin with the unlikeness, Scott's poetry was formed on the old Border ballad, modified by the medieval romance; in the note prefixed to *Marmion* he calls that poem a 'Romantic Tale,' and disclaims all idea of essaying 'epic composition.' When, therefore, Mr Matthew Arnold says of Scott's style that 'it is, tried by the highest standards, a bastard epic style,' it is only just to remember that Scott would himself have deprecated the application of those 'highest standards.' But it is true that, as the same critic says, Scott's style has an inherent inability for maintaining the Homeric level of nobleness; it necessarily shares that defect with the ballad form on which it is founded. Mr Arnold has quoted these lines (from *Marmion* VI. 29) as typical of Scott:

The element of contrast.

> Tunstall lies dead upon the field,
> His life-blood stains the spotless shield:
> Edmund is down—my life is reft—
> The Admiral alone is left.

He makes two remarks upon them,—that the movement, though rapid, is jerky; and that this external trait points to a deeper spiritual diversity, which the lines also reveal,—Scott's incapacity for the grand manner of Homer. This example is, however, utterly unfair to Scott. First, the 'jerkiness' of these lines does not represent the normal movement of Scott's verse where it is most Homeric,—they belong to the broken utterances of the wounded Marmion, as, recovering from his swoon, he hurriedly tells the disastrous tidings of the field to those around him,—their abruptness is purposed[1]:—next, the whole passage is infinitely far from representing Scott's nearest approach to

[1] A critic having observed this, Mr Arnold rejoins ('Last Words on translating Homer,' p. 67) that 'the best art, having to represent the death of a hero, does not set about imitating his dying noises.' But Marmion's words are not 'dying noises'; and poetry is surely permitted to represent abrupt speech.

the manner of Homer.   Adequately to represent that, we
might rather quote, from the same Canto, the magnificent
description of Flodden, beginning—

> At length the freshening western blast
> Aside the shroud of battle cast;
> And, first, the ridge of mingled spears
> Above the brightening cloud appears,
> And in the smoke the pennons flew,
> As in the storm the white sea-mew—

or, from the *Lay*, William of Deloraine's ride from Brank-
some to Melrose; or Dacre's defiance to the warriors of
Scotland—

> 'And let them come,' fierce Dacre cried;
> 'For soon yon crest, my father's pride,
> 'That swept the shores of Judah's sea,
> 'And waved in gales of Galilee,
> 'From Branksome's highest towers display'd,
> 'Shall mock the rescue's lingering aid'—

or, from the *Lady of the Lake*, a farewell not unworthy to
be compared with the parting of Hector and Andromache
in the sixth book of the *Iliad*,—the passage in which
Duncan's widow sees her young son go forth to be the
champion of their house :—

> In haste the stripling to his side
> His father's dirk and broadsword tied;
> But when he saw his mother's eye
> Watch him in speechless agony,
> Back to her open'd arms he flew,
> Press'd on her lips a fond adieu—
> 'Alas!' she sobb'd,—'and yet, be gone,
> 'And speed thee forth, like Duncan's son!'
> One look he cast upon the bier,
> Dash'd from his eye the gathering tear,
> Breathed deep to clear his labouring breast,
> And toss'd aloft his bonnet crest;
> Then, like the high-bred colt, when, freed,
> First he essays his fire and speed,
> He vanish'd, and o'er moor and moss
> Sped forward with the Fiery Cross.

Or—to take but one instance more—the lines, picturing the career of the Fiery Cross, in which Homer's favourite image of a fire raging in the hills is joined to much of Homer's magic in the use of local names—

> Not faster o'er thy heathery braes,
> Balquhidder, speeds the midnight blaze,
> Rushing in conflagration strong
> Thy deep ravines and dells along,
> Wrapping thy cliffs in purple glow,
> And reddening the dark lakes below;
> Nor faster speeds it, nor so far
> As o'er thy heaths the voice of war....

But it is not by a few detached verses that either the unlikeness or the affinity between Homer and Scott can be measured: both must be judged by the spirit of the whole. The unlikeness, as we have seen, depends on the inherent limitations, not merely of the ballad form, but of the ballad tone; it may be briefly expressed in the proposition that a translation of Homer into the metres and style of Scott could never be successful.

The element of analogy. The affinity, on the other hand, is profounder and more essential. On any view as to the origin of the Homeric poems, it is certain that the age of Achaean prowess lay behind the Homeric poet, but was still so near to him—either in time, or through tradition—that he could realise it with entire vividness. Scott stood in a similar relation to a past age of warlike and romantic adventure. This was due to the peculiar condition of Scotland at the date of his birth in 1771. Those literary influences which tend to make the difference between an *Aeneid* and an *Iliad* were in full force, indeed, at Edinburgh, but they were little felt, as yet, in Scotland at large. The memories and feelings of an earlier time still survived, with extraordinary freshness, in the life of the people. Old men could still tell of stirring deeds associated with the risings of 1745 and 1715; in many a Scottish home some episode of stubborn devotion was dear to the descendants of those who had died for the Covenant; and, in the Border country, ballad and legend still enabled men to feel the mental atmosphere of yet more distant days, when the bale-fire, signalling some inroad from the south, used to flash from peel to peel along the valleys of the Ettrick and the Yarrow, the Teviot and the Tweed. From childhood Scott had breathed this atmosphere and had known these scenes. His strong genius was in the largest sense Homeric, as being in natural sympathy with the heroic. Thus, by a combined felicity of moment and temperament, he was in touch with that past. Those features of his poetical style which are most liable to academic criticism are just those which show how far he had escaped from what is most anti-Homeric in an age of books. As Principal Shairp has well said, 'It is this spontaneity, this naturalness of treatment, this absence of effort, which marks out Scott's poetry as belonging essentially to the popular, and having little in common with the literary, epic[1].' Nowhere else, perhaps, in modern literature could any one be found who, in an equal measure with Scott, has united these three conditions of a true spiritual analogy to Homer;—living realisation of a past heroic age; a genius in native sympathy with the heroic; and a manner which joins the spontaneous impulse of the balladist to a higher order of art and intellect. *Summary.*

12. Fresh, direct, and noble, the Homeric mode of presenting life has been singularly potent in tracing certain types of character which ever since have stood out clearly before the imagination of the world. Such, in the first place, are the heroes of the two epics,—Achilles, the type of heroic might, violent in anger and in sorrow, capable also of chivalrous and tender compassion; Odysseus, the type of resourceful intelligence joined to heroic endurance,—one in whom the power of Homer is seen even better, perhaps, than in Achilles, since the debased Odysseus of later Greek poetry never succeeded in effacing the nobler image of his *The Homeric characters.*

[1] *Aspects of Poetry,* ch. XIII. p. 394.

Homeric original. Such, again, are the Homeric types of
women, so remarkable for true and fine insight—Andromache, the young wife and mother, who, in losing Hector,
must lose all; Penelope, loyal under hard trial to her
long-absent lord; the Helen of the *Iliad*, remorseful,
clear-sighted, keenly sensitive to any kindness shown her
at Troy; the Helen of the *Odyssey*, restored to honour in
her home at Sparta; the maiden Nausicaa, so beautiful
in the dawning promise of a noble womanhood,—perfect
in her delicacy, her grace, and her generous courage.
From Agamemnon to Thersites there is no prominent
agent in the Homeric epic on whom Homer has not set
the stamp of some quality which we can feel as distinctive.
The divine types of character are marked as clearly, and in
the same manner, as the human;—Zeus, the imperious but
genial ruler of the Olympian family,—intolerant of competing might, but manageable through his affections or his
appetites; Hera, his wife, who never loses sight of her
great aim,—the advancement of the Greek cause,—but
whose sometimes mutinous petulance is tempered by a
feminine perception of the point at which her lord's
character requires that she should take refuge in blandish-
ments; Apollo, the minister of death, the prophet, active in
upholding the decrees of his father Zeus, and never at
discord with him; Athene, who, unlike her brother Apollo,
is often opposed to the purposes of Zeus,—at once a mighty
goddess of war, and the goddess who presides over art
and industry.

Their typical value. 13. Of all such Homeric beings, divine or human, we perceive the dominant qualities and the general tendencies; but
they are not individualised beyond a certain point. Perhaps
the persons whom we seem to know best are the intensely
human Zeus and Hera, who furnish the only Homeric
example of domestic wrangling. The epic form, as compared with the dramatic, is necessarily at a disadvantage for
the subtler delineation of character; but, further, it was the
special bent of the Greek genius, in poetry as in plastic art,

to aim at lucid expression of primary motives, and to refrain
from multiplying individual traits which might interfere with
their effect; a tendency which is seen even in Greek
drama. This typical quality in Homeric portraiture has
been one secret of its universal impressiveness. The
Homeric outlines are in each case brilliantly distinct,
while they leave to the reader a certain liberty of private
conception; he can fill them in so as to satisfy his own
ideal : and this is one reason for the ease with which
Homer's truth to the essential facts of human life has
been recognised by every age and race.

14. The speeches of the Homeric persons illustrate this. Their ex-
They faithfully express the general attributes of the pression
speakers; but—supposing that we already know what in speech,
these attributes are—we seldom feel that the speech has
given us fresh insight of a closer kind: what we do
feel is rather that we have heard a speech thoroughly
appropriate to a given type of person in a given situation.
As an example, we might refer to the great speeches in
the ninth *Iliad*, where Odysseus, Ajax, and Phoenix come
as envoys from the Greeks to Achilles, and he—in perhaps
the most splendid example of Homeric eloquence—rejects
their prayer. Oratorical power, and the faculty of debate
—as a master of both has observed—are there seen
in their highest form. The speeches are also admirably
suited to the type of character which each speaker represents; but they add none of those minor traits by which
the secrets of individuality are revealed.

A similar limit is observable in those cases where a or in
person's inward thoughts are clothed in words, and given thought.
as a speech which he addresses to his own soul. These
audible thoughts are usually in the nature of comments
on the main point of the situation, and are such as might
have been made by a sympathetic bystander; they are com-
parable to the utterances of the Chorus in Greek Tragedy[1].

[1] The regular formula is, ὀχθήσας δ' ἄρα εἶπε πρὸς ὃν μεγαλήτορα θυμόν
(in which ὀχθήσας, 'troubled,' is a general term, denoting, according to

Divine
and human
action.

15. The profound human interest of the Homeric poems is enhanced by another feature in which they stand altogether alone—their mode of blending divine and human action. The Homeric gods meet mortals in hand-to-hand fight, they wound them or are wounded by them, they aid or thwart them, advise or deceive them, in visible presence; and it is the unique distinction of Homer that all this is managed without ever making the deities less than divine, or the mortals more than human. Homer alone has known how to create a sphere of action in which man's nature is constantly challenged to prove its highest capacity by the direct pressure of a supernatural force, while the gods are not lowered, but exalted, by meeting men on common ground. If we would feel how the Homeric communications between heaven and earth reconcile perfect ease and grace of inter-course with celestial dignity and religious awe, let us contrast them with the abrupt interventions of the *deus ex machina* in some plays of Euripides, or, again, with such a relationship of gods and men as the literary epic is apt to represent,—the *Aeneid*, for example, where Jupiter is little more than an idealised Roman Senator, and the agency of Olympus generally, instead of being vitally interwoven with the organism of the poem, is rather a mechanical adjunct.

Homeric
use of
simile.

16. A literary estimate of Homer owes particular notice to one abounding source of variety, vividness, and beauty. The Homeric use of simile is so characteristic, it plays so important a part in the poems, and it has so largely in-fluenced later poetry, that it is well worthy of attentive consideration. The first point to observe is that Homeric simile is not a mere ornament. It serves to introduce

circumstances, grief, anxiety, terror or anger). It is used in the *Iliad* of Achilles (18. 5, 20. 343, 21. 53), Hector (22. 98), Odysseus (11. 403), Menelaus (17. 90), Agenor (21. 552). In the *Odyssey* it occurs thrice, always of Odysseus (5. 298, 355, 407). The menacing thoughts of Poseidon against Odysseus are twice introduced by a similar formula (κινήσας δὲ κάρη προτὶ ὃν μυθήσατο θυμόν, 5. 285. 376).

something which Homer desires to render exceptionally impressive,—some moment, it may be, of peculiarly intense action,—some sight, or sound, full of wonder, or terror, or pity,—in a word, something *great*. He wishes to prepare us for it by first describing something similar, only more familiar, which he feels sure of being able to make us see clearly. Thus the Homeric similes are responses to a demand made on the narrator by the course of the narrative; they indicate a spontaneous glow of poetical energy; and consequently their occurrence seems as natural as their effect is powerful. In the eighteenth book of the *Iliad* Athene invests Achilles with the aegis, and encircles his head with 'a golden cloud,' from which she makes a flame to blaze. This gives occasion for one of the most beautiful similes in Homer (*Il.* 18. 207):—

> As from an island city, seen afar,
> The smoke goes up to heaven, when foes besiege;
> And all day long in grievous battle strive
> The leaguered townsmen from their city wall:
> But soon, at set of sun, blaze after blaze,
> Flame forth the beacon-fires, and high the glare
> Shoots up, for all that dwell around to see,
> That they may come with ships to aid their stress:
> Such light blazed heavenwards from Achilles' head[1].

The comparison is between the flame flashing from the golden cloud above the head of Achilles and the beacon-fire which, in the gloaming, flares out beneath its column of smoke. The circumstances of the island siege serve as framework for the image of the beacon. This is frequently the case in Homeric simile. When Homer compares *A* to *B*, he will often add details concerning *B* which have no bearing on the comparison. For instance, when

---

[1] This version is from an admirable translation of 'The Similes of Homer's Iliad' by the Rev. W. C. Green, late Fellow of King's College, Cambridge (Longmans, 1877). In v. 211 I have ventured to substitute 'Flame forth' ($\phi\lambda\epsilon\gamma\epsilon\theta o\upsilon\sigma\iota\nu$) for 'Are lit,' because I conceive the fires to have been *lit* before.

the sea-god Poseidon soars into the air from the Trojan
plain, he is compared to a hawk (*Il.* 13. 62),—

> That from a beetling brow of rock
> Launched in mid air forth dashes *to pursue*
> *Some lesser bird along the plain below:*

but Poseidon is not pursuing any one; the point of simi-
litude is solely the speed through the air. Such admission
of irrelevant detail might seem foreign to that direct aim at
vividness which is the ruling motive of Homeric simile; but
it is, in fact, only another expression of it. If *A* is to
be made clearer by means of *B*, *B* itself must be clearly
seen; and therefore Homer takes care that *B* shall never
remain abstract or shadowy; he invests it with enough
of detail to place a concrete image before the mind. The
hawk, for example, to whom Poseidon is likened, is more
vividly conceived when it is described as doing a particular
act characteristic of a hawk,—viz. pursuing another bird.

'Secure of the main likeness,' Pope says, 'Homer makes
no scruple to play with the circumstances;' but, while this
is true in the sense just noticed, we must remember that the
Homeric 'playing with circumstances' is never an aimless
luxuriance. The poet's delight in a picture, and the Hellenic
love of clear-cut form, are certainly present; but both are
subordinate to a sense that the object which furnishes the
simile must be made distinct before the simile itself can be
effective. In this respect Dante sometimes offers a striking
resemblance to Homer. It is generally believed that Dante
had no direct knowledge of Homer; but, even if it had
been otherwise, the particular resemblance of which we are
now speaking is manifestly due to a natural affinity of
spirit,—to the earnest desire of vividness,—and not to
literary imitation. Dante compares the boiling pitch of
Malebolge to the boiling pitch in the Arsenal of Venice
(*Inf.* XXI.). And, in order that the Arsenal may be more
clearly placed before our minds, he rapidly mentions the
various tasks with which the workers in it are busy,—
how one man is building a new boat, while another is

Irrelevant
detail.

Com-
parison
with
Dante.

caulking an old one,—how one is hammering at the prow, another at the poop,—how others are making oars, or twisting ropes, while others mend mizen or mainsail. These labours have no analogy to the sufferings of the lost in the Infernal Lake; but they help us to see the very place where the pitch is boiling at Venice; and the description of them is therefore thoroughly Homeric. A contrast is afforded by the Hebraic similes of the Old Testament, which, as a rule, tersely mark the point of comparison, and dispense with non-essential details. There are, of course, exceptions; as when Job, comparing the inconstancy of friends to the failure of water, makes such failure more vivid—in a truly Homeric manner—by describing the disappointment of wanderers in the desert, who reach springs only to find them dry :—'the caravans of Tema look for them, the companies of Sheba rest their hope on them: they are ashamed of their trust, they come hither and blush' (Job vi. 15—20). *Contrast with Hebrew poetry.*

17. The *Iliad* contains about a hundred and eighty detailed similes,—the *Odyssey*, barely forty; and the proportion is such as might be expected when the broad difference between the two epics is considered. Full of adventure and marvel as is the *Odyssey*, it has far fewer moments of concentrated excitement than are presented by the warlike action of the *Iliad;* in particular, it lacks all those numerous occasions for simile which in the *Iliad* are given by the movements of masses. But the spirit of the comparisons is essentially the same. When Charybdis swallows the raft of Odysseus, he saves himself by clutching a wild fig-tree which overhangs the whirlpool. There he clings, 'like a bat,' waiting till the depths of the vortex shall give up his raft; and the keenness of his prolonged suspense is emphasised by a simile. 'At the hour when a man rises up from the assembly, and goes to supper,—one who judges the many quarrels of the young men that seek to him for law,—at that same hour those timbers came forth to view from out Charybdis' (*Od.* 12. 439)[1]. *Why simile is rarer in the Odyssey.*

[1] I. . . . . that these three verses, *Od.* 12. 439—441,

18   The range of Homeric simile is as wide as the life known to the poet. Some of the grandest images are suggested by fire—especially, fire raging in a mountain forest—by torrent, snowstorm, lightning, or warring winds. Among animals, the lion is remarkable as furnishing no fewer than thirty comparisons to the *Iliad*,—the finest of all, perhaps, being that in which Ajax, defending the corpse of Patroclus, is compared to a lion guarding his cubs, who 'glares in his strength, and draws down all the skin of his brows, covering his eyes'' (*Il.* 17. 135). The useful and ornamental arts afford other similitudes (which we shall have occasion to mention in the next chapter); others are drawn from the commonest operations or experiences of every-day life ; for Homer thinks nothing too homely for his purpose, if only it is vivid. The struggle of Greeks and Trojans for the body of Patroclus is likened to men tugging at a bull's hide which they wish to stretch for tanning (*Il.* 17. 389); the quick staunching of the War-God's wound by the divine healer, Paièon, is likened to the quick curdling of milk by the agency of fig-juice—the old Greek equivalent for rennet (*Il.* 5. 902); the stubborn Ajax, beset by Trojans, is likened to an ass trespassing on corn-land, and vainly belaboured with cudgels by boys (*Il.* 11. 557). This forcible use of homely imagery is no less Hebraic than Homeric ; it is enough to recall 2 Kings xxi. 13, 'I will wipe Jerusalem as a man wipeth a dish: he wipeth it and turneth it upside down,'—or the similes (which Homer also has) from the threshing-floor and the winnowing fan.

Special mention is due to a small group of peculiarly

were suspected in antiquity (though on grounds which seem very inconclusive), another example may be added—*Od.* 6. 232 ff., where the splendour given by Athene to the aspect of Odysseus is marked by the simile of the craftsman overlaying gold upon silver.

[1] It should be noted that a personal knowledge of lions would not necessarily presuppose an Asiatic Homer. In the 5th century B.C. lions still existed in Thessaly, Macedonia, and Thrace, according to Herod. 7. 125 f. His statement is confirmed by Xenophon (*Cyneg.* 11), and by Aristotle, a native of the region (*Hist. An.* 6. 31, 8. 28). See Geddes, *Problem of the Homeric Poems*, p. 268.

touching similes in the *Iliad*—taken, as if for contrast with camp and battle, from the life of children, or of the family. Apollo throws down the Greek wall as easily as a child destroys the sand-house which he has built on the sea-shore (*Il.* 15. 361); Achilles reproves Patroclus for weeping like a little girl running at her mother's side, clinging to her robe, and tearfully looking up, until the mother lifts her in her arms (*Il.* 16. 2). Achilles, burning the remains of Patroclus, grieves as a father burning the remains of a son who has died soon after marriage (*Il.* 23. 222). The evenly-poised battle is as the balance in the hands of a careful working-woman, weighing wool, 'that she may win a scanty wage for her children' (*Il.* 12. 435).

Subjective imagery, from sensation or thought, is extremely rare in Homer. Once there is a simile from a dream, in which the dreamer cannot overtake one who flies before him (*Il.* 22. 199). Once only in the *Iliad* have we a simile—but then a most beautiful one—from the action of the waking mind. Hera, speeding from Ida to Olympus, is likened, for swiftness, to the thoughts of a man who has travelled in many lands: 'He considers in his wise heart,—" *Would that I were there—or there!*"— and thinks wistfully of many things' (*Il.* 15. 82).[1] *(margin: Subjective imagery rare.)*

19. Homer sometimes illustrates the same object by two or more similes, presented in rapid succession. It is well to observe the condition under which this usually occurs, since imitations of the practice by later poets have sometimes been Homeric in semblance without being properly Homeric in motive. A good example is afforded by the passage which describes the Greeks thronging from their quarters by the ships to the place of assembly in the plain. Five comparisons are there contained in twenty-two verses (*Il.* 2. 455—476). As the Greeks issue from their huts in glittering armour, the poet likens them to *fire* devouring a great forest; as they noisily hasten forward on the plain, to a clamorous flight of *birds;* as, having reached the place of meeting, they stand in their assembled *(margin: Aggregation of similes —how used by Homer.)*

'swift as a wing, or as a

multitude, to countless *leaves;* as they are agitated by a
ripple of warlike excitement, to buzzing *flies;* and, as they
are marshalled in divisions by their leaders, to *flocks of
goats* parted by goat-herds. Fire—birds—leaves—flies—
goats;—each image marks a distinct moment; one rapidly
follows another in the order in which the phases of the
great spectacle itself are unfolded before Homer's imagination.   Homer's one anxiety is to make us see *each*
successive phase of that spectacle as vividly as he sees it :
if he can only do that, he does not care—as a literary
epic poet would have been apt to care—how incongruous
the similes, taken all together, may appear, or how closely
they are crowded together.   When Milton compares the
fallen angels, prone on the fiery flood, to autumn leaves
strewing a brook, *or* to sedge scattered on the Red Sea[1],
the images of multitude are alternative ; but in the Homeric
passage, while the general idea of multitude is common
to the images from birds, leaves, flies, and goats, each
image presents that idea in a different aspect.   Sometimes
one simile is almost unconsciously evolved from another.
In *Il.* 13. 492 the Trojans following Aeneas are compared
to sheep following the bell-wether; this suggests the joy felt
by the shepherd ; and this, in turn, is compared to the joy
felt by Aeneas.   It is a similar transition when Milton adds,
after speaking of the sedge on the Red Sea,—

> whose waves o'erthrew
> Busiris and his Memphian chivalry,—

and so evolves a new image for the confusion of the Arch-
Rebel's host.

The   20.   It may now be well to select some one integral
Twenty- portion or chapter of Homeric action,—to follow it in rapid
second
Book of outline,—and to see how it illustrates those leading cha-
the *Iliad*. racteristics which have been separately considered.   For
this purpose, no part of either epic can be more suitable
than the twenty-second book of the *Iliad*, where the story

---

[1] *Par. Lost* 1. 302 ff.

may be said to culminate in the slaying of Hector by Achilles. No other single book of Homer, perhaps, is more comprehensively typical.

Athene (in Olympus) is friendly to Achilles; Apollo, on the Trojan plain, is befriending Hector. In order to save Hector, Apollo has taken upon himself the semblance of a Trojan warrior, and has enticed Achilles away in pursuit. At last Apollo reveals himself to his pursuer :—'Wherefore, son of Peleus, chasest thou me with swift feet?'...'Me thou wilt never slay, for I am not subject unto death.' Achilles replies, in anger : 'Thou hast foiled me, Far-darter, most mischievous of all the gods...Verily I would avenge me on thee, had I but the power.' Achilles then rushes back over the plain to Troy,—'like some victorious steed in a chariot.'

Hector, 'bound by deadly Fate,' is meanwhile standing before the walls of Troy, at the Scaean Gates. His aged father, Priam, is on the walls, and can see Achilles rushing onward,—his armour flashing 'like the star that cometh forth at harvest-time,'—like Orion's Dog, that brings fever to men. Priam implores his son to come within the walls ; —'Have compassion on me also, the helpless one ;'—he rends his white hair,—but Hector is deaf to him,—and to his mother Hecuba, who also pleads with him from the walls :—'Hector, my child, have regard unto this bosom, and pity me, if ever I gave thee consolation of my breast.'

Achilles has now come close. 'As a serpent of the mountains upon his den awaiteth a man, having fed on evil poisons, and fell wrath hath entered into him,'—so Hector awaits the attack ; yet he is troubled, and his thoughts are told to us in words—'thus spake he to his great heart.' But Achilles is upon him, like a very god of war, 'brandishing from his right shoulder the Pelian ash, his terrible spear ; and, all around, the bronze on him flashed like the gleam of blazing fire, or of the Sun as he ariseth.' Hector turns to flight, and Achilles pursues him round the walls of Troy,— 'as a falcon upon the mountains, swiftest of winged things, swoopeth fleetly after a trembling dove.'

All the gods are gazing on them from Olympus, and now, seeing Hector hard-pressed, Zeus speaks among them. Shall we save Hector, he asks, or allow Achilles to slay him? Athene protests against the idea of saving Hector,—'a mortal, doomed long ago by Fate;' and Zeus answers,—'Be of good comfort, dear child: not in full earnest speak I; and I would fain be kind to thee. Do as seemeth good to thy mind.' Then Athene darts down to the battle-field, to help Achilles.

Now for the third time Achilles had chased Hector round the walls, when Zeus, in Olympus, 'hung his golden balances, and set therein two lots of dreary death,'—one for Achilles, one for Hector. Hector's scale sinks,—he is to die: and from that moment Apollo has no more power to help him.

Athene, on the plain below, now comes to the side of Achilles: 'Do thou stand still, and take breath; and I will go, and persuade this man to face thee in fight.' She takes the guise of the Trojan Deiphobos, Hector's brother, and pretends that she has come forth from Troy to aid him. Thus encouraged, Hector turns to confront Achilles,— defying him to combat, but proposing, before they fight, to make a chivalrous compact,—that, whichever may fall, the victor shall be content with stripping the armour from the vanquished, and shall restore the corpse, to receive the due rites from friends. Achilles sternly answers that there can be no compact between them, 'as between men and lions there is no pledge of faith,—as wolves and sheep cannot be of one mind.'

He hurls his spear,—Hector crouches, and it flies over his head;—Athene, unseen of Hector, restores it to the hand of Achilles. Hector now hurls his spear, but he, too, misses:—he calls to his trusty brother Deiphobos for a second spear—but Deiphobos has vanished! The truth flashes on Hector—'It was *Athene* who played me false'— and he knows that he is doomed. Drawing his sword, he rushes on Achilles, who, by a spear-thrust, mortally wounds him in the neck,—and he falls. 'I pray thee by thy life, and knees, and parents,' the dying man says, 'leave me not for dogs to devour by the ships of the Achaeans,'—but Achilles brooks no thought of ransom for the corpse. 'Entreat me not, dog, by knees or parents: would that my heart's desire could so bid me myself to carve thy flesh, and eat it raw, for the evil thou hast wrought me, as surely there is none that shall keep the dogs from thee.' Then, with his last breath, Hector warns his slayer of wrath to come from the gods, in the day when he also shall be slain at those same Gates of Troy; 'and the shadow of death came down upon him, and his soul flew forth of his limbs, and was gone to the house of Hades, wailing her fate, leaving her vigour and youth.'

Achilles strips the gory armour from the body, and binds the body to his chariot, and, lashing his horses to speed, drags it to the camp: the fierce rage for the death of Patroclus is still consuming his heart: while, in Troy, Priam and Hecuba make bitter lament, and all the folk of Troy fall to crying and moaning: 'most like it seemed as though all beetling Ilios were burning utterly with fire.'

But meanwhile Hector's wife, Andromache, was in her house in Troy, waiting for his return: 'in an inner chamber she was weaving a double purple web, and broidering therein manifold flowers.' She had bade her handmaids 'to set a great tripod on the fire, that Hector might have warm washing when he came home out of the battle,—fond heart!—and knew not how, far from all washings, bright-eyed Athene had slain him by the hand of Achilles.' Suddenly she heard the cry of Hector's mother, Hecuba, on the battlements; 'her limbs reeled, and the shuttle fell from her hands.' She rushed forth with two of her hand-maids: 'but when she came to the battlements and the throng of men, she stood still upon the wall, and gazed, and beheld him dragged before the walls: and night came on her eyes, and shrouded her.' The awakening from that swoon is followed by her passionate lament, for herself, and for her son: 'the day of orphanage sunders a child from his fellows.'

21.   In the swift action of this twenty-second book, we can recognise at least four general traits as pre-eminently Homeric.

(1) The outlines of character are made distinct in deed, in dialogue, and in audible thought.

(2)   The divine and human agencies are interfused: the scene passes rapidly from earth to Olympus, and again to earth: the gods speak the same language as men,—noble, yet simple and direct; the gods are superhuman in might,—human in love, in hate, and in guile.

(3)   Each crisis of the narrative is marked by a powerful simile from nature.

(4)   The fiercest scenes of war are brought into relief against profoundly touching pictures of domestic love and sorrow.

Perhaps the best proof of the enduring reality which Homer has given to his epic world is the fact that, in a world so different as our own, 'Homeric' is still an epithet which can be applied, not only to a style, but to an action or to a man.   Among those for whom the word 'Homeric' has a clear meaning, not a few, perhaps, have known some friend in whose character or conduct they have felt a certain affinity with the spirit which breathes in Homer.

One example may suffice.   After referring to the Homeric qualities which distinguish Clough's poem, *The Bothie of Tober-na-Vuolich*,—'its out-of-doors freshness, life, naturalness, buoyant rapidity,' its Homeric ring in such phrases as '*Dangerous Corrievrechan...where roads are unknown to Loch Nevish*'—Mr Matthew Arnold goes on to say of Clough himself,—'But that in him of which I think oftenest, is the Homeric simplicity of his literary life.'

Those general characteristics of Homer which it has been the purpose of this chapter to indicate are the chief reasons why the word 'Homeric' is fraught with a living suggestiveness, not shared by 'Virgilian' or 'Miltonic.' But there is also a further reason. Homer describes a certain phase of early civilisation. He portrays its politics, its religious and moral ideas, its material circumstances, its social manners. This picture is not a laboured mosaic or an archaeological revival. It is a naturally harmonious whole, and it completes the unity of impression which Homer leaves on the mind. We may now consider the principal features of this picture.

CHAPTER II.

THE HOMERIC WORLD.

The
Hellenic
type
already
mature.
1. THE Homeric poems are the oldest documents of Hellenic life. The Greek race, as first revealed by Homer, resembles the poetical art which discloses it. It is a matured type, which must have been gradually developed, though the antecedent phases of development are lost in a prehistoric darkness. The Homeric Greek exhibits all the essential characteristics and aptitudes which distinguish his descendant in the historical age. If his natural gifts are not yet in full exercise, they only wait for opportunity and circumstance. The broader aspects of the Homeric world are the same in the *Iliad* and in the *Odyssey*. But there are also differences, which, like certain traits of language, suggest that the *Odyssey* belongs to a somewhat later period than the *Iliad*.

General
unity
of the
picture.
These differences will be noted as they occur. On the other hand, each epic may, for our present purpose, be treated as a whole. Each, indeed,—as will be seen in Chapter IV.,—contains parts which did not belong to the original form of the poem. In the *Iliad* such additions have been numerous, and certainly have not all been contemporaneous; yet, even there, minor discrepancies in regard to plot and style do not affect the general consistency with which the salient features of the Achaean period are presented.

2. As the geography is the framework of the picture, Homeric
we may first glance at that.   Homer imagines the earth geography.
as a round plane, girdled by the deep and strong river
Oceanus—which, as far as Homer is concerned, seems to
have nothing to do with any dim idea of the Atlantic, but
to be a pure myth.   The 'bronze' or 'iron' sky is the con-
cave roof of the earth, propped by pillars which the giant
Atlas upholds[1].   On this large flat disc, the earth, there is
only one inner zone of which Homer has any distinct
notion.   This is the belt of countries around the Aegean
sea.   By the 'inner geography' of Homer we mean the geo- 'Inner'
graphy of this Aegean zone.   The 'outer geography' consists 'outer'
and
in hints of regions beyond that zone.   The 'outer geo- geogra-
graphy' is very scant and hazy.   So much is true of both phy.
poems.

3. On the western side of the Aegean, the *Iliad* shows *Iliad.*
a good knowledge of Greece.   There is not, however, any Inner
geogra-
collective name for it.   The Greeks are called the 'Achaeans,' phy.
'the Argives,' or 'the Danai[2].'   '*Hellas*' denotes merely a
district in the region afterwards called Thessaly[3].   The
name Thessaly does not occur in either poem, though the

[1] Mr Bunbury, in his *History of Ancient Geography* (1. 33), thinks
that the Homeric Atlas merely *guards* the pillars, and that the idea
of his *upholding* them began with later poets (Hes. *Theog.* 517 etc.).
But in *Od.* 1. 53 ἔχει δέ τε κίονας αὐτός, κ.τ.λ., the emphatic pronoun
favours the other view, which the name ἄ-τλας (upholder) itself suggests.   Atlas has been explained as the sea, on which, at the horizon,
the sky seems to rest.

[2] In *Il.* 2. 530 (Catalogue), but nowhere else, we have Πανέλληνας
καὶ Ἀχαιούς.

[3] *Il.* 2. 683 οἵ τ' εἶχον Φθίην ἠδ' Ἑλλάδα καλλιγύναικα.   Phthia
and Hellas are there two of five districts in Πελασγικὸν Ἄργος, which
belong to the kingdom of Peleus.   In *Il.* 9 (one of the perhaps later
books), 447, 478, 'Hellas' seems to have a larger sense, denoting the
whole N. region of Thessaly.   In *Od.* 1. 344 καθ' Ἑλλάδα καὶ μέσον
Ἄργος = 'in Northern and Southern Greece.'   Ἑλλάς = all Greece first
in Hes. *Opp.* 651.   Thuc. (1. 3) supposes that when the hero Hellen and
his sons had grown powerful in Phthiotis, the name *Hellenes* became
diffused through their being called in to help other states in war.

region is familiar to a part of the *Iliad*. The knowledge of western Greece includes Aetolia, with the great river Achelous, but excludes Acarnania and Epeirus (which is not found as a proper name). The poetical assumption in the *Iliad* is that the Achaean princes are still ruling in Peloponnesus, Agamemnon having his royal seat at Mycenae. 'Dorians' are not mentioned in the *Iliad*. The name 'Argos' denotes not only the town Argos, or the region of Argolis, but also, especially in the formula '*Achaean* Argos[1],' the whole or a great part of Peloponnesus (a name which Homer never uses). Similarly '*Pelasgian* Argos[2] seems to mean Thessaly, or the northern part of it. On the northern shores of the Aegean, the Thracian tribes are known, including the Paeonians who dwell on the Axius (*Vardar*), 'the fairest stream that waters the earth[3].'

In Asia Minor, the *Iliad* knows the topography of the Troad in some detail. The country afterwards called Lydia is 'Maeonia,' identified by the mention of Mount Tmolus[4]. On the coast from Mysia to Caria not one of the Greek colonies is mentioned[5]. The name of 'Ionians' occurs only once in Homer (*Il.* 13. 685), and in that passage it has been generally understood as referring to the Athenians. The references to the interior of Asia Minor (Phrygia, Paph-

---

[1] Ἄργος Ἀχαϊκόν, *Il.* 9. 141, 283: 19. 115: *Od.* 3. 251. In *Od.* 18. 246 Ἴασον Ἄργος also = Peloponnesus: and Ἄργος *alone* has this sense in *Od.* 1. 344, &c. In *Il.* 12. 70 the phrase ἀπ' Ἄργεος (repeated, 13. 227, 14. 70) seems to mean the whole of Greece. (Distinguish Homer's ἀπίη γαῖα (a far land) from later poets' Ἀπία γῆ = Peloponnesus.)

[2] Πελασγικὸν Ἄργος *Il.* 2. 681 (the only place in either poem where this combination occurs).

[3] *Il.* 2. 850.

[4] *Il.* 2. 866. In 20. 390 ff. the λίμνη Γυγαίη and the river Hermus are also named. Ὕδη there (383) seems to represent a site answering to that of Sardis.

[5] The name of *Miletus*, indeed, occurs (*Il.* 2. 868),—but it is a town of the Κᾶρες βαρβαρόφωνοι, who also possess Mycale, and the valley of the Maeander. In 2. 647 Miletus is a town of Crete.

lagonia, etc.) are slight and vague[1]. Among the Aegean islands, Crete and Rhodes are named, with a south-eastern group: also the group of the north-east, off the Troad—Tenedos, Imbros, Samothrace (called Samos), Lesbos, Lemnos. There is no mention of the Cyclades, nor of Chios or Samos.

The 'outer' geography of the *Iliad* asks but few words. To the north, there is a dim rumour of nomads who roam the plains beyond the Thracian hills, living on the milk of their mares[2]: yet the name 'Scythian' is not found. To the south, there is a rumour of 'swart faces' (Aethiopes), 'remotest of men': and of Pygmies, who dwell hard by the banks of the river Ocean[3]. Egypt is noticed only in a passing mention of the Egyptian Thebes[4]. The name 'Phoenician' occurs only once, but the cunning works of Sidon are more than once mentioned[5]. Tyre is not named.

*Iliad.
Outer
geogra-
phy.*

4. The 'Catalogue' of the Greek and Trojan allies (*Il.* 2. 484—877) has a peculiar character, and should be considered by itself, apart from the rest of the *Iliad*. The small

The 'Catalogue'—a document apart.

---

[1] A region somewhere to the east of Paphlagonia seems to be denoted by Ἀλύβη, 'the birthplace of silver,' the home of the Halizones (*Il.* 2. 857, cp. 5. 39),—identified by some of the ancients with the country of the Chalybes. Neither poem mentions the Euxine, or the river Halys. (See Bunbury, *Anc. Geo.* i. 37.)

[2] Ἱππημολγῶν | γλακτοφάγων, *Il.* 13. 5.

[3] The *Il.* mentions the Aethiopes only when it is needful to send the *gods* on some very distant excursion (to feast on the Aethiopian offerings)—1. 428, 23. 206. The 'Pygmies' (3. 6) are curiously illustrated by M. Schweinfurth's account of a race of dwarfs (Akka) in Central Africa (*Travels in the Heart of Africa* ii. ch. xvi.): Bunbury i. 48.

[4] *Il.* 9. 381 f. Θήβας | Αἰγυπτίας, ὅθι πλεῖστα δόμοις ἐν κτήματα κεῖται: it has a hundred gates, and at each 200 men 'go forth with horses and chariots.' Orchomenus (in Boeotia) and Apollo's temple in 'Pytho' (Delphi) are the other typically rich places (*ib.* 381, 405).

[5] Phoenicians *Il.* 23. 744: Sidon 6. 289 (embroidered robes, ἔργα γυναικῶν | Σιδονίων): 23. 743 (a silver cup, Σιδόνες πολυδαίδαλοι εὖ ἤσκησαν).

groups of verses, strung together in a jerky manner, show
the style of the Hesiodic school, which produced other
'Catalogues' of this kind, and which had its chief seat in
Boeotia. Accordingly the poet of the Catalogue makes
Boeotia the most important part of Greece. He puts it first,
and names more towns in it than in any other region[1]. The
story that Solon inserted a verse (558) in order to support
the Athenian claim to Salamis seems at least to indicate
that, as early as *circ.* 600 B.C., the Catalogue had canonical
authority as a Domesday Book of Greece. At the same
time the story suggests the kind of motive, and also
the ease, with which interpolations may have been made
down to a relatively late period. And there can be no
doubt that the Catalogue actually contains such additions.
But, in the main, it may be as old as 800—700 B.C., or
older. The Achaean empire of Agamemnon, with its
capital at Mycenae, extends beyond the Peloponnesus:
Boeotia and Thessaly are populous, while Athens is obscure: Greek settlers have reached Crete and Rhodes, but
are not heard of on the coasts of Asia Minor. In these
broad features the map of the Catalogue is probably
historical, though we cannot date it[2]. But it certainly was
not originally intended for its present place in the *Iliad*.
The Hesiodic poet who composed it appears to have been
thinking of the Greek ships as mustering on the shores
of his own Boeotia, before they left Aulis for Troy[3] And
in two special points the Catalogue seems to be at variance
with popular tradition. It places the Boeotians in Boeotia;
but, according to the popular Greek tradition, their im-

[1] 29 in all. From Boeotia the poet of the Catalogue passes to the
regions around it—then to Peloponnesus and the regions adjacent to
it on the N.W.—then to Crete—and then back to Thessaly. Among
the places in Greece Proper not mentioned in the Catalogue are Delphi,
Eleusis, Megara, Pisa, Pharsalus, Larissa.

[2] Cp. Freeman, *Hist. Geography of Europe*, and D. B. Monro
in the *Historical Review*, no. 1.

[3] Hence ἄγε νῆας, νέες ἐστιχόωντο, etc., which would be strange if
the ships had for ten years been drawn up on land at Troy.

migration took place sixty years *after* the Trojan war[1]. It is true, we do not know the authority for this tradition, nor can we press it, as to the fact; but at least the absence of the name Thessaly from the *Iliad*, while the region is so well-known, agrees with the tradition. Again, the Catalogue places Tlepolemus,—a Heracleid, and therefore a Dorian,— in Rhodes[2]. Dorians are mentioned nowhere else in the *Iliad*; and their presence in Rhodes rather suggests their presence in Peloponnesus, since it was from Sparta that the Dorian colonisation of the Aegean islands seems to have begun. The passage relating to Tlepolemus may, of course, be a later interpolation.

5. This being the area which the *Iliad* recognises, it may be asked—'How far does the poem show a *personal* knowledge of its scenes?' The answer must be that there are two main threads of local association. Parts of the *Iliad* bear the impress of northern Greece in the imagery of wild woodlands and hills; in the prominence given to the horse, which is characteristic of Thessaly; and in the presence of Mount Olympus as the dominant feature of the landscape[3]. Other parts of the *Iliad* show local colouring borrowed from the valley of the Caÿster near Ephesus, or from that 'Icarian sea' which washed the sea-board of south-western

Traces of personal knowledge.

---

[1] The mythical chronology placed events in this order:—1184 B.C. Troy taken: 1124, Boeotians driven Southward into 'Boeotia' by the Thessalian immigrants from Epeirus: 1104, Achaean rule in the Peloponnesus overthrown by the Dorians. Thuc. (I. 12) noticed this difficulty in the Catalogue, and got over it by supposing that Homer's Boeotians were only a sort of advanced guard (ἀποδασμός). It is curious that the Catalogue (v. 750) seems to put Dodona in *Thessaly*, instead of Epeirus.

[2] *Il.* 2. 655. His followers are διὰ τρίχα κοσμηθέντες—a hint of the three Dorian tribes (Hylleis, Dymânes, Pamphyli).—Cp. Pind. *Pyth.* 5. 68 where the Dorian colonisers of Thera set out from Sparta.

[3] See Geddes, *Problem of the Homeric Poems*, chapters XVIII, XIX, XX, where this whole topic is ably treated. The traits from northern Greece belong mainly to Grote's 'Achilleid' (*Iliad* minus books 2—7, 9, 10, 23, 24). The character of Thessaly as especially the equestrian land is illustrated by the frequency of the horse on the coins of Crannon.

Asia Minor. We also find the Niobe myth localised at Mount Sipylus on the Lydian border[1].

Odyssey. Inner Geography.

6. In the *Odyssey*, the coast of Ionia is better known. We hear for the first time of Chios, and of 'windy Mimas', the neighbouring promontory on the Ionian mainland[2]. The poet knows the altar of Apollo in Delos, the central resort of early Ionian worship[3]. 'Dorians' are once mentioned, in Crete[4]. In Greece Proper we still hear of 'Pytho', as in the *Iliad*, not yet of Delphi[5]. As to the islands on the west side of Greece—Ithaca and the adjacent group—the poet knew some of their general characteristics. Ithaca is rugged and rocky, as he says—suited to goats, and not to horses. But it is not a 'low' island, and his description of its position, relatively to its neighbours, is hard to reconcile with the supposition that he was personally familiar with it[6].

Odyssey. Outer geography.

7. In the 'outer' geography of the *Odyssey*, we find that the Phoenician traders are now thoroughly familiar visitors.

[1] The Asia Minor traits belong chiefly to books 2—7, 9, and 24. River Caÿster and 'Asian' meadow (first extant trace of the name 'Asian'), *Il.* 2. 461 : Icarian sea, *ι.* 145 : Mt Sipylus, 24. 615. I omit the argument of Dr Geddes (p. 281), from *Il.* 2. 535, Λοκρῶν οἱ ναίουσι πέρην ἱερῆς Εὐβοίης (that the poet is looking westward from Ionia), because this occurs in the *Catalogue*, which, as plainly of Boeotian origin, I should distinguish from book 2. 1—483.

[2] *Od.* 3. 172 ὑπένερθε Χίοιο, παρ' ἠνεμόεντα Μίμαντα.

[3] *Od.* 6. 162.

[4] *Od.* 19. 177. Δωριέες τε τριχάικες, usually explained as 'divided into three tribes;' but perhaps rather 'with waving locks (or crests)', fr. θρίξ, and ἄισσω (rt. αικ), as Mr Monro thinks: cp. κορυθάιξ, πολυάιξ.

[5] *Od.* 11. 581.

[6] Ithaca is distinctly placed to the *west* of Cephallenia (Σάμη) and far apart from it (*Od.* 9. 25 f.). Ithaca is really to the north-east of Cephallenia, and is divided from it only by a narrow strait. Then Cephallenia is said to form a *group*, apart from Ithaca, with *Zacynthus* (Zante !), and Dulichium—which Mr Bunbury identifies with Leucadia (Santa Maura) : *Anc. Geo.* i. 69. (I agree with Mr W. G. Clark, *Peloponn.* p. 206, that Santa Maura is much too small, and not in the right position for Dulichium.) The best description of Ithaca in relation to Homer is to be found in Mr W. J. Stillman's papers, 'On the Track of Ulysses,' in the *Century* Magazine for Sept. and Oct., 1884. See also Bunbury, *Anc. Geo.* i. 68 s.

Voyages to Egypt seem also familiar, though 'the river Egyptus' is the only name for the Nile. The 'swart-faces' of the *Iliad* are thus far more defined, that the *Odyssey* knows two divisions of them—eastern and western Aethiopians. Libya is named for the first time. The 'Sicilians'[1] are mentioned; and in the last book (which has been regarded as a later addition to the poem) we find 'Sicania'[2] (an older name for 'Sicily'). Odysseus, on sailing from Troy, is first driven to the land of the Cicones on the coast of Thrace, and then crosses the Aegean to Cape Malea (the S.E. point of the Peloponnesus); hence he is driven out to sea by evil winds. From that moment, till he finally reaches Ithaca, his wanderings belong to the realm of fancy. The 'Lotus-eaters' were doubtless suggested to the poet by sailors' stories of a tribe on the north-coast of Africa who lived chiefly on the fruit of the lotus-tree[3]. Scylla and Charybdis were suggested by a rumour of perils run by mariners in the straits of Messina[4]. Further than this we cannot go. When the early Corinthian settlers in Corcyra became skilful seamen, they set up the claim that Corcyra was the Homeric home of the seafaring Phaeacians. This was the common creed of the old world, and still lives

Wanderings of Odysseus —imaginary.

---

[1] Σικελοί, *Od.* 20. 383 (in 24. 211 etc. the old attendant of Laertes is a Σικελή).

[2] Σικανίη *Od.* 24. 307. The Σικανοί were early immigrants from Iberia, καὶ ἀπ' αὐτῶν Σικανία τότε ἡ νῆσος ἐκαλεῖτο, πρότερον Τρινακρία καλουμένη (Thuc. 6. 2). The Σικελοί were later immigrants from Italy.

[3] *Od.* 9. 82 ff. Her. 4. 177. Scylax (*Periplus* 110) places them near the lesser Syrtis (Gulf of Khabs). Polybius 12. 2 describes the lotus (*rhamnus lotus*) from personal knowledge as yielding a fruit which, when prepared, resembled the fig or date,—and also as yielding wine.

[4] Thuc. 4. 24 ἡ μεταξὺ Ῥηγίου θάλασσα καὶ Μεσσήνης...ἔστιν ἡ Χάρυβδις κληθεῖσα τοῦτο—owing, as he says, to the dangerous eddies and currents. Admiral Smyth has described these (*The Mediterranean*, pp. 178—182): cp. Bunbury, *Anc. Geo.* i. 61, who remarks that 'anything in the nature of a whirlpool' has ever been subject to exaggeration—instancing the Norwegian Maelström and the Corrievrechan in the Hebrides.

in Corfu[1]. But even this has no real warrant from Homer. The *Odyssey* knows 'Thesprotia,' the part of southern Epeirus over against Corcyra, yet never names it in connection with Scheria, the land (never called the island) of the Phaeacians. It is futile to aim at mapping out the voyage of Odysseus as definitely as 'the voyage of Magellan or Vasco de Gama[2].' The whole impression left by the *Odyssey* is that a poet, who himself knew only the Aegean zone, wove into imaginary wanderings some touches derived from stories of the western Mediterranean brought by Phoenician traders, who had reached the south of Spain as early as about 1100 B.C.[3]

Sum-
mary.

Homeric
polity.

8. Not a word in Homer shows acquaintance with the great monarchies on the Euphrates or the Tigris. The names of Assyria and Babylon are never heard. Civilisation, outside of the Aegean, is represented solely by Egypt and Phoenicia[4]. Remembering the despotic character of kingship in the oriental empires—that character which Herodotus has so graphically depicted in Xerxes—we cannot fail to be impressed by the contrast which the Homeric world reveals. Here, as in the East, monarchy is the prevalent form of government. But it is a monarchy which operates mainly

---

[1] Thuc. i. 25. Canóni Bay in Corfu (so called from the cannon mounted there) is shown as the spot where Odysseus met Nausicaa ('Chrysida,' in the local version).

[2] Bunbury, *Anc. Geo.* i. 50, whose remarks on this subject are judicious. Almost all the fabulous tribes and places of the poem have been prosaically localised. Thus :—the land of the Cyclopes=Sicily (Eur. *Cyclops* assumes this): Laestrygones=Sicily (Greek view), or=Formiae in Campania (Roman view): isle of Aeolus=Stromboli (one of the 'Aeoliae insulae,' or Lipari group) : isle of Calypso=Gaudos (Gozo, close to Malta on the N. E.): Circè's isle=the promontory (!) of Circeii on the Italian coast—&c.

[3] Cp. Bunbury, *Anc. Geo.* i. 6 l.

[4] In *Od.* 11. 520 ἑταῖροι Κήτειοι (*v. l.* κήδειοι) fall at Troy with Eurypylus. These comrades of the Mysian hero have been rashly claimed as Hittites by some ingenious writers. It is hardly necessary to observe that the name of that people (the *Khita* of the Egyptian monuments) would not appear in Greek as Κήτειοι.

by reasonable persuasion, appealing to force only in the last resort. Public questions are brought before the whole body of those whom they concern. The king has his duties no less than his privileges. At this early age—while in each non-Hellenic monarchy 'all were slaves but one[1]'— the Hellenes have already reached the conception of a properly political life.

9. 'Basileus[2],' 'leader of the people,' 'duke,' is the title Ki of the royal office. It includes 'chiefs' or 'kings' of different relative rank: thus Agamemnon, the suzerain, is 'most royal[3].' Every basileus rules by right hereditary and divine: Zeus has given the sceptre to his house. The distinguishing epithet of the Homeric kings, 'Zeus-*nurtured*,' (διοτρεφής) means generally, 'upheld and enlightened by Zeus,' but is further tinged with the notion of the king's

---

[1] Eur. *Hel.* 276 τὰ βαρβάρων γὰρ δοῦλα πάντα πλὴν ἑνός: whereas the early Greek monarchies were founded on *consent* (ἑκούσιαι, as Arist. *Pol.* 3. 10. 11 says).

[2] Curtius would derive it from rt. βα and Ion. λευ=λαο (cp. Λευτυχίδης), a compound like Στησί-χορος: cp. ξευξίλεως (Soph. fr. 129 Nauck), ᾧ ὑπεζευγμένοι εἰσὶν οἱ λαοί. [Eustathius says, p. 401. 11, ξευξίλεως εἴρηται παρὰ τοῖς μεθ' Ὅμηρον ὁ βασιλεύς.] Another deriv. from βα and λευ=λᾱϝα (λᾶας), 'one who mounts a stone,' refers to the Teutonic and Celtic custom that the king should show himself to the people on a high stone—a custom not proved for early Greece. See Curt. *Etym.* § 535 (5th ed., Eng. tr. by Wilkins and England, 1886, vol. I. p. 439).

[3] *Il.* 9. 69, the only instance of βασιλεύτατος. The compar. βασιλεύτερος occurs only thrice in *Il.*, (9. 160, 392: 10. 239), and once in *Od.* 15. 533. While βασιλεύς is always a *title*, like 'duke,' ἄναξ in Homer is a descriptive epithet, like 'noble.' Mr Gladstone (*Homeric Studies*, I. 543) holds that the formula ἄναξ ἀνδρῶν is applied only to *patriarchal* chiefs—i.e. to βασιλῆες who were also heads of ruling families or clans. It seems hard to make this out. The formula is used of 1. Agamemnon: 2. Anchises: 3. Aeneas: 4. Augeias: 5. Euphetes; 6. Eumelus. I would suggest a metrical reason. Every one of these names = | – – – ; hence, in the Homeric hexameter, ἄναξ ἀνδρῶν was a peculiarly convenient introduction for them; and, out of some 50 places where the formula occurs, it precedes the 2nd half of the 5th foot in all but one (*Il.* 1. 7).

descent from a god or demi-god. The king is (1) leader in war, (2) supreme judge, (3) president of the council and of the popular assembly. (4) In public sacrifices, as head of the state, he takes the same part which the head of a family takes in private sacrifice. But he has not otherwise a sacerdotal quality[1]. A demesne (τέμενος) is assigned to him from the public land[2], and he discharges functions of public hospitality.

Dikè and themis.

10. Homer has no word for 'law[3].' The word *dikè* ('justice') means 'a way pointed out,' and so the 'course which usage prescribes[4].' The word *themis*, again, means, 'what has been laid down,' *i.e.*, first, a decision in a par-

---

[1] Aristotle (*Politics* 3. 14. 12, speaking of the kings of the heroic age): κύριοι δ' ἦσαν τῆς τε κατὰ πόλεμον ἡγεμονίας καὶ τῶν θυσιῶν, ὅσαι μὴ ἱερατικαὶ (*i.e.* sacrifices requiring a priest acquainted with special rites—like those of the Eumolpidae), καὶ πρὸς τούτοις τὰς δίκας ἔκρινον. The *sacrificial* function alone (he adds) remained associated with the name of 'king' in most Greek states (as in the case of the archon basileus at Athens); while at Sparta the *military* function was left to the 'kings'. Cp. Thuc. I. 13 ἐπὶ ῥητοῖς γέρασι πατρικαὶ βασιλεῖαι.

[2] In an interesting paper on 'The Homeric Land System' (*Journ. Hellen. Stud.* VI. 319), Prof. W. Ridgeway holds that the Homeric poems indicate the 'Common-Field' system of agriculture,—the public land being portioned out, in temporary tenure, among the members of the community, while the hereditary king's τέμενος was an exceptional instance of property in land. He shows that πολυλήιος = rich in ληίς (live stock, as opp. to inanimate κτήματα), not in λήιον (standing corn); and explains the term οὖρα (ἡμιόνων, βοῶν, *Il.* 10. 351) as an ancient unit of land-measure,—viz., the distance between the first and last furrows of a day's ploughing. But it is more difficult to assume that ἐπιξύνῳ ἐν ἀρούρῃ (*Il.* 12. 422) means the public field of a community. It seems rather to mean simply a field in which the holdings of the two disputants were conterminous.

[3] Homer has only νομός (pasture), never νόμος.

[4] Curt. *Etym.* § 14. The use of δίκη as = 'way,' 'fashion' (cp. the adverbial δίκην) occurs in *Od.* (as 11. 218 ἀλλ' αὕτη δίκη ἐστὶ βροτῶν). The plur. in Hom. = 'judgments,' as *Il.* 16. 543 ὃς Λυκίην εἴρυτο δίκῃσί τε καὶ σθένεϊ ᾧ. In *Od.* 9. 215, which describes the savage Cyclops as οὔτε δίκας εὖ εἰδότα οὔτε θέμιστας, the former = 'dooms,' while the latter has its derived sense, precepts of justice. Cp. Maine, *Ancient Law*, ch. I.

ticular case, 'a doom'; then, the custom founded on former dooms. The plural *'themistes'* denotes a body of such precedents. The Homeric king is entrusted by Zeus with 'themistes' in the sense that he upholds those judicial precedents on which the rights of his people rest. A bad king is one who gives 'crooked judgments¹.' The Council Council. (βουλή) consists of a small number of 'elders,' whom the king convenes for the purpose of laying business before them². The Assembly (ἀγορή) includes all the free men Agora. of the realm.

11. The *Iliad* describes the life of a Greek camp. The *Iliad.* Council is there composed of a few prominent chiefs or kings, who hold the same relation to the suzerain, Agamemnon, as local elders to a local king. The Assembly is the body of the fighting men; the chiefs speak before it, and the Assembly expresses its sense by shouts or murmurs.

The *Odyssey* describes civil life in a society partly *Odyssey.* deranged by the ten years' absence of its heads at Troy. In some respects the monarchical system of the *Iliad* might seem to be undergoing a change. (1) Though the hereditary principle is still acknowledged in the *Odyssey*, there are hints that it is less absolute and inviolable³. (2) The Agora

---

¹ Zeus has given into the king's keeping σκῆπτρόν τ' ἠδὲ θέμιστας (*Il.* 9. 99). The judges uphold judgments by the authority of Zeus— δικασπόλοι, οἵ τε θέμιστας | πρὸς Διὸς εἰρύαται, *Il.* 1. 238. Corrupt rulers: *Il.* 16. 387 οἳ βίῃ εἰν ἀγορῇ σκολιὰς κρίνωσι θέμιστας, | ἐκ δὲ δίκην ἐλάσωσι, θεῶν ὄπιν οὐκ ἀλέγοντες.

² Gladstone, *Hom. Stud.* III. 98: 'Upon the whole, the Βουλή seems to have been a most important auxiliary element of government; sometimes as preparing materials for the more public deliberations of the Assembly, sometimes intrusted, as a kind of executive committee, with its confidence; always as supplying the Assemblies with an intellectual and authoritative element, in a concentrated form, which might give steadiness to its tone, and advise its course with a weight equal to so important a function.' In *Il.* 9. 70 ff. we have an instance of a question referred to a council of γέροντες, as to a committee, *after* an ἀγορή.

³ The suitors assume that Odysseus is dead (*Od.* ʼ. 183); the hereditary claim of Telemachus is admitted (1. 387 ὅ τοι γενεῇ πατρώιόν

seems a less passive body than in the *Iliad*. It appears
as an effective organ of civic discussion[1]. But the evidence
on these points is very slender; and allowance must be
made for the special conditions presupposed by the subject
of the *Odyssey*.

Homeric religion. 12. The basis of Homeric religion is the feeling that
'all men have need of the gods' (*Od.* 3. 48), and that the
gods are quickly responsive to this need, if they are duly
worshipped. Sacrifice and prayer are the appointed means
of seeking their help, or appeasing their anger. The Homeric
sense of the divine placability is well expressed in the
words of the aged knight Phoenix to the implacable
Achilles (*Il.* 9. 496 ff.): 'Achilles, tame thy high spirit;
neither beseemeth it thee to have a ruthless heart. Nay,
even the very gods can bend, and theirs withal is loftier
Sacrifice. majesty and honour and might. Their hearts by incense
and reverent vows and drink-offering and burnt-offering
men turn with prayer, so oft as any transgresseth and
Sin and doeth wrong. Moreover Prayers (Λιταί) are daughters
Prayer. of the great Zeus, halting and wrinkled and of eyes
askance, that have their task withal to go in the steps
of Atè[2]. For Atè is strong and fleet of foot, wherefore she far outrunneth all prayers, and goeth before them
over all the earth, doing hurt to men; and Prayers follow
behind to heal the harm.' The loftiest forms which human
prayer to Heaven assumes in Homer are seen when

ἐστιν); and yet the suitor Antinous hopes (*ib.* 386) that Zeus will
not 'make Telemachus king'. Mr Gladstone remarks (*Hom. Stud.* III.
51) that this seems to imply the need of some formal act, 'either ap-
proaching to election, or in some way involving a voluntary act on the
part of the subjects or a portion of them.'

[1] In *Od.* 2 Telemachus appeals to the Agora of the Ithacans to
vindicate his rights, and a debate takes place. In *Od.* 24. 420 ff. it is
debated by the Ithacans in the Agora whether the suitors shall be
avenged.

[2] ἄτη (ἀάω) is 'hurt' (done to the mind). Cp. Milton, *Samson* 1676,
'among them He a spirit of phrenzy sent, | Who hurt their minds'.
Ἄτη is the power which infatuates men (sometimes as a punishment for
insolence) so that they become reckless in offending the

Hector, going out to war, prays to all the gods that a noble life may be in store for his infant son (*Il.* 6. 476); and where Achilles prays to 'Zeus, lord of Dodona, Pelasgian, dwelling afar,' that his comrade Patroclus may return safe from the fight (*Il.* 16. 233). In sacrifice, as in prayer, the Homeric man ordinarily communes with the gods directly, not through priests. The priest (ἱερεύς), as dis- Priests. tinguished from the soothsayer (μάντις), never appears in Homer save as the guardian of a local shrine[1].

13. In later Greek poetry Fate is sometimes definitely Fate. opposed, and superior, to the will of the gods. This is never the case in Homer. Fate and the gods appear as concurrent and usually harmonious agencies; there is no attempt to separate them distinctly, or to define precisely the relation in which they stand to each other. The idea of Fate is expressed chiefly by two words, both meaning 'portion,'—αἶσα and μοῖρα. The personified Αἶσα weaves the thread of a mortal's destiny, and assigns it to him at birth. Like αἶσα, μοῖρα may be either good or evil; but the personified Μοῖρα is regularly associated with the Death-god, Thanatos[2]. Two other words denote the *death*-doom; πότμος ('what falls to one'), and κήρ ('destruction'); the personified Κήρ (sometimes plural) is the goddess who brings a violent death, especially in battle. The 'three Fates' are a post-Homeric conception, found first in Hesiod[3].

The Erinyes in Homer are avenging powers who up- Erinyes.

---

[1] Such was the priest of Apollo at Chrysè in the Troad (*Il.* 1. 37); the priest of Hephaestus in the Troad (*Il.* 5. 10),—the priest of Apollo at Ismarus in Thrace (*Od.* 9. 198), etc. There are only two places where Homer speaks of 'priests' in the plur.: (1) *Il.* 9. 575, where the Aetolians send θεῶν ἱερῆας ἀρίστους to implore help from Meleager—*i.e.* priests of the chief local shrines: (2) *Il.* 24. 221 ἢ οἱ μάντιές εἰσι θυοσκόοι, ἢ ἱερῆες, where special rites are in view. In *Il.* 16. 234 the Selli at Dodona are not called ἱερῆες, but ὑποφῆται of Zeus, the declarers of his will.

[2] In *Il.* 24. 209 Μοῖρα is the *weaver* of a death-doom.

[3] *Theog.* 218. Plural 'Fates' occur only in *Il.* 24. 49 τλητὸν γὰρ Μοῖραι θυμὸν θέσαν ἀνθρώποισιν. In *Od.* 7. 197 πείσεται ἄσσα οἱ αἶσα κατὰ κλῶθές (v. l. κατακλῶθές) τε βαρεῖαι | γεινομένῳ νήσαντο λίνῳ, these 'spinners' are merely 'the half-personified agency of αἶσα,' as Mr

hold the right, alike among gods and among men. They
punish all crimes against the family; especially they execute
the curses of injured parents on children. They do not
allow the aged or the poor to be wronged with impunity.
They bring retribution for perjury. In a word, they are the
sanctions of natural law. The immortal steed Xanthus,
suddenly endued with human speech by the goddess Hera,
spoke to Achilles, and revealed his doom; then 'the
Erinyes stayed his voice' (*Il.* 19. 418).

The gods in the Odyssey. 14. As compared with the *Iliad*, the *Odyssey* shows a
somewhat more spiritual conception of the divine agency.
The vivid physical image of Olympus and the Olympian
court, as the *Iliad* presents it, has become more etherial. It
is a far-off place, 'where, as they say, is the seat of the gods
that standeth fast for ever. Not by winds is it shaken, nor
ever wet with rain, nor doth the snow come nigh thereto,
but most clear air is spread about it cloudless, and the
white light floats over it. Therein the blessed gods
are glad for all their days' (*Od.* 6. 42 ff.). 'The gods, in
the likeness of strangers from far countries, put on all
manner of shapes, and wander through the cities, beholding
the violence and the righteousness of men' (*Od.* 17. 485).

Divine agency more spiritual. The gods of the *Iliad* most often show their power on
the bodies or the material fortunes of man; it is com-
paratively seldom that they guide his mind, by inspiring
a thought at a critical moment. In the *Odyssey* the latter
form of divine agency becomes more prominent. 'When
Athene, of deep counsel, shall put it into my heart, I will
nod to thee,' says Odysseus to his son (*Od.* 16. 282).
Faith in their help has become a more spiritual feeling.
'Consider whether Athene with Father Zeus will suffice for
us twain, or whether I shall cast about for some other
champion.' 'Verily,' Telemachus answers, 'the best of
champions are these two thou namest, though high in the

Merry remarks; comparing, as other examples of personification
stopping short of mythology, ἅρπυιαι, the personified storm-winds
(*Od.* 1. 245), and κραταιίς (*Od.* 12. 124).

clouds is their seat' (*ib.* 260 ff.). While the notion of the Other
gods has been thus far spiritualised, the notion of the forms
of the
supernatural generally takes many fantastic forms[1], associated super-
with that outer Wonderland, beyond the Aegean zone, of natural.
which sailors had brought stories. It is here that we find
those beings or monsters who are neither gods nor men—
Calypso, Circe, Polyphemus, Proteus, Aeolus, Scylla, the
Sirens.

15. The Homeric notions of right and wrong have a Homeric
simplicity answering to that of the religion, but are strongly ethics.
held. They begin with the inner circle of the family. The The
ties of the family are sacred in every relation,—between family.
husband and wife, parent and child, kinsman and kinsman.
Polygamy is not found among Greeks. The picture of the
Trojan Hector and Andromache in the *Iliad*—the pictures
of Menelaus and Helen, Alcinous and Arēte, above all,
Odysseus and Penelope, in the *Odyssey*—attest a pure and
tender conception of conjugal affection. The prayer of
Odysseus for the maiden Nausicaa is this :—'May the gods
grant thee all thy heart's desire : a husband and a home,
and a mind at one with his may they give—a good gift, for
there is nothing mightier and nobler than when man and
wife are of one heart and mind in a house' (*Od.* 6. 180 ff.).
Dependents of the family are included in the recognised
duty of kindness and help. So are those who have a claim

---

[1] *E.g.* the herb 'moly', given by Hermes to Odysseus as a charm
against Circe's evil spells (*Od.* 10. 302) ; the 'imperishable veil' of Ino,
which saved Odysseus from drowning (*ib.* 5. 346) ; the flesh 'bellowing
on the spits', when the oxen of the Sun were being roasted by the companions of Odysseus (*ib.* 12. 395); the Phaeacian ship suddenly turned to
stone (*ib.* 13. 163); the *second-sight* of the seer Theoclymenus, when he
forebodes the death of the suitors (compared by Mr Lang to the visions
of Bergthora and Njal in the *Story of Burnt Njal* ii. 167) :—'Shrouded
in night are your heads and your faces and your knees, and kindled is
the voice of wailing, and all cheeks are wet with tears, and the walls
and the fair beams of the roof are sprinkled with blood' (*Od.*
20. 351 ff.). In the *Iliad* the nearest analogies to such marvels are the
speaking horse (19. 407), the self-moving tripods of Hephaestus (18. 376),
and his golden handmaids, who can move, speak and think (*ib.* 418).

Strangers and suppliants. on hospitality: 'for all strangers and beggars are from Zeus' (*Od.* 6. 208). The suppliant (ἱκέτης) must be protected, even when he seeks refuge from the consequences of blood-shed (*Il.* 16. 573); for the Zeus of Suppliants has him in keeping (*Od.* 13. 213), and will punish wrong done to him (*Il.* 24. 570).

Slavery. 16. Slavery in Homer wears a less repulsive aspect than in later periods of antiquity. It is the doom for prisoners of war, however noble their birth: and instances are also mentioned of children, belonging to good families, being kidnapped by pirates or merchants (*Od.* 15. 403 ff.). It is recognised as an awful calamity: 'Zeus takes away the half of his manhood from a man, when the day of slavery overtakes him' (*Od.* 17. 322). But the very feeling for human dignity which this implies may have helped to temper the slave's lot. The *Odyssey* furnishes examples of devotedly attached slaves, and there is no Homeric instance of a cruel master. Homeric slavery seems to be domestic only, the slave being employed in the house or on the land: we do not hear of serfs bound to the soil[1]. Besides the slaves (δμῶες) there are also free hired labourers (θῆτες: *Od.* 4. 644).

Limit to the sphere of themis. 17. Themis, the custom established by dooms, acts as a restraining force within the largest circle of recognised relationships. But outside of that circle—when the Greek has to do with a mere alien—themis ceases to act, and we are in an age of violence. Excommunication, political and social, is expressed by the form, 'outside of clan, custom, and hearth'[2]. The life of a man-slayer was forfeit to the kinsmen of the slain, who might, however, accept a fine (ποινή) as satisfaction. Speaking generally,

[1] In *Od.* 2. 489, indeed, ἐπάρουρος has been taken as = *adscriptus glebae;* but it need not be more than an epithet describing the particular kind of work on which the θής was employed.

[2] *Il.* 9. 63 ἀφρήτωρ, ἀθέμιστος, ἀνέστιος. Hence, and from 2. 362 f., I had inferred that, above the Homeric family, was the unity of the clan (φρήτρη), and then of the tribe (φῦλον): 1st ed., p. 54. But I grant that such a relationship cannot be proved for the Homeric age. Homer knows no gentile *sacra.*

we may say that the Homeric Greeks appear as a gentle and generous race in a rude age. There is no trace among the Homeric Greeks of oriental vice or cruelty in its worst forms. Their sense of decency and propriety is remarkably fine—even in some points in which their descendants were less delicate. If the Homeric man breaks themis *Aidōs.* in any way, he feels that others will disapprove. This feeling is called *aidōs.* Hence, therefore, *aidōs* has as many shades of meaning as there are ways in which themis can be broken;—'sense of honour,' 'shame,' 'reverence,' etc. And the feeling with which he himself regards a *Nemesis.* breach of themis by another person is called *nemesis,*— righteous indignation. The *Odyssey,* in comparison with *Odyssey* the *Iliad,* shows more traces of reflection on questions of *compared with Iliad.* right and wrong. There are some additions to the stock of words for expressing the religious or moral feelings[1].

18. The civilisation based on these ideas and feelings *The Ho-* was very unlike that of the later Greek world. The Homeric *meric civi-lisation.* man already exhibits, indeed, the clear-cut Greek type of humanity: he has its essential qualities, mental and moral. But all his surroundings bespeak an age of transition. Crude contrasts abound. Luxuries and splendours of an eastern cast are mingled with elements of squalid barbarism. Manners of the noblest chivalry and the truest refinement are strangely crossed by traits of coarseness or ferocity. There are moments when the Homeric hero is almost a savage[2].

---

[1] Thus the following words occur in the *Odyssey,* but not in the *Iliad:*—(1) ἀγνή, epithet of Artemis, of Persephone, and of a festival, ἑορτή: (2) ὁσίη, 'piety' (the only part of ὅσιος found in either poem): (3) θεουδής, 'god-fearing', as epithet of νόος or θυμός: (4) νοήμων (found in *Il.* only as a proper name),='right-minded' (always with δίκαιος),— nearly = the later σώφρων, which does not occur in Homer. The word δίκαιος is frequent in the *Odyssey,* while the *Iliad* has only the superlative (once) and the comparative (twice), but the positive nowhere.

[2] Thus the Homeric man, even the noblest, is liable to savage out-bursts of fury,—like that in which the Macedonian Alexander slew his friend Cleitus,—though not, as in that case, kindled by wine. Patroclus

Archaeo-   19. Homer gives some general notion of the extent to
logical
evidence. which the useful and ornamental arts had been developed;
and in some points this literary evidence can now be supplemented by evidence from monuments of archaeology[1].
The poet naturally assumes that his hearers are familiar
with the products to which he refers. Hence the indications which he gives are often slight. Nor can any
real help be derived from the scenes depicted on vases
or reliefs of the classical Greek age, which clothe
Homeric life in the garb of the sixth or fifth century B.C.
The only monuments which can be trusted for the
illustration of Homer are those of an earliei date. As
the Homeric poems show, the field over which such
testimony may be sought is a wide one. Agamemnon
received a breast-plate from the king of Cyprus. Menelaus
received a mixing-bowl from the king of Sidon. Helen's silver
work-basket on wheels came from Egyptian Thebes. A Phoenician merchant showed a necklace of amber and gold to the
mother of Eumaeus. Priam offered Achilles a Thracian cup[2].

Use of   20. The power of working stone is implied in the
stone.   Homeric mention of mill-stones, quoits, and sepulchral

slew the son of Amphidamas 'in wrath over a game of knuckle-bones'
(*Il.* 23. 88). Achilles, the very embodiment of chivalry, fears lest the
wild beast within him should leap forth, and he should *slay* Priam—the
aged and helpless king, his guest, and his suppliant (*Il.* 24. 568—586).

[1] This evidence has been brought into relation with the evidence of the Homeric text by Dr W. Helbig in his compact and
comprehensive work, *Das Homerische Epos aus den Denkmälern erläutert*
(Leipzig, Teubner, 1884).

[2] The chief sources of archaeological evidence for Homer are discussed
by Helbig, pp. 1—59. They are (1) Phoenician: (2) archaic Greek and
Italian: (3) Northern—*e.g.*, an archaic bronze hydria has been found at
Grachwyl in Switzerland. In the Aegean zone, the chief groups of
relevant 'finds' have been at 1. Hissarlik: 2. Thera: 3. Ialysos in
Rhodes: 4. Mycenae (where Helbig would put the remains before the
Dorian conquest,—*i.e.* earlier than *circ.* 1100 B.C.—but not *long* before
the Homeric times): 5. Spata in Attica: 6. The Dipylon at Athens,
where—in graves of a later age (*circ.* 700 — 500 B.C.) than the five preceding groups—vases have been found with designs more nearly Homeric
than any others known,—though the ships depicted are un-Homeric in
one point, as having beaks (which do not occur before 800— 700 B.C.:
pp. 54—59).

slabs (στῆλαι). The chambers in Priam's palace are
built of 'polished stone'; and so is Circe's house (*Od.*
10. 210). But the use of wood in house-building of the
humbler sort was probably more general than that of stone.
Homer nowhere mentions stone statues, or figure-sculpture
on stone. He knows no treatment of stone for decorative
purposes beyond hewing and polishing (denoted by the
word ξεστός)[1].

21. The house of the Homeric chief is most clearly exem- *The*
plified by the house of Odysseus[1], the general arrangement *Homeric house.*
of which is shown in the accompanying plan[2]. It was sur-
rounded by a high and massive stone wall, probably of
the rude and irregular structure known as 'Cyclopean'.
In this defensive wall there was only one opening, viz. the
front gate, with large and solid folding-doors. Outside
the wall, on each side of the gate, stone seats were
placed. On passing through this gateway (πρόθυρον) in
the outer wall, the visitor found himself in a court-yard
(αὐλή, ἕρκος). This was open to the air. It was not paved. *The*
It was, in fact, like a farm-yard, and quite as dirty[3]. Small *court.*
chambers (θάλαμοι), built at the sides of the court-yard,
against the outer wall, served as farm-buildings, as sleeping-
rooms for male slaves, and sometimes even for members of
the family[4]. In the midst of the court-yard stood the altar
of 'Zeus of the Court' (Zeus Herkeios), the symbol of
domestic unity[5].

22. Standing at the front gate, where he entered, *The*
the visitor sees a portico, supported by pillars, run- *aethusa and pro*
ning along the inner side of the court-yard, opposite to *domus.*

---

[1] Helbig, pp. 71—73.

[2] Based on that given by Mr John Protodikos in his essay *De
Aedibus Homericis* (Leipsic, 1877).

[3] Argos, the dog of Odysseus, lay on a huge dung-heap in the court-
yard of the house (*Od.* 17. 297).

[4] In two cases, at least, an unmarried son of the house has a θάλαμος
in the αὐλή--Phoenix (*Il.* 9. 471 ff.) and Telemachus (*Od.* 19. 48).

[5] *Od.* 22. 334: here the master of the house offered sacrifice. In
Soph. *Ant.* 487 ὁ πᾶς Ζεὺς Ἑρκεῖος = 'the whole family.'

him.   This portico is the 'aethusa' (αἴθουσα), specially so
called.   The space covered by it is called the *prodomus*

MYXOΣ ΔOMOY

ΘAΛAMOΣ   OΔYΣΣEΩΣ

ΘHΣAYPOΣ

ΘAΛAMOΣ
OΠΛΩN

ΓYNAIKΩNITIΣ

ΛAYPA

ΛAINOΣ OYΔOΣ

EΣXAPA   OPΣOΘYPA

MEΓAPON

ΛAYPA

MEΛINOΣ OYΔOΣ

AI ΘOY   ΣA
ΠPOΔOMOΣ

AYΛH

AIΘOYΣA AYΛHΣ   AIΘOYΣA AYΛHΣ

ZEYΣ EPKEIOΣ

THE HOMERIC HOUSE OF THE ODYSSEY.

(πρόδομος) or 'fore-hall,' as being immediately in front
of the great hall, to which it served as a kind of vestibule.
Hence *aethusa* and *prodomus* are sometimes used con-
vertibly ; as when a person who sleeps *under* the aethusa is
said to sleep *in* the prodomus.   Guests, even of high
distinction, were sometimes lodged there for the night[1].

---

[1] As Telemachus and Peisistratus, in the house of Menelaus at
Sparta.   Helen orders beds to be prepared for them ὑπ᾽ αἰθούσῃ (*Od.* 4.

The term 'aethusa' itself was a general one, being merely
the epithet of a portico which is open to the sun's rays
(αἴθειν). Another portico, similar to that of the *prodomus*, ran along the opposite side of the court, on each
side of the gateway (πρόθυρον), and, sometimes at least,
along the two other sides of the court also, which then had
a colonnade running all round it,—the *peristyle* (περίστυλον)
of later times. Hence the Homeric phrase, 'he drove out
of the gateway and the echoing portico' (*Il.* 24. 323).
Hence, too, the *prodomus* (with its portico) can be distinguished from the αἴθουσα αὐλῆς, which then means the
colonnade on the opposite side, or the other sides, of
the court (*Il.* 9. 472 f.).

23. From the *prodomus* a door led into the great hall The
(μέγαρον, δῶμα). In the house of Odysseus, this door has a meg
threshold of ash (μέλινος οὐδός, *Od.* 17. 339), while the
opposite door, leading from the great hall to the women's
apartments, has a threshold of stone (λάϊνος, *Od.* 20. 258).
Each threshold, as appears from the story, was somewhat
raised above the level of the floor. In one of the side-walls
of the hall, near the upper end, was a postern (ὀρσοθύρη),
also raised above the floor, and opening on a passage
(λαύρη) which ran along the outside of the hall, communi-
cating both with the court and with the back part of
the house. At the upper end of the hall was the
hearth (ἐσχάρη), at which all the cooking was done; for
the hall served both as kitchen and as dining-room. Not
only the guests but the retainers of the Homeric prince
live and eat with him in the hall,—a number of small
tables (one for every two persons, as a rule) being ranged in
it from end to end; in the house of Odysseus, upwards
of sixty such tables must have been in use. In this
respect the home-life of the Achaean basileus resembled
that of the medieval baron or the Scandinavian chief.

297), and they sleep ἐν προδόμῳ (*ib.* 302). So αἰθούσῃ in *Il.* 24. 644
= προδόμῳ *ib.* 673. If Odysseus, in his humble disguise, is fain to take
a rough 'shake-down' in αἴθουσα, the slight is not in the place but in
the mode (*Od.* 20. 1).

24. The women's part of the house was an inner court, immediately beyond the great hall, with which it was in direct communication by the door with the stone thresh-

The women's apart- ments.

old. The women's apartments are sometimes collec- tively called *thalamos*[1]. They included the private room, or rooms, of the mistress of the house (to which, in Penelope's case, access was given by stairs), and the work- rooms of the women slaves. In the house of Odysseus, the strong-room or treasury for precious possessions ($\theta\eta\sigma\alpha\nu\rho\delta s$), and the armoury ($\theta\dot{\alpha}\lambda\alpha\mu os$ $\ddot{o}\pi\lambda\omega\nu$), were also in this region. The phrase $\mu\nu\chi\dot{o}s$ $\delta\dot{o}\mu ov$, 'innermost part of the house,' is sometimes so used as to indicate a part beyond the women's court. Here, in the house of Odysseus, was probably the chamber, built by himself, enclosing the bed of which the head-post was an olive-stump (*Od.* 23. 192),—the sign by which he finally convinced Penelope of his identity[2].

Analogy to later Greek house.

Thus the general plan of the Homeric house is essentially that of the Greek house in historical times. There is an outer court,—the Homeric *aulé*, the later *an-*

[1] From the collective *thalamos*—as a whole part of the house—dis- tinguish the plur. $\theta\dot{\alpha}\lambda\alpha\mu oi$, said of the small chambers against the walls of the *court-yard*. So from *megaron*, in its special sense—the public hall—distinguish $\mu\dot{\epsilon}\gamma\alpha\rho\alpha$, said of work-rooms for the women in the thalamos (*Od.* 19. 16).

[2] See Protodikos, p. 60. Some points in regard to the Odyssean house remain doubtful. (1) What was the circular $\theta\dot{o}\lambda os$ in the $\alpha\dot{v}\lambda\dot{\eta}$? (*Od.* 22. 442). Perhaps, as some of the ancients thought, and as Protodikos thinks (p. 24), a $\tau\alpha\mu\iota\epsilon\hat{\iota}ov$,—*i.e.* a sort of pantry, in which plates, dishes, cups, etc., were kept. (2) What were the $\dot{\rho}\hat{\omega}\gamma\epsilon s$ $\mu\epsilon\gamma\dot{\alpha}\rho oi o$? (*Od.* 22. 143). I have elsewhere (*Journ. Hellen. Stud.*) given reasons for thinking that they mean the 'narrow passages,' leading from the $\dot{o}\rho\sigma o\theta\dot{v}\rho\alpha$ to the back-part of the house. The Neo- Hellenic $\dot{\rho}o\hat{v}\gamma\alpha$ is used in a like sense, and seems to be descended from the Homeric word (evidently once a familiar one). The Low Latin *ruga* (Fr. *rue*) is not a probable source for it. (3) What were the $\mu\epsilon\sigma\dot{o}\delta\mu\alpha\iota$? (*Od.* 19. 37.) Probably the main (or longitudinal) beams in the roof of the megaron, while $\delta o\kappa oi$ were the transverse beams; as Protodikos holds (p. 37). Buchholz (*Hom. Realien*, p. 109) reverses the relation of $\delta o\kappa oi$ and $\mu\epsilon\sigma\dot{o}\delta\mu\alpha\iota$.

dronītis. There is an inner court for the women, with rooms round it,—the Homeric thalamos, the later *gynae-conītis.* And between the two there is the principal room of the house, in which the host and his guests eat,—the Homeric *megaron* or *doma*, the later *andron*[1].

25. The public hall (megaron) in the house of Odysseus, —a typical palace,—is not floored with wood or stone. The floor is merely earth trodden to hardness. There is, however, a long raised threshold of ash-wood inside the door leading to the court-yard, and a similar threshold of stone inside the door leading to the thalamos. In the megaron of Alcinous, the walls are covered with plates of bronze,— a mode of ornamentation which had come into the Hellenic countries from Asia, and which continued to be used in the East for many centuries. Traces of it appear in the Treasuries of Mycenae and Orchomenus. Portions of the wood-work in the Homeric palace, especially doors and door-posts, may also have been overlaid with gold or silver. The cyanus (κύανος), which adorned the cornice in the hall of Alcinous (*Od.* 7. 87), was formerly interpreted as bronze or blue steel. But there is now little doubt that it was a kind of blue glass paste, used as an artificial substitute for the natural ultramarine obtained by pulverising the sapphire (lapis lazuli)[2]. The brilliant effect of the metallic wall-plating and other decoration in the palace of Alcinous is marked by the phrase, 'a radiance of the sun or of the moon' (*Od.* 7. 84), which is also applied to the palace of Menelaus at Sparta (*Od.* 4. 45). The poet of the *Iliad*, on the other hand, ascribes such

[margin: Interior fittings and decoration, etc.]

----

[1] With regard to the house at Tiryns, see Note at the end of the book. The origin and age of that house are doubtful; but it certainly is not the Homeric house of the *Odyssey*.

[2] See Helbig, pp. 79—82. The explanation was first suggested by R. Lepsius. The *locus classicus* is Theophrastus περὶ λίθων § 55, who distinguishes the natural κύανος (αὐτοφυής), or lapis lazuli, from the artificial (σκευαστός): Fragments of an alabaster frieze, inlaid at intervals with small pieces of blue glass, were found at Tiryns. Their age is uncertain.

decoration to no mortal's house—perhaps simply because he has no occasion to describe the interior of
a palace; but he calls the house of the god Poseidon
'golden', and that of the god Hephaestus 'brazen'. Metal-
plating on wood or other material must be understood
by the epithet 'golden' or 'silvern' as applied to several
objects in both epics.   Such are the 'golden' sceptre,
wand, distaff, bread-basket, chair, etc.; the 'silvern' wool-
basket, chest, table, etc. The hall was at once lighted
and warmed by large braziers (λαμπτῆρες),—three of which
are brought in by the maid-servants of Odysseus at night-
fall; they light the fires with dry faggots, and take turns in
watching to replenish them (*Od.* 18. 307).   The smoke
from the braziers and the hearth sufficed to blacken
the bows, spears, and other arms hung on the walls (*Od.* 16.
290). The outlet for the smoke may have been an opening
in the roof, though Homer mentions nothing of the kind[1].

Social manners. 26. The social manners of the time, in the house of a chief
of the highest rank, may be gathered from the reception of
Telemachus and his friend (Nestor's son Peisistratus) at the
palace of Menelaus in Sparta.   The travellers, in a chariot
drawn by two horses, drive up to the outer gate of the
court-yard.   A retainer (θεράπων) informs the master of the
house, and is ordered at once to unyoke the horses, and to
conduct the strangers (whose names are as yet unknown)
into the house. Accordingly the horses are stabled, and the
strangers are led into the great hall—which astonishes them
by its splendour.   Thence they are ushered to baths.
Having bathed, anointed themselves with olive-oil and put
on fresh raiment, they return to the great hall, where their
host Menelaus receives them.   They are placed on chairs
beside him.   A hand-maid brings a silver basin and a
golden ewer, from which she pours water over their hands.
A polished table is then placed beside them.   'A grave

[1] Such a hole or smoke-vent (καπνοδόκη, Ion. for καπνοδόχη—the
Attic κάπνη or ὀπή) belongs to the earliest form of Graeco-Roman house:
cp. Her. 8. 137.—In *Od.* 1. 320 ἀνοπαῖα has been taken as 'up the smoke-
vent'; but probably it means simply 'upwards': see Merry *ad loc.*

dame' (the house-keeper) brings bread (in baskets), and 'many dainties'; while a carver places on the table 'platters of divers kinds of flesh'¹, and golden bowls for wine.　Menelaus then invites them to eat, and, as a special mark of honour, sets before them, with his own hands, a roast ox-chine.　He does not yet know who his guests are; but, when he mentions Odysseus in conversation, tears come into the eyes of Telemachus, who raises his purple mantle to hide them.

Menelaus is musing on this, when the mistress of the house enters the hall². Helen, in her radiant beauty, comes from the inner, or women's, part of the house—'the fragrant tha-lamos'—attended by three hand-maids. She takes a chair, to which a foot-stool is attached; at her side a maiden places a silver basket, on wheels, full of dressed yarn; and lays across it a golden distaff, charged with wool of violet blue. She and her lord converse with their guests until the night is far spent. Then supper is served, and Helen casts into the wine a soothing drug which she had brought from Egypt,—'a drug to lull all pain and anger, and bring forgetfulness of every sorrow.' Presently attendants, with torches, show the two guests to their beds in the porch,—

---

¹ In the Homeric world, fish is not mentioned as a delicacy—rather it is regarded as the last resource of hunger (*Od.* 12. 329 ff., *Od.* 4. 368). The similes from fishing point to the use of fish by poor people who could command no other animal food.

⁹ Helen in her own house at Sparta is the best example of the Homeric woman's social position—as Nausicaa is the best proof that the poet perfectly apprehended all that is meant by the word 'lady'. In comparing the Homeric place of woman with her apparently lower place in historical Greece, two things should be borne in mind. (1) The only Homeric women of whom we hear much are the wives of chiefs or princes, who share the position of their husbands. The women of whom we hear most from the Attic writers belong to relatively poor households: their social sphere is necessarily more confined. (2) The intellectual progress made between 800 and 500 B.C. was for the men, and only in exceptional cases for the women. The Homeric woman of 950 B.C. was probably a better companion for her husband than the Attic woman of 450 B.C.

where bedsteads have been set, with purple blankets, and coverlets and thick mantles thereon (*Od.* 4. 20—305).

A contrast.

If we contrast this picture with that of the suitors in Ithaca we feel the skill and delicacy of the poet's touch. In the house of Menelaus, Homer presents a scene of noble and refined hospitality; in the invaded house of Odysseus he means to describe a scene of coarse riot. When one of the suitors snatches up an ox's foot from a basket, and throws it at Odysseus—missing him, and hitting the wall (*Od.* 20. 299 ff.)—we are not to infer that incidents of this kind were characteristic of good Homeric society.

Homeric dress.

27. The dress of the Homeric man is a shirt or tunic (*chiton*)[1], and over that a mantle (*chlaina*)[2], which answers to the outer garment called *himation* in the classical age. The Homeric woman wears a robe (*peplus*) reaching to the feet. On her head she sometimes wears a high, stiff coif, (κεκρύφαλος), over the middle of which passes a many-coloured twisted band (πλεκτὴ ἀναδέσμη)[3], while a golden fillet glitters at the front. Either from the coif, or directly from the crown of the head, a veil (κρήδεμνον, καλύπτρη) falls over shoulders and back.

In imagining such a scene as Helen standing on the walls of Troy with Priam and the Trojan elders (*Il.* 3), the general picture (Helbig remarks) which we should conceive as present to the poet's mind is one dominated by the conventional forms and brilliant colours[4]

---

[1] In *Il.* 13. 685 the Ἰάονες (probably Athenians) are called ἑλκεχίτωνες, 'tunic-trailing'—*i.e.* wearing the long tunic which reached below the knee (χιτὼν τερμιόεις). This was once worn by Dorians as well as Ionians, but was never the ordinary garment of daily life—being worn only (1) by elders or men of rank, (2) by other persons on festal occasions. The Homeric poet, when he said ἑλκεχίτωνες, was perhaps thinking of an Ionian festival, such as that at Delos. See Helbig, pp. 119 ff.

[2] Or φᾶρος, *Od.* 6. 214.

[3] Schliemann assumed that the πλεκτὴ ἀναδέσμη was a golden frontlet. Helbig points out the error (p. 158), which the word πλεκτή itself refutes. A frontlet would have been ἄμπυξ.

[4] The Homeric vocabulary of colour marks vividly the distinction between *dark* and *light* (or *bright*), but very imperfectly the distinctions

of the East,—not by the free dignity and harmonious symmetry of mature Greek art. Priam and the elders of Troy wear close-fitting tunics, which in some cases reach to the feet—over these, red or purple mantles, which fall straight and foldless,—some of them embroidered with rich patterns,—the king's mantle, perhaps, with the picture of a fight. Their upper lips are shaven; they have wedge-shaped beards; their hair falls over their cheeks in long locks fastened with golden spirals. Helen wears a richly-embroidered robe (*peplus*), which fits close to her form; a costly perfume breathes from it; on her breast glitter the golden brooches which fasten the peplus; a necklace (ὅρμος) hangs down to her breast,—the gold forming in it a contrast with the dark-red amber. On her head is the coif, with glittering frontlet, and the veil falling over the shoulders[1].

28. The Homeric warrior has defensive armour resembling that of the heavy infantry soldier (*hoplite*) of later times. This defensive armour is an essentially Greek trait; it is not oriental. Thus the Ionian Aristagoras tells the Spartan Cleomenes that the barbarians, who fight with bows and short spears, go into battle wearing trousers and turbans[2]. The Homeric defensive panoply consists of helmet, cuirass (θώρηξ, formed of breast-plate and back-plate), greaves, belt[3], shield, and lastly the 'mitra,'—a girdle of metal,

Homeric armour.

between shades of colour. Thus he says of a robe which was κυάνεον that nothing was μελάντερον (*Il.* 24. 93): though κυάνεος properly = dark blue. He applies χλωρός both to *young herbage* (pale green), and to *honey* (as 'pale,' or perh. merely 'fresh-looking'). A striking parallel to his χλωρός is the Gaelic *urail*, as meaning (1) green of any shade, (2) 'flourishing,'—fresh, comely,—said of a face. Thus the character of the Homeric colour-sense is in accord with the character of Homeric art. The notion that 'Homer was colour-blind' has long been exploded.

[1] Helbig, p. 194.

[2] τόξα—αἰχμὴ βραχέα—ἀναξυρίδες—κυρβασίαι (Her. 5. 49).

[3] ζωστήρ. The word ζῶμα, as used in the *Iliad*, probably de-notes a projecting rim at the bottom of the θώρηξ, forming a 'waist' which served to hold the ζωστήρ in its place. In the *Odyssey* the ζῶμα has a somewhat different sense, denoting a kind of broad girdle some-

(or plated with metal,) protecting the body below the belt[1].
The mitra was not included in the panoply of later days.
The Homeric shield is round; but there are hints that
an oblong shield was familiar at least through poetical
tradition; thus the comparison of the shield of Ajax to
a tower (*Il.* 7. 219, etc.) implies that form[2]. The Homeric
warrior must be imagined as a somewhat clumsier figure
than the classical hoplite;—his armour heavier, more
angular, and fitting less neatly. The war-chariot—important
in Homeric fights—had gone out of Greek use before
700 B.C.[3]

Homeric
art.

29. The fine art of the Homeric age appears mainly as
decorative art, applied to objects in daily use, such as cups
and other vessels, furniture, armour, or dress. A difficult,
but interesting, question is to estimate the actual state
of art with which the Homeric poems were contemporary.
The following is an outline of the general view which many
archaeologists now accept. (1) The oldest objects of art
found in the graves at Mycenae are older than the Dorian
conquest of the Peloponnesus, *i.e.*, older than about
1100 B.C. Three main elements are present there; skilled
goldsmith's work, probably Phrygian; work of an early
indigenous Greek art, best represented by decorated
sword-blades; and, in a much smaller degree, Phoenician
work. (2) This earliest period is followed by an interval
of some three centuries (1100—800 B.C.) which in Greek
art, as in Greek history, is almost a blank. Then, about
800—750 B.C., a revival of art begins in the East, and
is carried by Phoenicians into Greece. This revived art

times worn instead of the θώρηξ when a lighter equipment was required.

[1] In *Il.* 4. 187 the μίτρη is made by χαλκῆες.

[2] Cp. Mr W. Leaf, in *Journ. Hellen. Stud.* IV. 283, who has
elucidated several points of Homeric armour. Among others, the
στρεπτὸς χιτών of *Il.* 5. 113 has been explained by him as a pleated
doublet worn under the cuirass, to protect the skin from the metal.

[3] In the war-poetry of Archilochus, Alcaeus and Tyrtaeus, there is
no reference to the use of the ἅρμα.

is represented especially by metal work, such as the Phoenician bronze bowls in the British Museum, and by pottery, such as the vases from Cameirus in Rhodes. (3) The Homeric notices of art belong mainly to the interval between 1100 and 800 B.C.; that is, to a period of comparative decadence, intervening between two periods of vigour. The Homeric art is nearest to the Mycenean[1], but later and ruder; while the influence of the eighth-century revival, if it has been felt at all, is as yet only incipient.

30. The most elaborate work of art in Homer is the Shield of Achilles (*Il.* 18. 478 ff.). The central part of the Shield (the ὀμφαλός, or boss) was adorned with representations of earth, heaven, sea, sun, moon, and stars. The outer rim of the shield represented the earth-girdling river Oceanus. Between the boss and the rim, successive concentric bands displayed various scenes of human life; a besieged city; a city at peace; ploughing; reaping; vintage; oxen attacked by lions; sheep at pasture in a glen; youths and maidens dancing. An ingenious reconstruction of the Shield, from Phoenician, Assyrian, Egyptian, and early Greek sources, has been given by Mr A. S. Murray[2]. He observes that the Shield, though a general picture of human life, gives no place to ships—an omission natural for Assyrians, but strange for Greeks—nor does it include any rite of Greek religious worship[3]. Helbig thinks that the particular scenes depicted on the Shield had been suggested to the poet by real works of art, but that the Shield as a whole is the work of his fancy. It proves the artistic feeling of the poet, but belongs to an age which was not yet ripe for

Shield of Achilles.

How far imaginary.

---

[1] Thus Nestor's cup (*Il.* 11. 632), with its two πυθμένες, is illustrated by some of the Mycenean cups, where the πυθμένες appear as golden supports connecting the handles of each cup with its stem.

[2] *History of Greek Sculpture*, ch. III. p. 44.

[3] The Chest of Cypselus, described by Pausanias, was of the 7th century B.C.; and on the Chest—in contrast with the Shield—the actors are not nameless, but are well-known persons of Greek mythology, with their names written beside them. See Murray, *op. cit.*, pp. 47, 61.

plastic expression of so complex a kind[1]. There can be no doubt that the Shield as a whole is a work of the imagination; the only question is how far actual works of art had inspired its details. One thing is certain. The poet knew that different metals could be inlaid, as he represents them on his Shield, so as to give variety of colour : his field is of gold, his vine-poles of silver, his fence of tin, etc. Some of the bronze sword-blades found at Mycenae—one of which was adorned with a lion-hunt—were overlaid with a dark metallic enamel, and in this figures cut in gold leaf were inserted,—the gold being artificially toned to different shades[x].

Other works.

The golden brooch ($\pi\epsilon\rho\acute{o}\nu\eta$) of Odysseus (*Od.* 19. 226) represented a hound holding a fawn in his fore-paws, and strangling it, while it writhed. This may have been suggested by a real work of art. The animals and fighting scenes wrought on the golden belt of Heracles (*Od.* 11. 610) recall some Rhodian vase-paintings[3]. But there is no other Homeric hint of that Greek art, dating from the 8th century B.C., which Phoenician work had stimulated; and the passage in which the belt occurs is, by general consent, one of the later parts of the *Odyssey*.

The remark made above, as to the right way of conceiving Homeric figures and dress, may probably be extended to the general effect of the Homeric house and of

---

[1] Generally, the Greek artistic sense in Homer is shown by (1) distaste for the formless and planless,—the monsters, such as Scylla, being non-Hellenic conceptions: (2) feeling for physical beauty, even in the old—as Achilles admires the comeliness of Priam (*Il.* 24. 631)—just as, later, old men chosen for their beauty shared in the Panathenaic procession ($\theta\alpha\lambda\lambda o\phi\acute{o}\rho o\iota$, Michaelis, *Parthenon*, pp. 330 f.): (3) especially, the admiration of the human *form* as seen (e.g.) in the corpse of Hector (*Il.* 22. 369, cp. Herod. 9. 25). Agamemnon is likened to Zeus for head and eyes, to Ares for girth, and to Poseidon for breast (*Il.* 2. 477). Yet Pheidias was the first who wrought out the Zeus of Homer.

[x] Prof. P. Gardner in *Macmillan's Magazine*, vol. LIV. p. 377; who refers to U. Koehler in *Mittheilungen Deutsch. Inst. Athen.* VII. 244.   [3] *Ib.* p. 378.

Homeric art. The modern spectator, if he could be placed Oriental stamp of Homeric art generally. in the dwelling of an Homeric king, might fancy himself at Nineveh in the palace of Sanherib, or at Tyre in the palace of Hiram, rather than in a Greek home[1].

31. Homer makes no reference to coined money. A Standards of value. 'talent's weight' of uncoined gold is sometimes mentioned[2]. The ox is the ordinary measure of values. Thus a female slave, skilled in embroidery, is worth four oxen; Laertes had given twenty for Eurycleia; a fine tripod is worth twelve; a suit of 'golden' armour is worth a hundred. Much-wooed maidens 'multiply oxen' for their fathers—by gifts from the successful suitors[3].

Some kind of alphabetic writing is probably indicated by Writing. the 'baneful tokens' in *Il.* 6. 168; but elsewhere in Homer the later word for 'writing' ($\gamma\rho\acute{\alpha}\phi\omega$) means only to 'scratch' or 'graze.' The subject of writing will be noticed again in Chapter IV.

The *Odyssey* has a word for a man who is skilled Craftsmen. in a profession or trade—'craftsman of the people' ($\delta\eta\mu\iota o\epsilon\rho\gamma\acute{o}s$). This term is applied to (1) soothsayers, (2) surgeons, (3) minstrels, (4) heralds, (5) artificers. Commerce Merchants. is not yet in high esteem with Greeks. Odysseus is nettled when a Phaeacian chief remarks that he is not like 'one skilled in games,' but rather like 'a master of sailors that are merchants' ($\pi\rho\eta\kappa\tau\hat{\eta}\rho\epsilon s$, *Od.* 8. 161).

32. Apart from the action of each epic, glimpses into

---

[1] Helbig, p. 318.

[2] It denotes no great value—as may be inferred from *Il.* 23. 751, where 'half a talent of gold' is only the third prize for running,—the second being an ox, and the first a silver bowl.

[3] See Butcher and Lang's *Odyssey*, Note 5, p. 410. 'The ἔδνα in Homer are invariably gifts made by the wooers to the father or kinsmen of the bride, that is, the bride-price, the *kalym* of the dwellers on the Volga. The Greeks of the Homeric age virtually bought their wives: cp. Aristotle, *Pol.* ii. 8 § 19, speaking of the barbaric customs of ancient Greece, τὰς γυναῖκας ἐωνοῦντο παρ᾽ ἀλλήλων.' The Homeric μείλια are gifts to the bride from her father: the wooer's gifts to her are called simply δῶρα. In Pindar ἔδνα already = φέρνη, the dowry.

the general life of the age are given by many of the
similes. These tell of the shipwright—for whom mules
drag timber from the hills—the chariot-builder, the stone-
mason, and the house-builder. A woman 'of Caria or
Maeonia' stains ivory with crimson, to make a cheek-piece
for the bridle of a chief's horse. The art of 'overlaying
gold on silver' is noticed. A doubtful fight suggests the
equipoise of scales in the hands of 'a careful working-
dame,' weighing wool, that by spinning 'she may earn a
scant wage for her children.' We see neighbours disputing
about a boundary, 'with measuring-rods in their hands.'
Or a skilled rider[1] is urging four horses together along a
highway towards a great town, and leaping from one horse
to another, while the folk marvel. A late hour in the
afternoon is the hour 'when a man rises up from the
marketplace and goes to supper,—one who judges the
many quarrels of the young men that seek to him for law[2].'

On the Shield of Achilles two scenes of townlife are given.
One is a joyous marriage procession, while torches blaze, and
the bridal chant rings clear. Another is a dispute for the
blood-price of a slain man, in the marketplace; the slayer
vows that he has paid; the kinsman of the slain denies it;
and the elders, seated on polished stones in a semicircle,
try the cause. In the rural scenes of the Shield—Ploughing,
Reaping, Vintage, Pasturage — we note the kindly and
joyous aspect of the country life. And then there comes
the picture of the dance:—'youths dancing, and maidens
of costly wooing, their hands upon one another's wrists.

---

[1] *Il.* 15. 679; the only mention of riding (κελητίζειν) in *Il.*: for in
10. 513 we need not assume that Odysseus and Diomede ride, rather than
drive, the horses of Rhesus. In *Od.* 5. 371 the shipwrecked Odysseus
bestrides a spar, κέληθ' ὡς ἵππον ἐλαύνων. In two other instances
a Homeric simile turns on a practice not ascribed to the Homeric
heroes: (1) the use of the trumpet, σάλπιγξ, *Il.* 18. 219: (2) boiling
meat in a caldron, λέβης, *Il.* 21. 362.

[2] *Od.* 12. 440—notable as an indication of time exactly like the
ἀγορὰ πλήθουσα (early forenoon) or ἀγορᾶς διάλυσις (early afternoon) of
the classical age.

Fine linen the maidens had on, and the youths well-woven tunics faintly glistening with oil.   Fair wreaths had the maidens, and the youths daggers of gold hanging from silver baldrics.' Now they move round in a swift circle— now they run in lines to meet each other. 'And a great company stood round the lovely dance in joy.'

33.   The Homeric Greeks burn their dead.   When the body has been laid on the pyre, sacrifice is offered, on a scale proportionate to the rank of the dead.   If he was a great chief, many oxen and sheep are slain, as well as some of his favourite horses and dogs, and their carcases are thrown on the pyre.   The corpse is wrapped in the fat of the victims; unguents and honey are also placed near it.   When the body has been consumed, the embers are quenched with wine.   The friends then collect the bones, washing them with wine and oil, or wrapping them in fat; cover them with fine cloths; and place them in an urn (λάρναξ).   The urn is then deposited in a grave (κάπετος); over this is raised a round barrow of earth and stones (τύμβος or σῆμα)[1], and on the top of the barrow is set an upright slab of stone (στήλη).   Until the body has received funeral rites, the spirit of the dead is supposed to be excluded from converse with the other shades in the nether world (*Il.* 23. 71). In practising cremation, the Homeric Greeks were in accord with the most ancient practice of the Indo-European peoples, except the Persians.   With the Semitic races, on the other hand, interment was the prevailing custom. Among the Greeks and Romans of the historical age cremation and interment were in contemporary use.

Funeral rites.

34.   The Homeric place of the departed is 'the house of Hades.' 'Hades,' 'the Unseen,' is in Homer always a proper name, denoting the god Pluto.   Between earth and

The state of the dead.

---

[1] Three fire-funerals are described with some detail;—*Il.* 23. 110 ff. (Patroclus): *Il.* 24 786 ff. (Hector): *Od.* 24. 63 ff. (Achilles).   The sacrifice of the Trojan prisoners at the funeral of Patroclus is exceptional—a trait of unique ferocity, intended to mark the frenzy of grief in Achilles.

the realm of Hades is an intermediate region of gloom, Erebus : while Tartarus, the prison of the Titans and other offenders against Zeus, is as far below Hades as he is below the earth.   In the realm of Hades the spirit (ψυχή) of the dead has the form, the rank, and the occupations which were those of the living man.   But the spirit is a mere semblance (εἴδωλον) or wraith ; 'the living heart is not in it' (*Il*. 23. 103) ; it is 'strengthless.'   The Homeric feeling on this point is illustrated by the use of the pronoun αὐτός.   As distinguished from the spirit in the nether world, the real self (αὐτός) is either the corpse left on earth (*Il*. 1. 4), or the man as he formerly lived (*Od*. 11. 574)[1].   So the Egyptian Book of the Dead[2] has a picture of the deceased man (the αὐτός) making prayers to the Sun-god, while his soul attends behind him.   When Odysseus wishes to call up the spirits of the dead, he digs a pit, a cubit square, into which flows the blood of the sheep which he sacrifices ; and the spirits, invoked by his prayers, then come up from Erebus to the drink-offering of blood (*Od*. 11. 36).   By drinking of the blood, the ghosts recover some of the faculties of the living, so that they can recognise Odysseus, and speak to him[3].

Homer knows not the 'Islands of the Blest :' these are first named by Pindar.   But in the far region of the sunset is 'the Elysian plain.'   'No snow is there, nor yet great storm, nor any rain ; but always the river Ocean sendeth

---

[1] Similarly in *Od*. 11. 602 αὐτός is the real Heracles, as he exists, after apotheosis, among the gods, in distinction from his eidolon in the house of Hades.

[2] Bunsen's *Egypt* (vol. 1. p. 26, transl.), quoted by Gladstone in *Homeric Synchronism*, p. 261.   The 'Book of the Dead,' or 'Funeral Ritual,' is 'a collection of prayers of a magical character, referring to the future condition of the disembodied soul' (R. S. Poole, in *Encycl. Brit.* VII. p. 721).   It has been published by Lepsius and by De Rougé, and translated by Birch.

[3] See *Od*. 11. 153, 390.   The drinking of the blood is not mentioned in every instance, but the poet evidently conceived it as the general condition : see Merry on *Od*. 11. 96.

forth the breeze of the shrill west to blow cool on men.'
There is Rhadamanthus, son of Zeus; and thither Menelaus
shall pass without dying, because Helen, the daughter of
Zeus, is his wife.   (*Od.* 4. 563 ff.)

Such are the chief traits of the Homeric age.   As a
general picture of that age, the Homeric poetry has the
value of history.   It is manifestly inspired by real life.
This is equally true whether the life is conceived as strictly
contemporary with the poet, or as known to him only
through a vivid tradition.

CHAPTER III.

HOMER IN ANTIQUITY.

Influence of the Homeric poems.

1. WE have now considered the general characteristics of the Homeric poems and of the Homeric age. The subject which next invites attention is the influence of Homer in Greek antiquity. That influence pervades Greek literature. But it is much more than literary. It enters into every part of Greek life. Eulogists of Homer, Plato tells us, used to say that he had been 'the educator of Hellas[1].' In a certain sense, such a claim can be made for every great national poet. The peculiarity of Homer's case is that, for him, the claim can be made with so much literal truth. There is no other instance in which the educative power of national poetry over a national mind has been so direct or so comprehensive.

Homer was long known to the Greek world solely, or chiefly, through public recitation. The spirit in which the public reciter conceived his office will be better understood if we begin by noting the Homeric references to minstrelsy.

---

[1] *Rep*. 606 E ὅταν Ὁμήρου ἐπαινέταις ἐντύχῃς, λέγουσιν ὡς τὴν Ἑλλάδα πεπαίδευκεν οὗτος ὁ ποιητής.

2. The *Iliad* nowhere mentions a minstrel (ἀοιδός[1]) reci- Min-
strelsy in
Homer. ting lays. It says, indeed, that the Thracian poet Thamyris boasted that 'he would conquer, though the Muses them- *Iliad.* selves should sing against him' (2. 597). He was 'coming from Eurytus of Oechalia' (in Thessaly) when the Muses met him and struck him blind. Here we seem to have a glimpse of a poet who (1) recites his own poetry, (2) is familiar with the idea of competition in singing, and (3) is the guest of chieftains. Achilles has no minstrel to entertain him in his tent, but plays the lyre himself, and sings to it 'the glories of heroes' (κλέα ἀνδρῶν, 9. 189). Patroclus was waiting in silence, till Achilles 'should cease from singing.'

The *Odyssey* assigns a recognised position to the pro- *Odyssey.* fessional minstrel (ἀοιδός). In the palace of Alcinous, king of Phaeacia, the blind minstrel, Demodocus, is led in by the king's 'herald' or chamberlain (κῆρυξ), and is set on 'a high chair inlaid with silver,' in the midst of the guests (8. 65). Demodocus sings the 'glories of heroes' (κλέα ἀνδρῶν, v. 73) to the lyre—choosing the episode of a quarrel between Odysseus and Achilles. Then the company go out to see athletic games. The next time that Demodocus sings at the feast, his theme is again from the 'Trojan lay': but Odysseus names the part which is to be sung—viz., the story of the wooden horse; and the minstrel '*took up the tale from that point*' (ἔνθεν ἑλών, 8. 500).

In Ithaca, during the absence of Odysseus, the min- strel Phemius was constrained by the suitors to sing to them at their feasts. He sang 'the pitiful return of the Achaeans' from Troy. This pained Penelope, and she begged him to change his theme; but Telemachus re-

---

[1] In *Il.* 24. 720 παρὰ δ᾽ εἶσαν ἀοιδούς, | θρήνων ἐξάρχους, the 'singers' placed by Hector's corpse merely 'lead the dirge,' while the women join in with their wail. The only other place where the *Iliad* has the word is a doubtful passage, 18. 604 μετὰ δέ σφιν ἐμέλπετο θεῖος ἀοιδός, | φορμίζων,—'was making music with his lyre' (for the dancers— in one of the scenes on the Shield). These words occur in no ms. They were inserted by Wolf from Athenaeus (v. p. 180 D), who blames Aristarchus for having struck them out (*ib.* p. 181 D).

marked that the minstrel could not be blamed for choosing
it—since men most applaud the song which is *newest* (1.
352). So the *Odyssey* knows at least two great themes for
minstrels,—(1) 'The Doom of Ilios' ('Ιλίου οἶτον, 8. 578),
and (2) the 'Return of the Achaeans' ('Αχαιῶν νόστον, 1.
326): and the latter is the 'newest.'

The similes from the art of the minstrel are striking.
(1) When the swineherd Eumaeus wishes to make Penelope
understand the charm of the newly-arrived stranger (Odysseus), he says:—'Even as when a man gazes on a minstrel,
whom the gods have taught to sing words of yearning joy
to mortals, and they have a ceaseless desire to hear him,
so long as he will sing;—even so he charmed me, sitting
by me in the halls' (*Od.* 17. 518 ff.). (2) Ease in stringing
a bow is thus described:—'Even as when a man that
is skilled in the lyre and in minstrelsy easily stretches a
cord about a new peg, after tying at either end the twisted
sheep-gut, even so Odysseus straightway bent the great bow'
(*Od.* 21. 406 ff.).

Such, then, are the essential traits of the minstrel,
or 'aoidos,' as we find him in the *Odyssey*:—(1) He is a
singer directly moved by 'the god' (ὁρμηθεὶς θεοῦ, *Od.* 8.
499), or by 'the Muse:' (2) he sings for a select company
of guests at the banquet in a great man's house: (3) he
accompanies his song on the lyre: (4) his song is a lay
of moderate length, dealing with some episode complete
in itself, taken from a larger story (such as the tale of
Troy). When his host asks him for a particular lay, the
minstrel begins 'from that point' in the larger story.

Post-Ho-
meric re-
citation.
Rhap-
sodes.

3. After the picture of the 'aoidos' in the *Odyssey*,
there is a gap in our knowledge. Then, early in the historical age, we meet with the public reciter, or '*rhapsode*'
(ῥαψῳδός), who claims, in a certain way, to represent the
Homeric aoidos. The earlier rhapsodes were sometimes,
doubtless, epic composers also; but it is not likely that this
was often the case after the sixth century B.C. 'Rhapsode'
is strictly 'a singer of stitched things,'—as Pindar (*Nem.* 2. 2)

paraphrases it, ῥαπτῶν ἐπέων ἀοιδός. 'To stitch verses together' was a metaphor for 'composing verses[1].' 'Rhapsode,' then, need not mean anything more than 'a reciter
of poetical compositions' (whether his own, or another's).
The word was, however, peculiarly suitable to the continuous flow of epic verse, as contrasted with a lyric strophe.
It has nothing to do with any notion of the epic being
pieced together from short lays.

4. The public recitation of the Homeric poems by
rhapsodes can be traced back to about 600 B.C., and was
doubtless in use from a considerably earlier time. It is found
at Sicyon in Peloponnesus,—at Syracuse,—at Delos,—at
Chios,—at Cyprus,—and at Athens. This shows how widely
the Homeric poems were diffused, from an early date,
throughout the Greek world, among Dorians and Ionians
alike. At Athens there was a special ordinance prescribing
that Homer should be recited (ῥαψῳδεῖσθαι) at the festival of
the Great Panathenaea, once in every four years[2]. This law
was probably as old as 600—500 B.C. It was further provided
that the competing rhapsodes at the Panathenaea should
recite consecutive parts of Homer, instead of choosing their
passages at random[3].

The passage in which Herodotus (5. 67) notices
the recitations at Sicyon is of interest as illustrating the
power of Homer over the popular Greek mind. Cleis-

---

[1] Hes. fr. 34 (Homer and Hesiod) ἐν νεαροῖς ὕμνοις ῥάψαντες ἀοιδήν
(cp. 'pangere versus'). ὕμνος itself is perh. ὕφ-νος (ὑφαίνω), 'web':
though in any case it seems unlikely that in Od. 8. 429 (ἀοιδῆς
ὕμνον ἀκούων) it was used with a consciousness of that sense.

[2] καθ' ἑκάστην πενταετηρίδα, Lycurgus Leocr. § 102.

[3] Acc. to Diogenes Laertius 1. 2. 57, Solon ἐξ ὑποβολῆς γέγραφε
ῥαψῳδεῖσθαι, οἷον ὅπου ὁ πρῶτος ἔληξεν, ἐκεῖθεν ἄρχεσθαι τὸν ἐχόμενον.
Acc. to the Platonic Hipparchus 228 B Hipparchus compelled the
reciters of the Homeric poems ἐξ ὑπολήψεως ἐφεξῆς αὐτὰ διιέναι :
i.e. in such a way that they should 'take one another up' consecutively.
The general sense of ἐξ ὑποβολῆς is clearly the same: the only question
is whether it means (1) 'from an authorised text,' or (2) 'with
prompting,'—each reciter having his proper cue given to him.

thenes, tyrant of Sicyon (600—570 B.C.), was bitterly
hostile to Argos. 'He put down the competitions of
rhapsodes,' Herodotus says, 'on account of the Homeric
poems, because Argives and Argos are celebrated almost
everywhere in them.' It has been thought that the
'Homeric poems' meant here were some poems specially
concerned with Argos, such as the lost epic called the
Thebais. But there is no reason why the reference should
not be to our *Iliad*, since in it 'Argives' is one of the collective names for the Greeks, and Agamemnon is lord of
'Argos and the isles.'

Homer-
idae.

5. In the island of Chios, there was a family or clan
called Homeridae, and it has generally been supposed that
they were rhapsodists; but this is doubtful. The Chian
Homeridae are first mentioned by Strabo (*circ.* 18 A.D.),
who says that they claimed descent from Homer, but does
not connect them with the recitation or study of Homeric
poetry. The term 'Homeridae,' as used by Pindar and
Plato, seems to have nothing to do with a gens in Chios, but
to mean simply 'votaries' or 'students' of Homeric poetry,
being equivalent to the more prosaic term 'Homerists'
('Ομήρειοι or 'Ομηρικοί)[1].

The
rhapsode
in the
fourth
century
B.C.

6. The hint in Herodotus as to Homer's power agrees
with the picture of the Homeric rhapsode in the Platonic
dialogue, the *Ion*. Here we see what the rhapsode's calling
was about 400—350 B.C. Ion, a native of Ephesus, is a professional rhapsode, who goes from city to city, reciting and ex-

[1] All that we know about 'Ομηρίδαι comes to this :—(1) The word
occurs first in Pindar *Nem.* 2. 2, 'Ομηρίδαι ῥαπτῶν ἐπέων ἀοιδοί, where it
has no special reference to a family in Chios. And the scholiast there
expressly recognises a general use of 'Ομηρίδαι to denote *rhapsodists* of
Homer who had no claim to be his *descendants ;* adding, however,
that 'Ομηρίδαι had *originally* meant such descendants—a statement for
which he perhaps had no ground except the form of the word itself.
Plato has the word 'Ομηρίδαι thrice (*Ion* 530 D, *Rep.* 599 E,
Phaedr. 252 B), always as = persons who concern themselves with the
Homeric poems. The scholiast on Plat. *Theaet.* 179 E (τῶν 'Ηρακλει-
τείων, ἢ ὥσπερ σὺ λέγεις, 'Ομηρείων), has 'Ομηρίδας φησὶ τοὺς 'Ηρακλει-

pounding Homer to large audiences. He has been attending
the festival of Asclepius at Epidaurus ; now he has come to
Athens to recite at the Panathenaea. On such occasions, the
rhapsode appeared on a platform (βῆμα), in a richly embroidered dress, with a golden wreath on his head. He recited Homer in a dramatic manner, with appropriate gesture
and declamation. Ion says that, when he recites, he feels
the strongest emotion: at the pathetic parts, his eyes fill with
tears ; at the terrors, his hair stands on end. He may have
an audience of 'more than twenty thousand;' and, after
all reasonable deduction, we must conclude that these
popular audiences were often very large indeed. As he
recites on his platform, the rhapsode beholds his own
moods reflected in the sea of upturned faces ; the hearers are
moved to wonder, to anger, or to tears. As Ion frankly puts
it to Socrates, a rhapsode whom his audience did not take
seriously—a rhapsode who merely made them *laugh*—would
have cause to look serious himself, for he would lose his pay.

The passage is a remarkable testimony to the intensity
with which the Greeks of the fourth century B.C. could still
enter into the spirit of Homer. They demanded that the
rhapsode should do something more than amuse them. He
must move them. He must bring the Homeric poetry home
to their hearts. On his part, the rhapsode Ion regards
himself and his professional brethren as more than reciters
or actors. They have an intellectual kinship with Homer ;
some measure of his spirit has descended on them. In
Ion's own phrase, they are 'possessed' by Homer. The
Platonic Socrates, with delicate irony, embodies this claim
in a simile. The Muse, says Socrates, is like the stone

τείους διὰ τὸ τῆς ἀεικινησίας δόγμα—showing that the *scholiast* understood 'Ομηρίδαι as='Ομήρειοι. (2) *A family or clan in Chios* called
'Ομηρίδαι is noticed by Strabo XIV. p. 645, who says that it was
so called ἀπὸ τοῦ ἐκείνου γένους, and that hence it was quoted by
the Chians in proof that Homer was a Chian. Harpocration. in
his lexicon, also mentions the Chian Homeridae, but notices that
their descent from Homer was not undisputed.

which Euripides has named the magnet, but which is usually called the stone of Heracleia. The poet is the first link in a magnetic chain; the audience is the last; the rhapsode is the link which connects them. The professional ancestors of Ion are such as Orpheus, or the Thamyris of the Iliad, or the Phemius of the Odyssey, whom Socrates calls 'the rhapsode of Ithaca.'

7. Ion devotes himself exclusively to Homer. He does not pretend to any thorough knowledge of Hesiod, for instance, or of Archilochus. Some rhapsodes, he says, give themselves to Orpheus or Musaeus; but the majority are occupied with Homer alone.

Was Homer ever sung? The rhapsode of Plato's time clearly did not *sing* Homer to music; the word ἄδειν is, indeed, used of Ion's performances (Plat. *Ion* 532 C, 535 A), but that word was applicable to any solemn recitation: thus Thucydides applies it to the reciting of an oracular verse (2. 53). Whether the *Iliad* or *Odyssey* was ever sung to music, is very doubtful. Once, certainly, there had been heroic lays which were really sung to the lyre. But the form of Homeric verse is ill-suited for that purpose. In the hymn to the Delian Apollo (verse 170) the reciter is supposed to carry a lyre: but this may have been conventional,—a symbol of legitimacy in the descent of the Homeric rhapsode's art from that of the 'aoidos.' Hesiod describes the Muses giving him a branch of laurel as the token of his vocation; and in the Hesiodic school of rhapsodists, at least, the wand or ῥάβδος—not the lyre—was usually carried.

The rhapsode as commentator. Besides reciting Homer, Ion interprets him. At the Panathenaea the competing rhapsodes recited continuously, each beginning where the last left off. Ion's comments, then, must have been given separately from his recitations, or else can have been combined with these only on occasions when he was the sole performer. It is evident from the Platonic dialogue that Ion's Homeric commentary had the form of continuous rhetorical exposition: he took pride in his fluency, and in the wealth, as he says, of his 'ideas about Homer.' 'I have embellished Homer so well', he declares, 'that his votaries ought to give me a golden crown.' Doubtless, like other men of that age, he dealt mainly with the allegories which a perverse ingenuity discovered in Homer.

8. The study of the poets in schools is described in Plato's *Protagoras*. When a boy goes to school, he is first taught his letters. As soon as he can read, he is introduced to the poets. The boys sit on benches, and the teacher 'sets before them' 'the works of good poets,' which they are required to learn thoroughly[1]. Evidently, then, the teaching was by manuscript copies which the boys had before them, and was not merely oral. The purpose was not only to form the boy's literary taste, or to give him the traditional lore: it was especially a moral purpose, having regard to the precepts (νουθετήσεις) in the poets, and to the praises of great men of old,—'in order that the boy may emulate their examples, and may strive to become such as they' (Plat. *Prot.* 326 A).

Homer in education.

9. From this point of view Homer was regarded as the best and greatest of educators. In Xenophon's *Symposium* (3. 5) one of the guests says :—' My father, anxious that I should become a good man, made me learn all the poems of Homer; and now I could say the whole *Iliad* and *Odyssey* by heart'. 'Homer, the prince of poets, has treated almost all human affairs. If any one of you, then, wishes to become a prudent ruler of his house, or an orator, or a general, or to resemble Achilles, Ajax, Nestor, or Odysseus'—let him study Homer (*ib.* 4. 6). Especially, as Isocrates says, Homer was looked upon as the embodiment of national Hellenic sentiment. No one else was so well fitted to keep the edge of Hellenic feeling keen and bright against the barbarian[2].

---

[1] Plat. *Prot.* 325 E παρατιθέασιν αὐτοῖς ἐπὶ τῶν βάθρων ἀναγιγνώσκειν ποιητῶν ἀγαθῶν ποιήματα καὶ ἐκμανθάνειν ἀναγκάζουσιν. ἐκμανθάνειν may imply committing portions to memory, a sense which the word has in *Legg.* 811 A.

[2] *Panegyricus* § 159.

Plutarch relates that Alcibiades, when a young man, once went up to a schoolmaster and asked him for a copy of Homer. The schoolmaster said that he had nothing of Homer's, whereupon Alcibiades struck him[1]. This story suggests the remark that, though Homer had a place in the education of very young boys no less than of older youths, it was better suited for the latter; and such, perhaps, was the view of the Homer-less schoolmaster. There is an amusing fragment of Aristophanes (from the 'Banqueters,' Δαιταλεῖς) in which an old man—a believer in the old orthodox system of education—examines his son on 'hard words in Homer' (Ὁμήρειοι γλῶσσαι), asking him 'what is meant by ἀμενηνὰ κάρηνα', and so forth. The young man, who represents new-fangled ideas and the new-born love of law-suits, retorts by examining his father on the archaic words in Solon's laws[2].

10.   In the *Frogs* of Aristophanes some of the poets are mentioned in connection with the special lessons which they severally teach. Orpheus teaches mystic rites, and abstinence from animal food. Musaeus gives oracles, and precepts for banishing pestilence. Hesiod is the poet of the husbandman. Homer is preeminently the poet of the soldier[3]. The rhapsode Ion, when cross-questioned by Socrates, is not absolutely certain that the study of Homer has made him a finished charioteer, or physician, or fisherman, or prophet; but he has no doubt whatever that it has made him a competent general. The Athenians, Socrates remarks, are sorely in need of such a general, and it is strange that they have not secured Ion's services; but Ion accounts for this by the Athenian prejudice against foreigners.

Plato's famous protest against the educational influence of the myths is pointed with especial force at Homer. But

---

[1] Plut. *Alcib.* 7 βιβλίον ᾔτησεν Ὁμηρικόν, εἰπόντος δὲ τοῦ διδασκάλου μηδὲν ἔχειν Ὁμήρου κονδύλῳ καθικόμενος παρῆλθεν.

[2] The point is curiously illustrated by Lysias (or. 10 §§ 15 ff.), who gives, from 'the old laws of Solon,' specimens of words obsolete in 400 B.C.

[3] Homer teaches τάξεις, ἀρετάς, ὁπλίσεις ἀνδρῶν (*Frogs* 1036).

it does not seem to have materially affected the place of Homer in Greek education. At the close of the first Christian century Dion Chrysostom speaks of the Homeric poems as still used in the teaching of children from the very beginning[1].

11. Herodotus remarks (2. 53) that Homer and Hesiod created the Greek theogony. They did this, he says, in four respects. They gave the gods their titles (ἐπωνυμίαι)—as Homer calls Zeus Κρονίδης, and Athene Τριτογένεια. They gave them their prerogatives (τιμαί),—as Poseidon is the sea-god, Ares the god of war, etc. They distinguished their arts or faculties (τέχναι), as Hephaestus is the artificer, Athene the giver of skill in embroidery, etc. They indicated their personal and moral characteristics, (εἴδη). The statement is true of Hesiod in the sense that the 'Theogony' is a storehouse of genealogical details. Homer affected the popular conception of the gods in a larger way. He traced types of divine character which established themselves in the Greek imagination. Sometimes, indeed, he was credited with a consciously didactic purpose in his delineation of the gods, even by writers who did not look for allegorical meanings. Thus Isocrates says that Homer feigns the gods deliberating, because he wishes to teach us that, if gods cannot read the future, much less can men[2].

Homer's influence on Greek religion.

12. A larger and a truer claim might be made for the work unconsciously wrought by the genius of the poet. Homeric mythology contains various elements, belonging to different stages of thought, and the fusion is imperfect. Coarse or grotesque traits are by no means wanting. But there is a complete absence of the grossest features common to all early mythologies. There are no amours of the gods in the shapes of animals; there is no Cronus swallowing his children, as in Hesiod. Such things abounded in the oldest Greek temple-legends, as Pausanias shows. Whatever the instinct of the great artist has tolerated, at least it

---

[1] εὐθὺς ἐξ ἀρχῆς, or. 11. p. 308.
[2] *Adv. Sophistas*, § 2.

has purged these things away. Further, Homer did the Greeks the inestimable service of making them conscious that their own religious sense was higher than their mythology,—a trait often observed in other races, and one which naturally tends to become more marked when it has received poetical expression.

The heroes. Homer was the ultimate authority concerning the heroes mentioned in the two great poems. Some of these heroes were objects of worship in the historical age. There is no trace in Homer of divine honours paid to men after death[1]. But the Homeric poems must have had a considerable influence, at least in a negative sense, on the various local cults of later times. As a general rule, the burden of proof would have been held to rest with any local priesthood who adopted a legend at distinct variance with Homer. On the other hand we must not overrate this restraining influence. In some cases, at least, it failed[2].

Greek view of Homer as a historian. 13. Homer was justly regarded by the Greeks as their earliest historian. But the historical character which they ascribed to him was not merely that which he could truly claim, as the delineator of their early civilisation. They held that his events and his persons were, in the main, real. This general belief was not affected by criticisms of detail, nor, again, by the manner in which the supernatural elements might be viewed. Thucydides differs from Herodotus in bringing down the Homeric heroes more nearly to the level of common men. But the basis of fact in Homer is fully as real to Thucydides as to Herodotus.

---

[1] Thus in the *Iliad* (3. 243) the Dioscuri are simply men who had died, and had been buried in Lacedaemon. The later notion of their alternate immortality appears in the *Odyssey* (11. 299—304). Hesiod first calls the heroes ἡμίθεοι (*Op.* 160); Homer never does so, except in *Il.* 12. 23, a verse which belongs to a late interpolation. He applies the name ἥρως (akin to Lat. *vir*) to any respected free man. The cult of ἥρωες is first mentioned by Pindar.

[2] A tomb of Castor was shown also at Argos (Plut. *Quaest. Gr.* c. 23). Again, the Homeric murder of Agamemnon (*Od.* 4. 530 ff.) and Oedipus-myth (11. 271 ff.) differ from the later versions.

Thucydides treats the Homeric Catalogue as a historical document,—exaggerated, perhaps, in its numbers, yet essentially authentic. He treats the Phaeacians as a historical people who had dwelt in Corcyra.

Appeals to the historical authority of Homer are not rare in Greek literature. Thus when the invasion by Xerxes was imminent, Sparta and Athens sent envoys to seek help from Gelon of Syracuse. Gelon said that he would help if he might lead. The Spartans replied that Agamemnon would groan if he could hear such a proposal; while the Athenians remarked that, according to Homer, it was Athens that had sent to Troy the best man of all to marshal an army,—Menestheus[1]. When the Athenians were contending with the Megarians for Salamis, they quoted *Iliad* 2. 558, where the Salaminian Ajax stations his ships with the Athenians (Arist. *Rhet.* i. 15). Pericles, in the Thucydidean funeral speech, says that the achievements of Athens render her independent of Homer's praise[2]. The point of the passage depends on the fact that Homer was the witness to whom Greek cities and families especially appealed in evidence of their prehistoric greatness; as Thucydides elsewhere contrasts the poor aspect of Mycenae in his own time with the past grandeur which Homer attests.

Ancient appeals to his authority.

14. As early as the seventh century B. C. other poems besides the *Iliad* and the *Odyssey* were popularly attributed to Homer. Callinus, who flourished about 690 B. C., believed Homer to be the author of an epic called the *Thebais*, as Pausanias tells us (9. 9. 5). It appears from Herodotus that an epic called the *Cypria* and another called the *Epigoni* were believed to be Homer's. Herodotus does not commit himself in regard to the *Epigoni*. But he denies the Homeric authorship of the *Cypria*, because he finds in it a statement which conflicts with the *Iliad*[3].

Poems ascribed to Homer in antiquity.

---

[1] Herod. 7. 159—161: cp. *Il.* 7. 125, 2. 552.

[2] Thuc. 2. 41 § 4: cp. 1. 10 § 1 (on Mycenae).

[3] Her. 2. 117 (*Cypria*): 4. 32 (*Epigoni*). In the *Cypria*, as Her. knew it, Paris reached Troy in 3 days from Sparta, whereas

This suggests how little these attributions probably regarded the evidence of style, language, or spirit. Unless there was some contradiction on the surface, the attribution could pass current, or could be left an open question. A comic poem called the *Margites* was ascribed to Homer by Aristotle[1]. Many other humorous pieces were called Homer's—the best known being the parody called the *Battle of the Frogs and Mice (Batrachomyomachia)*[2]. The so-called *Epigrams* anciently ascribed to him are short popular poems or fragments,—pieces of folk-lore which had acquired a half-proverbial character,—and, which, in some cases at least, are probably very old[3]. The 'Hymns' were also generally attributed to Homer. Thucydides (3. 104) quotes the Hymn to the Delian Apollo in

the *Iliad* (6. 290) sent him to Sidon—on the *same* occasion, as Her. assumes. Before the *Cypria* was incorporated into the Epic Cycle, it was altered (as we know from Proclus) in this very particular: a storm was brought in, which drove Paris to Sidon. The criticism of Her. had told.

[1] *Poet.* 4. The Μαργίτης was a feebly versatile person, who tried many things, but excelled in nothing. Only a few verses are extant, of which πόλλ᾽ ἠπίστατο ἔργα, κακῶς δ᾽ ἠπίστατο πάντα ([Plat.] *Alcib.* II. 147 B) is the most significant. The piece may have been as old as 700 B.C. Aristotle considers it the Homeric germ of comedy, as the serious epics were of tragedy.

[2] This mock-heroic piece, of which 305 verses are extant, cannot well be later than about 160 B.C., and was by some ascribed to Pigres, the brother (?) of Artemisia, *circ.* 475 B.C. It was doubtless on the strength of the really ancient *Margites* that later παίγνια were attributed to Homer.

[3] The 16 'epigrams,'—containing altogether 109 hexameter verses, —are subjoined to the older editions of Homer (as to Didot's). Of the 16, only 3 contain as many as 10 lines. The localities mentioned all belong to the West coast of Asia Minor (except that no. 16 speaks of Arcadia): viz. the Aeolian *Cymè* (2, 4): *Neonteichos*, a colony of Cymè on the river *Hermus* (1): Mount Ida (10): the Aeolo-Ionian *Smyrna*, and its river *Meles* (4): the Ionian *Erythrae*, opposite Chios (7), and Cape *Mimas* just N. of it (6): *Samos* (title of 12). Perhaps the most interesting is no. 4—a complaint by a poet who had come from Smyrna to Cymè,—had been ill-received,— and meditates emigrating.

reference to the Ionian festival at Delos, and expressly
identifies Homer with the 'blind man' there mentioned,
who 'dwells in rocky Chios.'

15. This leads us to the ancient notices of Homer's Notices
life. It is probable that nearly all of them are founded of Ho-
on poems which were generally ascribed to him, and which life.
were taken as containing bits of genuine autobiography.
This is clearly the case in regard to several of the legends
about his birth-place. The *Margites*, for example, spoke of
its author—'an old man, a divine singer,'—as coming to
Colophon. The Delian hymn sanctioned the claim of Chios.
One of the epigrams was held to vouch for Smyrna ; another
supported Cymè. Other competitors were Ios—a small
island of the Cyclades group, which stood alone in claiming
his grave—Rhodes—Salamis—Ithaca—Argos—Athens—
Thessaly—and Egyptian Thebes. But the favourites were
Smyrna, Chios, Colophon; and the ancient world gave a
decided preference to Smyrna[1]. Among the great Ionian
cities, Miletus is remarkable as *not* being connected by any
legend with Homer.

The extant Greek lives of Homer are all late,—pro- The
bably in no case earlier than about the second century A. D., 'Lives'.
a period fertile in rhetorical forgeries. The Life written
in Ionic which bears the name of Herodotus was obviously ascribed to him on the strength of the passage

---

[1] Antipater of Sidon (*circ.* 100 B.C.), in his epigram (*Anthol.
Planudea* 4. 296) puts the three strongest claimants first:—οἱ μέν σευ
Κολοφῶνα τιθηνήτειραν, Ὅμηρε, | οἱ δὲ καλὰν Σμύρναν, οἱ δ᾽ ἐνέπουσι
Χίον. Another epigram was ἑπτὰ πόλεις διερίζουσιν περὶ ῥίζαν Ὁμήρου, |
Σμύρνα, Ῥόδος, Κολοφών, Σαλαμίν, Ἴος, Ἄργος, Ἀθῆναι. Two other
versions of it, with lists partly different, occur in *Anthol. Plan.* 4. 297,
298. The best-known Latin couplet was 'Smyrna, Rhodos, Colophon,
Salamis, Chios, Argos, Athenae, | Orbis, de patria certat, Homere, tua'.
Egyptian Thebes is added in Lucian *Encom. Demosth.* § 9. Suidas gives
a prodigious list, including *Rome*. Strabo mentions Smyrna as τὴν ὑπὸ
τῶν πλείστων λεγομένην αὐτοῦ πατρίδα. See Geddes, *Problem of
Hom. Poems*, pp. 239 f. It is significant that the old myths (preserved
in the 'Lives') made Homer Μελησιγενής, | son of the river Meles at
Smyrna by a nymph Critheïs. Smyrna was Aeolo-Ionian.

in which he expresses a view as to Homer's age (2. 53),—
viz. that he had lived not much before 850 B. C. Some contemporaries of Herodotus, we may infer, assumed an earlier
date. It is to be noted that legend spoke of Homer's
poems as having been preserved and transmitted, not by a
son, but by a friend (some call him a son-in-law), Creophylus
of Samos—whose descendants, settled in Crete, afterwards
gave them to the Spartan Lycurgus. Here, perhaps, we may
recognise one of the earliest rhapsodes, who was also a poet.

Earliest traces of Homer.   The earliest trace of Homer in literature is the reference
to him in a lost poem of Callīnus, *circ.* 690 B. C., already
mentioned (§ 14) as reported by Pausanias. The earliest
mention of Homer's name in extant work is by the philo-
sopher Xenophanes of Colophon (*circ.* 510 B.C.), who says
that 'Homer and Hesiod have imputed to the gods all
that is blame and shame for men[1].' The earliest quotation from Homer is made by Simonides of Ceos[2], born
556 B.C., who quotes *Il.* 6. 148 as an utterance of 'the man
of Chios. '

Thus, while the belief of the ancient Greeks in
a personal Homer was unquestioning, his personality was
shadowy, and could be associated with inconsistent legends.
We have seen that a similar uncertainty prevailed as to
the criteria of his authentic work : any composition in
epic verse could be ascribed to Homer if it only seemed
sufficiently good of its kind. In a word, the attitude of
Greece towards Homer, before the Alexandrian age, was
wholly uncritical.

[1] *ap.* Sextus Empiricus *adv. Mathem.* 9. 193 πάντα θεοῖς ἀνέθηκαν
Ὅμηρός θ' Ἡσίοδός τε | ὅσσα παρ' ἀνθρώποισιν ὀνείδεα καὶ ψόγος ἐστί, |
κλέπτειν μοιχεύειν τε καὶ ἀλλήλους ἀπατεύειν. Timon the satirist
(270 B.C.) called Xenophanes Ὁμηραπάτης ἐπικόπτης (castigator of
Homeric fiction), unless, with Kühn, we read Ὁμηροπάτης (trampler on
Homer). Heracleitus, the contemporary of Xenophanes, is quoted by
Diog. Laert. 9. 1 as saying that Homer (and Archilochus) deserved to
be scourged (Heracl. fr. 119).

[2] Or Simonides of Amorgos (660 B.C.), as Bergk surmises from the
style (*Poet. Lyr.*, 3rd ed., p. 1146). Fr. 85 ἓν δὲ τὸ κάλλιστον Χῖος
ἔειπεν ἀνήρ· | οἵηπερ φύλλων γενεή, τοιήδε καὶ ἀνδρῶν.

16. But, though he was not yet a subject of critical study, he was already a cause of intellectual activity. In the sixth, fifth, and fourth centuries B.C. the Homeric poetry gave manifold occupation to ingenious or frivolous minds. Almost at the beginning of philosophical reflection in Greece the moral sense of some thinkers rebelled against the Homeric representation of the gods. The protest of Xenophanes has just been quoted. Hence arose the allegorising school of Homeric interpretation. Allegory afforded a refuge for the defenders of Homer. Theagenes of Rhegium, *circ.* 525 B.C., is mentioned as the earliest of the allegorizers[1]. He combined two modes of allegorizing which afterwards diverged,—the moral (or mental), and the physical: thus Hera was the air; Aphrodite was love. The moral allegorising was continued in the next century by Anaxagoras, who explained Zeus as mind, Athene as art. The physical mode was developed by Metrodorus of Lampsacus. Aristotle refers to the allegorizers as 'the old Homerists' (οἱ ἀρχαῖοι Ὁμηρικοί), and remarks that 'they see small resemblances, but overlook large ones' (*Metaph.* 13. 6, 7). The allegorizers of the classical age were equalled, or surpassed, in misapplied subtlety by the Neoplatonists of the third century A.D., who discovered their own mystic doctrines in Homer[2].

Allegorizing interpretation.

---

[1] Θεαγένης ὁ Ῥηγῖνος, ὁ κατὰ Καμβύσην γεγονώς, is named by Tatian *adv. Graec.* § 48 (quoted by Euseb. *Praep. Evang.* x. 2) at the head of a list of the earliest writers (οἱ πρεσβύτατοι) who dealt with inquiries as to Homer's 'poetry, birth, and date.' In Plato's time (cp. *Ion* 530 D) the highest repute for comment on Homer was enjoyed by Stesimbrotus of Thasos and Metrodorus of Lampsacus. They, as well as Theagenes and Anaxagoras, are among the commentators mentioned in the Venetian Scholia. Wolf well describes the method of the allegorizers: 'interpretatione sua corrigere fabulas atque ad physicam et moralem doctrinam suae aetatis accommodare, denique historias et reliqua fere omnia ad involucra exquisitae sapientiae trahere coeperunt' (*Proleg.* cxxxvi).

[2] Porphyrius (*circ.* 270 A.D.), the pupil of Plotinus, has left a choice specimen of this in his treatise Περὶ τοῦ ἐν Ὀδυσσείᾳ τῶν Νυμφῶν ἄντρου, an allegorizing explanation, from the Neoplatonic point of view, of the cave of the nymphs in the *Odyssey*.

17. Rhetorical dialectic also busied itself with Homer; sometimes by applying a kind of sophistical analysis, which aimed at detecting incongruities of thought or language. The sophist Protagoras (who applies this method to Simonides in Plato *Prot.* 339 A) objected to μῆνιν ἄειδε θεά, because Homer ought to have *prayed* the goddess to sing, instead of *commanding* her[1]. Sometimes, again, we hear of declamations on Homeric themes. Thus the sophist Hippias made Homer the subject of 'displays' at the Olympic festivals. In Plato's dialogue (*Hippias Minor*) he maintains that Achilles is the bravest, Nestor the wisest, and Odysseus the wiliest, of Homeric characters. Both these forms of treatment, the analytic and the declamatory, were probably used by the 'Homeromastix,' Zoilus of Amphipolis (*circ.* 280 B. C. ?), who was only the best known type of a class[2].

18. Another kind of interpretation applied to Homer was that which aimed at reducing the narrative to intelligible historical fact. Thucydides affords examples; as when he suggests that the Greek chiefs went to Troy, not because they had promised Helen's father to avenge her, but because the power of Agamemnon constrained them; or when he accounts for the ten years' resistance of Troy by the fact that the energies of the Greeks were partly given to providing themselves with food. We may suppose that this method was fully developed by Callisthenes (*circ.* 330 B.C.), who, in his history of Greece, devoted a separate book to the Trojan War. The same tendency often appears in later writers, as Polybius, Diodorus, Strabo, and Pausanias[3].

---

[1] εὔχεσθαι οἰόμενος ἐπιτάττει (Arist. *Poet.* 21.) See Spengel συναγ. τεχνῶν p. 45. Aristophanes burlesques the cavilling sophistical method in the verbal criticisms of Euripides on Aeschylus in the *Frogs*.

[2] Lehrs thinks that, of the works ascribed to Zoilus, the ψόγος Ὁμήρου was a declamation, while the κατὰ τῆς τοῦ Ὁμήρου ποιήσεως λόγοι ἐννέα (Suidas) were in the style of sophistical analysis.

[3] This 'pragmatizing' method is especially associated with the Sicilian Euhemerus (*circ.* 330 B.C.). But the distinctive point of his theory was that the *gods*, no less than the heroes, had been men,

Aristotle's comments on Homer, as illustrating the characteristics of epic poetry, have been noticed in Chapter I. (p. 4). He also wrote a treatise, now lost, on difficulties suggested by Homer[1].

19. But it was at Alexandria that Homeric criticism, in the proper sense, began. The materials for it, indeed, were for the first time brought together in such great libraries as those of Alexandria and Pergamum. Our knowledge of these materials is derived from the Homeric scholia.

The editions of Homer in the Alexandrian library were chiefly of two classes. (1) Editions known by the names of individual editors. The earliest recorded edition of this class is that by the epic poet Antimachus, of Clarus in Ionia (*circ.* 410 B. C.). Such editions are sometimes cited separately, by the editor's name; as ἡ Ἀντιμάχειος (*sc.* ἔκδοσις). Sometimes they are cited collectively, as 'the private editions' (αἱ κατ᾽ ἄνδρα)[2]. (2) The other great class consisted of editions known only by the names of cities. Such were the editions of Massalia, Chios, Argos, Sinope, Cyprus[3]. When cited collectively, these are called 'the

Alexandrian material for Homeric criticism.

who, after their deaths, were deified by admiring posterity. Thus such rationalising as that of Thucydides stops short of 'Euhemerism' proper.

[1] ἀπορήματα (or ζητήματα, or προβλήματα) Ὁμηρικά. Porphyry often refers to it in his own ζητήματα Ὁμηρικά: but the book from which he quotes cannot, as Lehrs thinks, have been the genuine work of Aristotle (*De Aristarchi Stud. Hom.* p. 222). The terms ἐνστατικοί ('objectors') and λυτικοί ('solvers', answerers) were especially applied to grammarians who impugned or defended points in Homer.

[2] Aristarchus had at least six such editions, ranging from the end of the 5th to the beginning of the 2nd cent. B. C.,—those of Antimachus, Zenodotus, Rhianus (the Alexandrian poet), Sosigenes, Philemon, and Aristophanes. Didymus (*circ.* 30 B. C.) had also that of Callistratus, and perhaps others. In Plut. *Alcib.* 7 a schoolmaster (*circ.* 420 B. C.) says that he has a Homer 'corrected by himself' (ὑφ᾽ αὐτοῦ διωρθωμένον). The anecdote suggests the scope which such διορθώσεις, at least in the earlier times, may have given to private caprice.

[3] ἡ Μασσαλιωτική, ἡ Χία, ἡ Ἀργολική, ἡ Σινωπική, ἡ Κυπρία (or Κύπριος). These five seem to have been the only 'civic' editions used

civic editions' (αἱ κατὰ πόλεις)[1]. There is no proof that they represented texts authorised for public use. It is more probable that their names merely indicated the places from which they had come, their revisers being unknown. Besides these two classes of editions, there were other texts designated as 'common' or 'popular' (κοιναί, δημώδεις). These are the same which are described as 'the more careless' (εἰκαιότεραι), being opposed to the more accurate or scholarly (χαριέστεραι).

The ancient vulgate.

Taken altogether, the copies known to the Alexandrians must have rested on an older *vulgate* text, of which the sources are unknown. This is indicated by the narrow limits of textual divergence. The Alexandrian critics notice only differences in regard to the reading of particular verses, or to omissions and additions of a very small kind. There is no trace of larger discrepancies or dislocations. Such, however, could not have failed to exist if there had not been a common basis of tradition.

20. The earlier activity of Homeric criticism at Alexandria belongs to the period from about 270 B. C. to 150 B. C., and is associated with three men—Zenodotus, Aristophanes, and Aristarchus.

Zeno-dotus.

Zenodotus, a native of Ephesus, was made Librarian of the Alexandrian Museum by Ptolemy Philadelphus, who reigned from 285 to 247 B. C. He published a recension of Homer, and a Homeric glossary ('Ομηρικαὶ γλῶσσαι). In the dawn of the new scholarship, he appears as a gifted man with a critical aim, but without an adequate critical method. He insisted on the study of Homer's style.; but he failed to

---

by Aristarchus. They are placed here in the order of frequency with which they are mentioned in the scholia. The editions of Massalia and Argos contained *Odyssey* as well as *Iliad*; in regard to the others, nothing is known on this point. The Cretan edition (Κρητική) probably was not used by Aristarchus. The Αἰολική (or Αἰολίς) is cited only for some variants in the *Odyssey*. See Ludwich, *Aristarchs Hom. Textkritik*, I. 4.

[1] Also αἱ ἀπὸ (or ἐκ, or διὰ) τῶν πόλεων: or simply αἱ τῶν πόλεων, or αἱ πολιτικαί.

place that study on a sound basis. One cause of this was
that he often omitted to distinguish between the ordinary
usages of words and those peculiar to Homer. In regard
to dialect, again, he did not sufficiently discriminate the
older from the later Ionic. And, relying too much on
his own feeling for Homer's spirit, he indulged in some
arbitrary emendations. Still, he broke new ground; his
work had a great repute; and, to some extent, its influence
was lasting.

21. Aristophanes of Byzantium (*circ.* 200 B. C.) was the Aristo-
pupil of Zenodotus, whom he followed (though not imme- phanes.
diately) in the office of Librarian. He, too, published a recension of Homer. There is no proof that his work was founded
on that of Zenodotus; and, in some respects at least, it seems
to have marked an advance. Aristophanes had more respect
for manuscript evidence. His wide erudition also enabled
him, in many cases, to defend readings which his prede-
cessor had too hastily condemned[1].

22. Aristarchus[2], a native of Samothrace, was a pupil Aristar-
of Aristophanes, and his successor in the headship of the chus.
Library. The first half of the second century B.C. is the
period to which his active life belonged, and the time of his
highest eminence might be placed about 160 B.C.

His contributions to Homeric study were of three kinds.
(1) συγγράμματα, *treatises* on special Homeric questions, sometimes polemical. (2) ὑπομνήματα, continuous *commentaries*

---

[1] In some cases where Zenodotus had expelled a verse from the
text (οὐδὲ ἔγραφε), Aristophanes was content to leave it in the text,
marking it with the obelus as spurious (ἀθετεῖν). The difference
between the two men is well illustrated by an example to which Lehrs
refers (p. 352). Anacreon describes a fawn as forsaken κεροέσσης...ὑπὸ
μητρός. Zenodotus wrote ἐροέσσης ('lovely'), on the ground that only
the males have horns. Aristophanes vindicated the text by showing
that the poets ascribe horns to hinds as well as to stags. Schol. Pind.
Ol. 3. 52: Aelian *Hist. An.* 7. 39.

[2] The principal authorities on Aristarchus are K. Lehrs *De Arist.
Studiis Homericis* (3rd ed., 1882); and A. Ludwich, *Aristarchs
Homerische Textkritik* (2 vols., 1884—5).

on the Homeric text. These seem to have been current, partly in a finished form, partly in the shape of rough notes, either made by himself for use in lectures, or taken down by his hearers. (3) ἐκδόσεις, *editions* of the Homeric text. He published two such[1]. The second appears to have been later than the commentaries, and to have closed his Homeric labours. In his text of Homer he used an apparatus of critical signs, forming a sort of critical short-hand or cipher, by which his readers could see at a glance when he thought a verse spurious,—when he thought that it was out of its right place,—or when it contained any point which he had illustrated in his commentaries. This system of signs had been partly used by the Alexandrians before him, and was further elaborated by later grammarians[2].

Characteristics of his work.

23. Aristarchus was the greatest scholar, and the best Homeric critic, of antiquity. Three general aspects of his work may be noted. (1) He carefully studied the Homeric

---

[1] Ammonius, the pupil of Aristarchus, wrote a tract, περὶ τοῦ μὴ γεγονέναι πλείονας ἐκδόσεις τῆς Ἀρισταρχείου διορθώσεως. Ludwich agrees with Lehrs in explaining this to mean, 'not more than *two.*' I confess that the explanation seems to me a little forced. Ammonius wrote also περὶ τῆς ἐπεκδοθείσης διορθώσεως. May he not have meant that the so-called second recension was only a modification of the first?

[2] The σημεῖα used by Aristarchus seem to have been six only. (1) The *obelus* (ὀβελός, or 'spit'), —, prefixed to a verse to indicate its condemnation as spurious (ἀθέτησις). This sign had already been used by Zenodotus and Aristophanes. (2) The *diplé* (διπλῆ), ⋗ (also ⊳, ⊳, or ⊲), a general mark of reference to the commentaries of Aristarchus, placed against a verse which contained anything notable, either in language or in matter. (3) The *dotted diplé*, (διπλῆ περιεστιγμένη,) ⋗, prefixed to a verse in which the reading of Aristarchus differed from that of Zenodotus. (4) The *asterisk* (ἀστερίσκος), *, when used alone, merely drew attention to a repeated verse. Thus it was prefixed to *Il.* 2. 180 because that verse is the same (*plus* δ') as 164. But if a repeated verse seemed to be spurious in one of the two places where it occurred, the *asterisk with obelus*, * —, was prefixed to that place. (5) The *antisigma*, Ɔ, and (6) the *stigmè* or dot (στιγμή), were used in conjunction. Aristarchus thought that *Il.* 2. 192 should be immediately followed by vv. 203—205. He prefixed the Ɔ to 192, and dots (for in Ven. A. the Ϲ must be an error, see Ludwich I. p. 209) to 203—205.

usages of words—recognising that criticism of the matter must be based on accurate knowledge of the language. Previous grammarians had dealt chiefly with rare or archaic words (γλῶσσαι). Aristarchus aimed further at defining the Homeric sense of familiar words—remarking (*e.g.*) that Homer always has ὧδε in the sense of 'thus' (never as = 'here' or 'hither'); that Homer uses βάλλειν of missiles, but οὐτάζειν of wounding at close quarters; φόβος, in the sense of 'flight'; πόνος, especially with reference to battle; Ὄλυμπος (in the *Iliad*), of the actual mountain. (2) In forming his text, he gave full weight to manuscript authority. When this test left him in doubt between two readings, he was guided by 'the usage of the poet[1].' So far from being rash in correcting the text, he appears to have been extremely cautious. In contrast with Zenodotus, he abstained from merely conjectural readings. He was even censured by later critics for excess of caution,—and perhaps with some reason[2]. (3) He commented on the subject-matter of Homer. He compared the Homeric versions of myths with those in other writers; and noticed characteristic points of the Homeric civilisation. He seems to have made a chart showing the topography of the Trojan plain and the Greek camp: and he notes (*e. g.*) that Homer means Thessaly by Ἄργος Πελασγικόν, and Peloponnesus by Ἄργος Ἀχαϊκόν[2].

Again, *Il.* 8. 535—537 had the *antisigma*, and 538—541 the *stigmè*, because the latter group seemed to repeat the sense of the former. The *stigmè* was also used alone as a mark of *suspected* spuriousness. Aristophanes used the κεραύνιον, T, as a collective *obelus* when several consecutive verses were adjudged spurious. The *dotted antisigma* ·)· was used by some to mark tautology. But these two signs were not Aristarchean.

[1] τὸ ἔθιμον τοῦ ποιητοῦ, Apollonius Dyscolus synt. p. 77 (Lehrs p. 360), who says that it was this which led Aristarchus to write πῶς δαὶ τῶν Τρώων φυλακαί, instead of πῶς δ' αἱ. (*Il.* 10. 408).

[2] Lehrs p. 363: 'Minime audax Aristarchus; imo mihi certum est si quid Aristarchus peccavit in contrarium peccasse.' Cp. *ib.* p. 359 (ὑπὸ περιττῆς εὐλαβείας οὐδὲν μετέθηκεν). Wolf (*Prolegomena* ch. 1) held that Aristarchus erred, through a too prosaic strictness (nimia

Didymus. 24. All that is now known concerning the work of Aristarchus has come down in a way which it is curious to trace. Early in the Augustan age, about 120 years after the death of Aristarchus, a treatise on his recension of Homer (περὶ τῆς Ἀρισταρχείου διορθώσεως) was written by Didymus, the Alexandrian grammarian, called Χαλκέντερος from his indefatigable industry. The object of Didymus was to ascertain the readings approved by Aristarchus. Why was such a work needed? It has been suggested that the authentic copies of the Aristarchean text may have perished by the fire in the Alexandrian War (47 B.C.). Such a supposition seems, however, hardly necessary. The criticism of Aristarchus had been gradually developed, and was embodied in a long series of works. It is possible that a clear and complete view of his opinions, with the grounds for them, could be obtained only by a careful collation of his various Homeric writings, and that this was the task which Didymus undertook.

Aristonicus. Aristonicus of Alexandria, a younger contemporary of Didymus, wrote a treatise on the critical signs employed by Aristarchus in the *Iliad* and the *Odyssey* (περὶ σημείων Ἰλιάδος καὶ Ὀδυσσείας). In this book he quoted the views of Aristarchus concerning the verses to which the various signs were prefixed.

Herodian and Nicanor. Herodian (*circ.* 160 A.D.) wrote a treatise on the prosody and accentuation of the *Iliad* (Ἰλιακὴ προσῳδία). Nicanor (130 A.D.) wrote a book on Homeric punctuation (περὶ στιγμῆς),—which, by the way, procured him the nickname of στιγματίας.

The Epitome. 25. About 200—250 A.D. it occurred to some student of the *Iliad* to make extracts from these four writers, Didymus, Aristonicus, Herodian, and Nicanor. He wove his extracts from them into a sort of continuous annotation on the Homeric text. Thus arose the Epitome of the four treatises, which, for shortness, we may call 'the Epitome.'

sobrietate acuminis), in *condemning* too much, but had the countervailing merit of *introducing* nothing rashly.

In the tenth century, a transcriber of the *Iliad* copied Codex Venetus A. the Epitome into its margin. By this time, the original form of the Epitome seems to have been a good deal disturbed, and some foreign elements had been mixed with it. The tenth century manuscript into which it was copied is the famous Codex Venetus A of the *Iliad*, no. 454 in the Library of St Mark at Venice[1]. The Epitome (especially the part of it relating to Didymus), as preserved in this one manuscript, is the principal source of all that we know in detail concerning the views of Aristarchus. This manuscript is also the only one which exhibits the critical signs of Aristarchus (§ 22). The scholia of A were first published by Villoison in 1788. They include scholia from other sources besides the Epitome. Of these we shall speak presently.

The recension of Aristarchus was never canonised in its entirety as a standard text. But his criticism seems to have had a much larger influence than that of any other single authority. It is probable that between about 200 and 400 A.D. a vulgate (the ancient common text modified in detail) was gradually formed by a comparison of his views, so far as they were known, with those of other critics[2]. The Aristarchean recension never canonised as a whole.

26. The division of the *Iliad* and the *Odyssey* into twenty-four books each, denoted by the letters of the alphabet, has sometimes been ascribed to Aristarchus, (who certainly used it in his recension,) sometimes to Aristophanes or to Zenodotus[3]. There is nothing to show who was the author of it. All we know is that it seems to have been already firmly established in the second half of the third century B.C. It is older, then, than Aristophanes or Aristarchus. The division into Books.

---

[1] The contents of the Epitome are thus described by its original author (cp. Ludwich I. p. 79) in a formula which the scribe of the Venetus A repeats at the end of each book :—παράκειται τὰ Ἀριστονίκου σημεῖα, καὶ τὰ Διδύμου περὶ τῆς Ἀρισταρχείου διορθώσεως, τινὰ δὲ καὶ ἐκ τῆς Ἰλιακῆς προσῳδίας Ἡρωδιανοῦ καὶ Νικάνορος περὶ τῆς Ὁμηρικῆς στιγμῆς.

[2] See W. Christ in the *Prolegomena* to his ed. of the *Iliad* (1884), p. 102.

[3] Cp. Ludwich II. p. 220, n. 195.

It is not demonstrably older than Zenodotus; but we cannot say more. One thing, at least, is plain. The arbitrary and mechanical neatness of the division bears the stamp of an age which sought to arrange its literary material in a way convenient for study and reference. This suits the view that the division originated at Alexandria in the third century B.C.

Writers of the fifth and fourth centuries B.C. indicate passages of Homer merely by mentioning the persons or events prominent in them. Thus, Herodotus (2. 116) denotes *Il.* 6. 289 ff. as 'the part where Diomede distinguishes himself' (ἐν Διομήδεος ἀριστηίῃ); Thucydides (1. 10) refers to the 'Catalogue' by ἐν νεῶν καταλόγῳ; Plato (*Crat.* p. 428 c) refers to *Il.* 9. 640 f. as occurring 'in the supplication' (ἐν λιταῖς); Arist. (*Poet.* 16) refers to *Od.* 8. 521 as ἐν Ἀλκίνου ἀπολόγῳ, (a title known also to Plato, *Rep.* 614 B, and properly confined to *Od.* bks. 9—12,) and to *Od.* 19. 386 ff. as ἐν τοῖς νίπτροις. Such descriptions sufficed for their purpose,—to recall a part of the poem to the memory; and, in most cases, coincide with the names of 'rhapsodies' or cantos into which the poem was divided for recitation[1]. Some recognised division of this kind is implied in the ancient regulations for a consecutive recitation at festivals (p. 77); and the record of it was preserved, at least for a time, after the alphabetical division into books had been adopted at Alexandria. The title of one canto sometimes covered more than one of our books; thus the Διομήδους ἀριστεία answered to book 5 and (part at least) of book 6. More often, one book comprises more than one canto; as book 2 includes the 'Dream' and the 'Catalogue.'

Crates and the Pergamene School. 27. The great library founded at Pergamum in Mysia by

[1] Several ancient titles of rhapsodies are preserved by Aelian *Var. Hist.* 13, 14. See Christ, *Proleg.*, pp. 1—7. Distinguish, as of a different class, phrases, invented for the occasion, by which short passages are sometimes indicated: as Thuc. 1. 9 ἐν τοῦ σκήπτρου τῇ παραδόσει (=*Il.* 2. 108 ff.): Arist. *Hist. An.* 9. 32 ἐν τῇ τοῦ Πριάμου ἐξόδῳ (=*Il.* 24. 316 ff.): Strabo 1. 17 ἐν τῇ πρεσβείᾳ (=*Il.* 3. 222 f.): Paus. L. 18. ᵕ ἐν Ἥρας ὅρκῳ =(*Il.* 15. 36 f.).

Eumenes II., early in the second century B.C., soon became a rival to the older institution at Alexandria; and a like rivalry developed itself between their schools of Homeric interpretation.   Crates, a native of Mallus in Cilicia, who was librarian of Pergamum in the time of Aristarchus, published Homeric commentaries[1].   The broad differences between the two schools turned mainly on two points.

(1) The Alexandrian school, represented by Aristarchus, was essentially a school of accurate grammatical scholarship. In particular, the Alexandrians aimed at laying down strict rules of declension and conjugation.   Now, Crates was far from denying the existence of ascertainable laws in language: like other Stoics, he gave much attention to correct idiom (Ἑλληνισμός).   But he maintained that the Alexandrians pushed their love of regularity too far.   While they insisted on the rules applicable to forms of words, Crates dwelt on the exceptions.   This is expressed in the statement that Aristarchus was the champion of 'analogy' (ἀναλογία), and Crates of 'anomaly' (ἀνωμαλία)[2].

'Analogy' and 'anomaly'.

(2) Aristarchus, as we have seen, did not neglect the questions arising immediately out of Homer's text, such as those of topography or antiquities.   But Crates went much further afield.   He conceived that Homeric criticism ought to embrace a mass of problems, philosophical, historical, or physical, which Homer suggested.   He found in Homer, not only allegories, but astronomical and cosmical theories which agreed with those of Stoic writers.   In his view, Homer's aim was not merely that of a poet (ψυχαγωγία), but pre-eminently that of a teacher (διδασκαλία), an opinion which enjoyed popularity in later times.   The readings of Crates are often mentioned, and are sometimes ingenious. But he and his school had comparatively little influence

---

[1] Ludwich (I. p. 43) agrees with Wachsmuth (*De Cratete Mallota*, p. 31, 1860) in doubting whether an *edition* of Homer was published by Crates.

[2] Wachsmuth *De Cratete* p. 15.   Gellius 2. 25 (where he refers to Crates and Aristarchus): ἀναλογία est similium similis declinatio... ἀνωμαλία est inaequalitas declinationum consuetudinem sequens.

on the Homeric text. Some pungent verses[1] record their scorn for the 'verbal scholarship' of Alexandria.

Demetrius. 28. Among other ancient scholars who dealt with Homer, Demetrius of Scepsis in the Troad (*circ.* 190 B.C.) deserves mention, on account of the fame enjoyed in antiquity by his labours on Homeric topography. His Τρωϊκὸς διάκοσμος, 'The Marshalling of the Trojans,' was a work in 30 books on the catalogue of the Trojan forces in *Iliad* 2. He agreed with the general opinion of the best ancient judges in rejecting the claim of the Greek Ilium (Hissarlik) to represent the site of Homeric Troy. His work, which is often quoted by ancient writers, appears to have united multifarious and exhaustive learning with a high degree of critical acuteness.

Eustathius. Midway between the ancient and modern studies of Homer, we find the great compilation of Eustathius, archbishop of Thessalonica in the latter half of the 12th century. It is entitled, Παρεκβολαὶ εἰς τὴν Ὁμήρου Ἰλιάδα καὶ Ὀδυσσείαν, *i.e.* 'excerpts' bearing on the poems[2]. The excerpts are made from a very large number of earlier writers, and include matter of every kind which can illustrate either the language or the subject-matter of Homer.

Scholia. 29. Many traces of ancient work on Homer, which would otherwise have been wholly lost, are preserved in the scholia, which, especially in the case of the *Iliad*, are most important. The scholia in the Codex Venetus (A) of the *Iliad* come mainly from two sources. (1) One of these is the Epitome of the four treatises, described above. The scholia from this source are the most valuable of all. (2) The other source appears to have been a large body of commentary, selected from various authors, and compiled

---

[1] By Herodicus (*ap.* Athen. p. 222 A), who describes the Aristarcheans. as 'buzzing in corners, busy with monosyllables': γωνιοβόμβυκες, μονοσύλλαβοι, οἷσι μέμηλεν | τὸ σφὶν καὶ σφωὶν καὶ τὸ μὶν ἠδὲ τὸ νίν. (Aristarchus had pointed out that Homer uses only μιν, not νιν.)

[2] παρεκβάλλειν meaning, 'to make extracts in the course of one's reading.'

later than the time of Porphyrius (*circ.* 270 A.D.), of whose
'Homeric Problems' much use was made.   In contrast
with the Epitome, the scholia from this second source deal
less with textual criticism, and more with allegorising
interpretations, mythology, or criticism of poetical style.
These scholia are found not only in Venetus A, but also,
with modifications, in some other MSS.[1]   For scholia on the
Odyssey, the most important MS. is the Harleianus, no.
5674 in the British Museum, of the thirteenth century.

30.   The results of inquiry into the ancient study of Our text
Homer, as briefly given in the foregoing pages, have more of Hom(
than a historical interest; more, too, than a critical value
in relation to particular points.   They establish a general
conclusion of the highest importance in regard to the
whole existing text of Homer[2].   It is as follows.

---

[1] These are: B=Codex Venetus no. 453 (11th, or perh. 10th,
cent.): V=cod. Victorianus no. 16 in the Munich Library (16th cent.?),
which has only scholia, without text: the cod. Townleianus in the
British Museum, which has been regarded as the source of V: and
L=codex Lipsiensis. See Ludwich 1. pp. 83 ff. The shorter scholia
variously known as the 'brevia,' 'vulgata,' 'minora,' or 'Didymi,'
(found in many MSS., and first published in 1517,) are almost worth-
less.

[2] The most important MSS. of the *Iliad* are the following. (1)
A=codex Venetus A, in Library of St Mark, no. 454 (10th cent.), a
parchment folio of 327 leaves. Some of the ancient leaves (19 in all)
have been lost in different places, and replaced by a late hand. Its
unique interest consists in the scholia, and the critical signs of
Aristarchus (as described above). Its text of the *Iliad* differs from that
of all our other MSS. in being more strongly influenced by the readings
of Aristarchus. (2) B: see last note. (3) C=Laurentianus 32. 5, in
the Laurentian Library at Florence (10th or 11th cent.). (4)
D=Laurent. 32. 15 (11th cent.): perhaps the best after A. (5) The
Townleianus: see last note.—Some fragments exist, older than A, but
of no critical importance; viz.: (1) three papyrus fragments, found in
Egypt, two of which are prob. of the 1st century B.C. (2) 800 lines
from different parts of the *Iliad*, in a 6th cent. MS. (the *Codex
Ambrosianus*), edited at Milan by Mai in 1819. (3) A *Syrian
palimpsest* (in the Brit. Museum) of the 6th or 7th cent., containing
3873 lines from books 12—16, and 18—24. For the text of the

We saw that the editions used by Aristarchus represented an older common text, or vulgate, and that one
of these editions was that of Antimachus (*circ.* 410 B.C.), in
which the variations appear to have been only of the same
small kind as in the rest.   Hence there is the strongest
reason for believing that the common text of 200 B.C.
went back at least to the fifth century B.C.   But Aristarchus
caused no breach in the transmission of that common text.
He made no wild conjectures or violent dislocations.   He
handed on what he had received, with such help towards
exhibiting it in a purer form as careful collation and study
could give ; and so, with comparatively slight modifications,
it descended to the age from which our MSS. date.   Our
common text, then, we may reasonably believe, is fundamentally the same as that which was known to Aristarchus ;
and therefore, in all probability, it rests on the same basis
as the text which was read by Plato and Thucydides.

Odyssey, the best MSS. are the *Harleianus* (see above in text); and
the *Augustanus* (*Monacensis*), no. 519 B in the Munich Library, of the
13th cent. according to the catalogue, but more probably of the 14th or
15th.   See La Roche, *Homer. Textkritik*, p. 481.

CHAPTER IV.

The Homeric Question.

1.   From an early time down to the fourth century B.C. other poems besides the *Iliad* and the *Odyssey* were currently ascribed to Homer (p. 85). The Alexandrian criticism of the third century B.C. arrived at the conclusion that the *Iliad* and the *Odyssey* were his only genuine works. At that point the ancient scrutiny of Homeric authorship may be said to have stopped. A few doubters went further; but they were almost unheeded.

The existence of ancient χωρίζοντες or 'Separaters'— who assigned the *Iliad* to Homer, and the *Odyssey* to another author—is known chiefly from the allusions to their opinion in the scholia of the Codex Venetus. The scholium on *Iliad* 12. 45 mentions a reading given by Aristarchus ἐν τῷ πρὸς τὸ Ξένωνος παράδοξον, in his 'Treatise against the Paradox of Xenon.' The other name mentioned in this connection is that of Hellanicus, a grammarian who was the elder contemporary of Aristarchus. It might be inferred from the existence of such a phrase as οἱ χωρίζοντες that Xenon and Hellanicus were merely the most prominent members of a literary sect which shared their view[1]. But we know nothing of their argument, except that it must have turned partly on style. They produced no effect on the ancient world. Seneca refers to the question in a tone which shows that it was well known in the first

The Chorizontes.

---

[1] See Bernhardy, *Gk. Lit.* II. 114.

century A.D., but that he regarded it as an unprofitable subtlety[1]. Suidas (*circ.* 1100 A. D.) is still able to say that the *Iliad* and *Odyssey* are undisputed[2] works of Homer. Ancient criticism was not, indeed, a stranger to the idea of 'many Homers'[3]. But that phrase had nothing to do with any modern theory of a composite authorship for the *Iliad* and the *Odyssey*. The 'many Homers' were merely poets who sought to associate their independent work with an illustrious name.

The modern 'Homeric Question.'

2. To the modern mind the *Iliad* and the *Odyssey* present two main problems. (1) The first is the fact of their existence. Greek literature opens with these finished masterpieces. We are certain that ruder work had gone before, but we know nothing of it. This phenomenon was less striking to the old Greeks than it is to us, since they knew no literature but their own. It is fully appreciated only when a comparison with other early literatures shows it to be unparalleled.

(2) The second problem depends on the inner characteristics of the poems. Each of them forms an organic and artistic whole. Yet each contains some parts which appear to disturb the plan, or to betray inferior workmanship. How can we account at once for the general unity and for the particular discrepancies?

These two problems—the external and the internal—are the basis of 'the Homeric question'[4]. The modern

---

[1] *De Brevitate Vitae* c. 13 (eiusdemne auctoris essent Ilias et Odyssea).

[2] ἀναμφίλεκτα (*s. v.* Ὅμηρος): justly noticed by Geddes as a proof that the Chorizontes 'were virtually silenced, and Antiquity refused to listen to them,' *Problem of the Homeric Poems*, p. 6.

[3] Ὅμηροι γὰρ πολλοὶ γεγόνασι ζήλῳ τοῦ πάλαι τὴν κλῆσιν λαμβάνοντες, Proclus (commentator on Hesiod), *ap.* Gaisford *Poet. Min. Gr.* iii. scholia, p. 6, quoted by Geddes (*Problem of the Homeric Poems* p. 7), who adds Eustathius 4, ὡς δὲ καὶ πολλοὶ Ὅμηροι. Proclus was arguing that Hesiod's competitor in the traditional 'contest' was not *the* Homer, but a Phocian Homer of later date.

[4] Cp. Volkmann, *Geschichte und Kritik der Wolfschen Prolegomena zu Homer*, c. 1.

discussion of the Homeric question, in a critical sense, began with Wolf's *Prolegomena* (1795).

3.   Before Wolf, we meet, indeed, with expressions of opinion by other scholars which might be regarded as partly anticipating his view.   But these, in so far as they were not mere conjecture, were based on the ancient tradition that the poems of Homer had been scattered until Peisistratus caused them to be collected.   A famous passage in Josephus (*circ.* 90 A.D.) was also suggestive. 'The present use of alphabetical writing,' Josephus says, 'cannot have been known to the Greeks of the Trojan war. The Greeks have no literature older than Homer; and Homer lived after the war. *And they say* (φασίν) *that even Homer did not leave his poetry in writing, but that it was transmitted by memory* (διαμνημονευομένην), *and after-wards put together from the separate songs* (ἐκ τῶν ᾀσμάτων ὕστερον συντεθῆναι): *hence the number of discrepancies which it presents*'[1].

Surmises before Wolf.

Here, Josephus does not merely reproduce the tradition of a collection by Peisistratus : he states that, in the received belief of the Greeks, Homer did not use writing ; that the poems had been transmitted only by memory ; and that this fact accounted for their inconsistencies.

4.   It was by such hints that the moderns before Wolf were guided.   Isaac Casaubon (1559-1614), referring in a note on Diogenes Laertius (9. 12) to the passage just quoted from Josephus, remarked that we could scarcely hope for a sound text of Homer, no matter how old our MSS. might be.   The Dutch scholar Jacob Perizonius in his *Animad-versiones Historicae* (1684) accepted the account given by Josephus, and brought it into connection with other ancient notices.

Bentley, in his 'Remarks' on the 'Discourse of Free-Thinking' by Anthony Collins (1713), supposes that a poet

---

[1] Josephus κατὰ 'Απίωνos 1. 2 p. 175 (Bekk.).   He is maintaining that no argument against the antiquity of the Jews can be drawn from the silence of Greek writers.

named Homer lived about 1050 B.C., and 'wrote' both the *Iliad* and the *Odyssey*. Each consisted of several short lays, which Homer recited separately. These lays circulated merely as detached pieces, until they were collected in the time of Peisistratus (*circ.* 550 B.C.), into our two epics[1].

5. Giambattista Vico, of Naples (born 1668), touched on the origin of the Homeric poems in some notes (1722) with which he supplemented his treatise on 'Universal Law'. Here his point was much the same as Bentley's in answer to Collins,—viz., that the Homeric poetry is not a conscious effort of profound philosophy, but the mirror of a simple age. In the second edition of his *Scienza Nuova* (1730) he went further. He there maintains that 'Homer' is a collective name for the work of many successive poets. These, in the course of many generations, gradually produced the poems which the Peisistratidae first collected into our *Iliad* and *Odyssey*. But, said Vico, though there were many Homers, we may say that there were pre-eminently *two*—the Homer of the *Iliad*, who belonged to North-east Greece (*i.e.* Thessaly), and the Homer of the *Odyssey*, who came later, and belonged to South-west Greece (*i.e.* the Western Peloponnesus and adjacent islands). Vico did not bring critical proofs of his propositions. He had no influence on Wolf or the Wolfians. Yet his theory must at least be regarded as a remarkable example of divining instinct[2].

[1] Cp. 'Bentley,' in 'English Men of Letters,' pp. 146 ff. Collins had maintained that the *Iliad* was 'the epitome of all arts and sciences,' and that Homer 'designed his poem for eternity, to please and instruct mankind.' Bentley replies, 'Take my word for it, poor Homer, in those circumstances and early times, had never such aspiring thoughts. He wrote *a sequel of songs and rhapsodies*, to be sung by himself for small earnings and good cheer, at festivals and other days of merriment; the *Ilias* he made for the men, and the *Odysseïs* for the other sex'. The phrase, '*a sequel*,' is ambiguous: as he goes on to say, 'These *loose songs* were not collected together in the form of an epic poem till Pisistratus' time, above 500 years after,' he perhaps did not mean, 'a *connected* series.'

[2] Professor Flint, in a monograph on Vico (1884), pp. 173—178, gives

But the work which had most effect, before the ap- Robert
pearance of the *Prolegomena*, was undoubtedly Robert Wood.
Wood's '*Essay on the Original Genius of Homer*' (1769)[1].
In one chapter he discussed the question whether the art
of writing was known to Homer, and answered it in the
negative. This view had never before been enforced by
critical argument. F. A. Wolf (born in 1759) read Wood's
essay in his student-days at Göttingen, and refers to it with
some praise in the *Prolegomena*[2]. Wood's doctrine about
writing became, in fact, the very keystone of Wolf's theory.

6. Wolf's 'Prolegomena'—a small octavo volume of Wolf's
280 pages—appeared at Halle in 1795, with a dedication to *Prole-*
David Ruhnken, as 'chief of critics'[3]. After some general *gomena*

a full and clear account of his Homeric theory. Without going so far
as to hold that Vico's 'discovery of the true Homer' (as he himself
called it) was 'a complete anticipation of the so-called Wolfian theory'
(p. 176), I agree in thinking that adequate justice has scarcely been done
to Vico. Wolf, some time after he had published the *Prolegomena*, had
his attention drawn to Vico by Melchior Cesarotti (translator of Homer
and Ossian). The review of Vico which he wrote in the *Museum
der Alterthumswissenschaft* I. 1807, pp. 555 ff., is contained in his *Kleine
Schriften* II. pp. 157 ff.

[1] Heyne, who was then by general consent the foremost 'humanist'
of Germany, reviewed Wood's Essay in enthusiastic terms (1770):
'We have to this day seen no one who has penetrated so deeply into
Homer's spirit.' The first German translation appeared in 1773, the
second (revised) in 1778,—both by Prof. Michaelis of Göttingen, where
F. A. Wolf finished his studies in 1779. Wolf (*Proleg.* xii) quotes the
2nd *English* edit. of 1775.

[2] c. xii., where, speaking of Wood's 'celebratissimus liber,' he
remarks (in a foot-note), 'plura sunt scite et egregie animadversa, nisi
quod subtilitas fere deest, sine qua historica disputatio persuadet, non
fidem facit.

[3] The volume of 'Prolegomena' is called 'I.', and we read 'Pars
Prima' at p. xxiv: but the second part, which was to have dealt with
the principles of Homeric textual criticism, was never published. It was
not Wolf's first contribution to Homeric studies, though he was only
36 when it appeared. In an essay addressed to Heyne (1779) he had
indicated his views as to the age of writing in Greece, which can be
traced also in his introductions to the *Iliad* and *Odyssey*, published in
1784. This was before the publication of the Codex Venetus by

remarks on the critical office in regard to Homer's text, Wolf
proceeds to discuss the history of the poems from about 950
B. C.—which he takes as the epoch of matured Ionian poetry
—down to the time of Peisistratus (about 550 B. C.).   The
four main points which he seeks to prove are the following.

(1) The Homeric poems were composed without the
aid of writing, which in 950 B.C. was either wholly
unknown to the Greeks, or not yet employed by them
for literary purposes[1].   The poems were handed down
by oral recitation, and in the course of that process suffered many alterations, deliberate or accidental, by the
rhapsodes.   (2) After the poems had been written down
circ. 550 B. C., they suffered still further changes.   These
were deliberately made by 'revisers' (διασκευασταί), or by
learned critics who aimed at polishing the work, and bringing it into harmony with certain forms of idiom or canons
of art.   (3) The *Iliad* has artistic unity ; so, in a still higher
degree, has the *Odyssey*[2].   But this unity is not mainly due

Villoison (1788).   Wolf greatly overrated the difference between the
ancient copies which the scholia of Venetus A disclosed; and reviewing
Villoison's edition in 1791, he spoke of it as *proving* that Homer
had long been transmitted by memory alone.

   [1] He insists that poems on such a scale as our Iliad and Odyssey
could not have been composed without writing.   Suppose it done,
however, the composer would have had no public, since he would have
had no readers :—' *The poems would have resembled a huge ship, built, in
some inland spot, and in days before naval science, by a man who had
neither engines and rollers for launching it, nor even a sea on which to
try his craft.*' (*Proleg.* c. xxv.)

   [2] Thus he says (*Proleg.* c. xxxi) that the 'carmina' which compose
the *Iliad* and *Odyssey*, 'though separated by the distance of one or two
centuries' [indicating that Wolf would have placed the latest rhapsodies
about 750—700 B.C.], 'deceive us by a general uniformity and resemblance of character.   All the books have the same tone, the same
moral complexion, the same stamp of language and of rhythm.'—And so
(*Proleg.* c. xxvii) he says that, in the *Odyssey* especially, the '*admirabilis
summa et compages* pro praeclarissimo monumento Graeci ingenii habenda
est,' but adds (c. xxviii) that this consummate piecing together is just
what we should *not* expect from an early poet who merely recited
single rhapsodies (singulas tantum rhapsodias decantantem).

to the original poems; rather it has been superinduced by their artificial treatment in a later age. (4) The original poems, from which our *Iliad* and our *Odyssey* have been put together, were not all by the same author.

7. But Wolf was far from denying a personal Homer. He supposes that a poet of commanding genius,—whom he often calls Homer,—'began the weaving of the web,' and 'carried it down to a certain point.' Nay more: this Homer wove *the greater part* of the songs which were afterwards united in the *Iliad* and the *Odyssey*. This is said in the *Prolegomena*[1]. But it is said still more emphatically in the *Preface* to his edition of the *Iliad*, published at nearly the same time[2]. '*It is certain that, alike in the Iliad and in the Odyssey, the web was begun, and the threads were carried to a certain point, by the poet who had first taken up the theme...Perhaps it will never be possible to show, even with probability, the precise points at which new filaments or dependencies of the texture begin: but this, at least, if I mistake not, will admit of proof—that we must assign to Homer only the greater part of the songs, and the remainder to the Homeridae, who were following out the lines traced by him.*'

Wolf recognised a personal Homer.

8. Nothing in this passage is more striking than Wolf's prophetic sense that it would never be possible to show exactly where different hands in the poems begin and end. When Wolf conceded 'the greater part' of the poems to one

---

[1] *Proleg.* c. xxviii *ad fin.* Atque haec ratio eo probabilior fiet, si ab ipso primo auctore filum fabulae iam aliquatenus deductum esse apparebit.—*Ib.* c. xxxi. At nonne omnibus erit manifestum...totas rhapsodias inesse quae Homeri non sunt, id est eius, a quo maior pars et priorum rhapsodiarum series deducta est?

[2] *Praefat.* p. xxviii. Quoniam certum est, tam in Iliade quam in Odyssea orsam telam et deducta aliquatenus fila esse a vate qui princeps ad canendum accesserat...forsitan ne probabiliter quidem demonstrari poterit, a quibus locis potissimum nova subtemina et limbi procedant: at id tamen, ni fallor, poterit effici, ut liquido appareat Homero nihil praeter maiorem partem carminum tribuendam esse, reliqua Homeridis, praescripta lineamenta persequentibus.

great poet, he was moved by his *feeling* for their internal characteristics—for the splendid genius, and the general unity. The whole argument for his *theory*, on the other hand, was essentially external. It was based on certain historical considerations as to early Greek civilisation and the development of poetical art. He has himself told us, in memorable words, how he felt on turning from his own theory to a renewed perusal of the poems. As he steeps himself in that stream of epic story which glides like a clear river, his own arguments vanish from his mind; the pervading harmony and consistency of the poems assert themselves with irresistible power ; and he is angry with the scepticism which has robbed him of belief in one Homer[1].

Objections to Wolf's view of writing.

9. In Wolf's theory, the fundamental proposition is the denial that a *literary* use of writing was possible for Greeks about 950 B. C. This proposition is, however, by no means so certain as Wolf held it to be.

The following points may be noticed. (1) It is true that the extant evidence from inscriptions does not go above the 7th century B. C. But it cannot be assumed that the monumental use of writing preceded its application to ordinary affairs. The opposite supposition would be more reasonable. And if the Greek writing on the earliest extant marbles is clumsy, this does not necessarily prove that the Greeks were then unfamiliar with the art of writing, but only that they had not yet acquired facility in carving characters on stone[2]. Long before that time, they may

---

[1] Preface to the Iliad, p. xxii: quoties...penitus immergor in illum veluti prono et liquido alveo decurrentem tenorem actionum et narrationum : quoties animadverto ac reputo mecum quam in universum aestimanti unus his carminibus insit color...vix mihi quisquam irasci et succensere gravius poterit, quam ipse facio mihi.

[2] Mr Hicks, in his excellent *Manual of Greek Historical Inscriptions*, observes (p. 1): 'Certainly the cramped and awkward characters of the earliest extant marbles prove that writing must have been an unfamiliar art in Greece as late as the 7th century B.C.' But, not to mention the earliest 'Cyclic' poems, it is certain that writing was

have attained to ease in writing on softer and more perish-
able materials, such as leaves, prepared skins[1], wood, or
wax.

(2) Commercial intercourse between the Greeks and
the Phoenicians, from whom the Greeks obtained their
alphabet, must have been frequent from about 1100 B. C., or
earlier still. The Phoenicians, as Josephus testifies, had
from the earliest age applied the art of writing, not only 'to
the recording of their public acts,' but also 'to the business
of daily life' (εἴς τε τὰς περὶ τὸν βίον οἰκονομίας καὶ πρὸς τὴν
τῶν κοινῶν ἔργων παράδοσιν)[2]. It would be strange if a
people so quick-witted as the Greeks, while advancing in
other parts of civilisation, had delayed to follow this example till so comparatively late a time in their development
as the 7th century B. C.

(3) We know, too, that long epic poems (some of those
known as the 'Cyclic'), which never enjoyed the same kind
of popularity as 'Homer,' came down from the 8th century
B. C.: and it is most improbable that these relatively obscure works should have been preserved without the aid
of writing. Such were the *Cypria* ascribed to Stasīnus, and
the *Aethiopis* of Arctīnus. It is certain that writing was used
by Archilochus and other poets of the early 7th century.
Wolf himself, indeed, admits the occasional use of writing
by poets as early as 776 B. C.[3]

already used by poets who lived in the early part of that century,—as
we shall see.

[1] Humboldt (*Atlas* p. 66) remarks that the old Mexican 'manuscripts'
are written on deer-skin, cotton cloth, or paper made from the maguy
plant, and suggests that, among the Greeks also, the use of prepared
skins may have preceded that of paper. We know that it preceded the
use of *papyrus*. Wolf's conjecture that the use of such skins (διφθέραι)
for writing came into Greek from the East only *circ.* 776 B.C. ('sub
epochum Olympiadum,' *Proleg.* p. lxii) lacks proof, and is against all
probability.

[2] κατὰ ᾿Απίωνος I. 6.

[3] Wolf is a thoroughly candid inquirer. In this case, while
admitting that Arctīnus and others of the early 8th century *wrote* their
poems, he seeks to distinguish such instances from an admission '*de*

(4) The balance of probabilities seems to be in favour of the view that the 'baneful tokens' (σήματα λυγρά) of *Iliad* 6. 168 denote some kind of alphabetical or syllabic writing[1]. But even if we granted that no allusion to writing occurs in the *Iliad* or *Odyssey*, no valid argument could be drawn from a silence which, in heroic poetry meant for recitation, may have been conventional.

(5) Herodotus, speaking of a Greek inscription which he saw at Thebes, supposes it to date from many centuries before his own time[2]. A similar belief as to the high antiquity of writing among the Greeks sometimes seems to be implied in the Greek literature of the 5th and 4th centuries B. C.[3]

(6) Recent researches have invalidated the argument

universa Graecia et paullo tritiore usu artis institutoque conscribendorum librorum' (*Proleg.* p. lxx). But (1) why is the line to be drawn precisely at 776 or 800 B.C.? And (2), supposing an earlier though not general use, why should not 'Homer' have been one of the few who used writing?

[1] πόρεν δ' ὅ γε σήματα λυγρά, | γράψας ἐν πίνακι πτυκτῷ θυμοφθόρα πολλά, | δεῖξαι δ' ἠνώγειν ᾧ πενθερῷ. On the tenth day the king of Lycia ᾔτεε σῆμα ἰδέσθαι (176), and 'when he had received the σῆμα κακόν' (178), set about slaying Bellerophon. Now, as Kreuser long ago pointed out (*Vorfragen über Homeros*, p. 202, 1828), πτυκτῷ implies that the σήματα (or σῆμα) could have been understood by Bellerophon himself; while πολλά suggests words rather than picture-writing. Ulrici (*Geschichte der Hellenischen Dichtkunst* 1. 226) argued that δεῖξαι is inapplicable to a letter: but why? As Thirlwall says (*Hist. Gr.* I. 502 ed. 1855) it could mean, '*produce*' (or better, perhaps, '*present*'). Mr Monro (note on *Il.* 6. 168, ed. 1884) inclines, with Mr Isaac Taylor (*Alphabet* II. 117), to the view in the text.

[2] Her. 5. 59 ταῦτα ἡλικίην εἴη ἂν κατὰ Λάϊον τὸν Λαβδάκου (*i.e.* considerably earlier than the Trojan war, according to the mythical chronology). It is obviously immaterial what the age of the ἐπίγραμμα really was. The point is that Herodotus felt no difficulty about his guess, but makes it in a matter-of-course way.

[3] Thus Eur. *Hipp.* 451 makes the Nurse say that the loves of the gods are known to all who have γραφὰς τῶν παλαιτέρων—plainly meaning (I think) writings, not paintings. So in *I. A.* 35 Agamemnon writes a letter. But this topic of the indirect literary evidence is so largely a question of tone and particular context that space excludes it here.

that the poems must have been made long before they were written because they often imply a *sound* (the 'digamma') which is not known to have been represented by a *letter* in any ancient MS. of Homer[1].

(7) The idea, 'a literary use of writing,' needs definition. If it is taken to mean, 'the wide circulation of writings by numerous copies, for a reading public,' certainly nothing of the kind seems to have existed before the latter part of the 5th century B. C. But suppose that a man had made a number of verses in his head, and was afraid of forgetting them. If he could use 'the Phoenician signs' well enough to keep his accounts (for instance), or other memoranda, why should he not write down his verses? That, in fact, is what Wolf allows that some men did as early at least as 776 B. C. The verses might never be read by anybody except himself, or those to whom he privately bequeathed them: but his end would have been gained.

10. Hence, with regard to the Wolfian theory, we have to discriminate between three things, which rest on different levels of probability,—memorial composition, oral publication, and oral transmission. Summary.

(*a*) As to memorial composition, it would be rash to deny that an exceptionally gifted man could have composed both our *Iliad* and our *Odyssey* without the aid of writing. Similar feats of memory are alleged[2]. (*b*) As to oral publication, it is certain that the Homeric poems were for centuries known to Greece at large mainly through the recitation of detached parts. (*c*) But a serious difficulty is raised by the theory of an exclusively oral transmission. The difficulty does not primarily concern the capacity of the human

[1] See below, § 39.

[2] The German poem *Parzival*, a romantic epic of more than 24,000 verses, was composed in the 13th century by Wolfram von Eschenbach, a poor knight, who confesses that he could neither read nor write. Lachmann appeals to this instance. But, before applying it to the Homeric question, it would be pertinent to know whether Eschenbach commanded the aid of an amanuensis.

memory. The true difficulty is that an approximately accurate tradition, through centuries, of such vast works,
without help from writing, implies an *organisation* of which
there is no trace.   The nearest analogies which can be
produced (as from India) presuppose a religious or sacerdotal basis.   We have to conceive of Homeric priesthoods
or colleges, in which, from generation to generation, lives
were concentrated on this task.   But such an idea is wholly
foreign to the free spirit in which Hellenic life and art were
developed; nor does it consist with what we know of the
wandering rhapsodes.

The general conclusion, then, is as follows.   It cannot
be proved that the Homeric poems were not committed to
writing either when originally composed, or soon afterwards.
For centuries they were known to the Greek world at large
chiefly through the mouths of rhapsodes.   But that fact
is not inconsistent with the supposition that the rhapsodes
possessed written copies.   On the other hand, a purely oral
transmission is hardly conceivable.

The
story
about
Peisis-
tratus.

11. Next to the argument from writing, Wolf's mainstay
was the story that the scattered poems of 'Homer' had
been first collected and written down at Athens in the time
of Peisistratus.   The story is both doubtful and vague.   It
occurs in no ancient writer before Cicero, and in no Greek
writer before Pausanias[1].   According to another tradition,

---

[1] Cic. *De Orat.* 3. 34. 137 qui primus Homeri libros, confusos
antea, sic disposuisse dicitur ut nunc habemus.   Pausan. 7. 26 Πεισίστρατος ἔπη τὰ Ὁμήρου διεσπασμένα τε καὶ ἄλλα ἀλλαχοῦ μνημονευόμενα
ἤθροιζετο.   One of the Βίοι Ὁμήρου (which are all, probably, of the
Christian era) quotes an inscription from a statue of Peisistratus at
Athens, in which he is made to say of himself—τὸν Ὁμηρον | ἤθροισα,
σποράδην τὸ πρὶν ἀειδόμενον.   It is most unlikely that such a statue
existed (after 510 B.C., at least), and the inscription is probably a late
rhetorical figment—possibly the prime source of the story which first
appears in Cicero.   A scholium on Plautus, found after Wolf's time and
edited by Ritschl (*die Alexandr. Bibliothek* p. 4) gives the story in a
somewhat more circumstantial form : *Pisistratus sparsam prius Homeri
poesim...sollerti cura in ea quae nunc exstant redegit volumina, usus ad
hoc opus divinum industria quattuor celeberrimorum et eruditissimorum*

which has older authority, it was Lycurgus who, about 776 B. C., first brought to Greece Proper a complete copy of the Homeric poems, previously known there only by scattered fragments[1]. Even if the story about Peisistratus is accepted, it does not disprove the original unity of the poems. When, for ages, rhapsodies had been recited singly, doubts might have arisen as to their proper sequence and their several relations to the plan of the great epic. It would satisfy the vague shape in which the story has reached us, if we regarded Peisistratus, not as creating a new unity, but as seeking to preserve an old unity which had been obscured[2].

hominum, videlicet Concyli (?), Onomacriti *Atheniensis*, Zopyri *Heracleotae, et* Orphei *Crotoniatae.* This was taken from a comment by Tzetzes (12th cent.), first published by Keil: Ὁμηρείους δὲ βίβλους... συντέθεικαν σπουδῇ Πεισίστρατος [? Πεισιστρατίδαι] παρὰ τῶν τεσσάρων τούτων σοφῶν· ἐπὶ κογκύλου, Ὀνομακρίτου τε Ἀθηναίου, Ζωπύρου τε Ἡρακλεώτου καὶ Κροτωνιάτου Ὀρφέως. Another form of the same statement has been published by Cramer from a Paris MS.: οἱ δὲ τέσσαρσί τισι τῶν ἐπὶ Πεισιστράτου διόρθωσιν ἀναφέρουσιν, Ὀρφεῖ Κροτωνιάτῃ, Ζωπύρῳ Ἡρακλεώτῃ, Ὀνομακρίτῳ Ἀθηναίῳ καὶ καγ ἐπὶ κογκυλω (sic). In the margin of the Par. MS. is Ἀθηνοδώρῳ ἐπίκλην [ἐπίκλησιν] Κορδυλίωνι: which probably means that Athenodorus Cordylion, a Pergamene grammarian of the 2nd cent. B.C., was taken to be the source of the statement. It has been conjectured that the corrupt words ἐπὶ κογκύλου and καγ ἐπὶ κογκυλω conceal ἐπικὸν κύκλον, and, being taken for a man's name, gave rise to the tradition of a *fourth* commissioner. But all this is doubtful. See Volkmann, pp. 333 ff. Onomacritus was 'a soothsayer, and editor (διαθέτης) of the oracles of Musaeus,' who was expelled from Athens by Hipparchus, son of Peisistratus, because the lyric poet, Lâsus of Hermione, had caught him in the act of interpolating an oracle (ἐμποιέων ἐς τὰ Μουσαίου χρησμόν—Her. 7. 6).

[1] Plutarch's view is that, *circ.* 776 B.C., the Greeks of Greece Proper knew the Homeric poems only by 'a dim rumour,'—a few persons possessing fragments,—until Lycurgus brought a complete copy from Crete, where the poems were preserved by the descendants of Homer's friend, Creophylus:—ἦν γάρ τις ἤδη δόξα τῶν ἐπῶν ἀμαυρὰ παρὰ τοῖς Ἕλλησιν, ἐκέκτηντο δ' οὐ πολλοὶ μέρη τινά, σποράδην τῆς ποιήσεως, ὡς ἔτυχε, διαφερομένης (*Lycurg.* c. 4). The tradition about Lycurgus was noticed as early as the 4th century B.C. by the historian Ephorus, and Heracleides Ponticus.

[2] Ritschl, accepting the Peisistratus story, so took it.

12. The Homeric poems, said Wolf, show art: 'but it is clear that this art is, in a way, comparatively near to nature; it is drawn from a native feeling for what is right and beautiful; it is not derived from the formal methods of a school[1]'. There we see the mark of Wolf's age, which was in revolt against the pedantic rules of pseudo-classicism. 'Art' was now associated with abstract canons on the 'unities,' and so forth: it was the synonym of frigid conventionality. 'Nature' was everything that put 'art' to shame; 'nature' was freedom, originality, genius[2]. The confusion of ideas involved in this antithesis long helped to complicate the Homeric question in Germany. Wolf was penetrated by the idea that the original Homeric poetry was the primitive poetry of the Greek people in its first youth, instinct with 'the divine force and breath of natural genius[3]' He justly says that 'Homer and Callimachus, Virgil, Nonnus and Milton,' are not to be read in the same spirit[4].

[1] *Proleg.* c. XII. p. xlii. In 1735 Thomas Blackwell, Professor of Greek at Aberdeen, had published his 'Inquiry into the Life and Writings of Homer.' It made a considerable impression both at home and abroad, because it hit the mind of the age by tracing Homer's excellence to the happy concurrence of *natural* conditions.

[2] This period of 'Sturm und Drang' ('storm and stress') was so nick-named from a drama of that title by F. M. V. Klinger (born 1752). Volkmann, in his work on Wolf already cited, regards the impulse as having come to Germany from the English literature of the 18th century:—'Genius and originality, those well-known watchwords of our Sturm-und-Drang period, are ideas propagated to us from England' (p. 14). Cp. G. H. Lewes, *Story of Goethe's Life*, p. 79: 'There was one universal shout for nature. With the young, nature seemed to be a compound of volcanoes and moonlight; her force explosion, her beauty sentiment. To be insurgent and sentimental, explosive and lachrymose, were the true signs of genius. Everything established was humdrum. Genius, abhorrent of humdrum, would neither spell correctly, nor write correctly, nor demean itself correctly. It would be German— lawless, rude, natural. Lawless it was, and rude it was,—but natural? Not according to Nature of any reputable type.'

[3] *Proleg.* p. cclv '*iuveniliter ludenti* populo...divina ingenii vi ac spiritu.'

[4] *ib.* p. xliii.

But it was an error on the other side to compare Homer
with the ruder forms of primitive song in other lands[1].
Our own early ballads, for instance, are rich in the pure
elements of natural poetry; in genuine pathos, especially,
they are often unsurpassed.   But the *Iliad* and the *Odyssey*
evidently show a larger mental grasp; they breathe a spirit
of finer strain; they belong to an order of poetry which
comes later in the intellectual growth of a people[2].   When
we endeavour to define Wolf's notion of a 'primitive' poet,
we find only one clear point.   He is a poet who, being
unable to write, and composing for hearers, not for readers,
makes only *short* poems.

13.   The permanent influence of Wolf's work has been Elasti-
due not only to the power with which his theory was stated, city of
but also to the tact with which he refrained from making it theory.
too precise.   His literary sense, keenly alive to those
inner traits which give each epic a general unity, mode-
rated his use of the external arguments.   He did not
attempt to define exactly how much the original poet had
done,—where the other poets come in,—or how they differ.

[1] The poems of 'Ossian' had been published by Macpherson in
1760—65. Wolf remarks that 'Homer—*i.e.* the old poetry of the
Ionians'—stands on a higher level than 'the Celtic songs of Ossian';
but he hints at two points of analogy :—(i) the poems are not all of one
age; (ii) they have not come down in their original form (*Proleg.*
p. cclv). Heyne on *Il.* 16. 53 (ed. min.) compared Homer's similes
with Ossian's.

[2] Wolf made many powerful converts among the German critics ;
but he was less successful with the poets. Schiller called the theory
'barbaric.' Wieland, though interested, was unconvinced. Klopstock
was decidedly adverse. Goethe went with Wolf at first (1796), but in
1798 wrote to Schiller, 'I am more than ever convinced of the unity and
indivisibility of the poem' (the *Iliad*). And in the little tract called
' Homer once more' (Homer noch einmal) that appears as his final
view (1821). Voss, at once scholar and poet, was also unpersuaded.

This illustrates Thirlwall's remark that critics who have studied
the details of the Homeric poems have usually favoured a manifold
authorship, while those who have dwelt rather on the general outlines
have tended to maintain an original unity. Poets usually look at Homer
in the latter way.

Hence 'Wolfian' is a somewhat elastic term, including several different shades of opinion. It has sometimes been applied too narrowly, and sometimes too widely.

The distinctively 'Wolfian' doctrine is simply this,—that the Homeric poems were put together, at the beginning of the Greek literary age, out of shorter unwritten songs which had come down from a primitive age. How many of these short songs we are to conceive as due to *one man*, was a minor point. Wolf's own belief, as we have seen, was that the poet who *began* the series of songs also composed *most* of them, and that the later poets continued the general line of his work.

Develop-
ments
of it.

The genuine developments of Wolf's theory have shown one of two general bents. One bent has been to make the first poet of the series *less* influential than Wolf did: this is represented by Lachmann. The other bent has been to make him still *more* influential: this is represented by Hermann.

Lach-
mann.

14. Lachmann dissected the *Iliad* into eighteen separate lays[1]. He leaves it doubtful whether they are to be ascribed to eighteen distinct authors. But, at any rate, he maintains, each lay was originally more or less independent of all the rest[2]. His main test is the inconsistency of detail. A primitive poet, he argued, would have a vivid picture before his mind, and would reproduce it with close

---

[1] *Betrachtungen über Homers Ilias* (Berlin, 1874).

[2] The only distinct exception admitted by Lachmann is his 16th lay (=*Iliad* bks. 18—22), which was intended as a sort of sequel to the 15th (=*Il.* 15. 592 to end of xvii), though by another poet. Generally, however, he concedes that, after the 11th book of the *Iliad*, the distinctness of the songs is less well-marked. Thus they all agree in representing Agamemnon, Odysseus, and Diomedes as placed *hors de combat*.

Grote says that any admission as to the later songs being adapted to the earlier is 'a virtual surrender of the Wolfian hypothesis' (*Hist. Gr.* vol. II. p. 233 *note* 1). This is not so. Wolf conceived the later poets as carrying on the 'threads' of the first and chief weaver (see p. 109). Wolf's criticism on Lachmann would have been that the latter underrated the general unity which the epics now exhibit.

consistency. He also affirms that many of the lays are utterly distinct in general spirit[1]. Lachmann had been prepared for analysing the *Iliad* by previously trying his hand on the *Nibelungenlied*, in which he discovered twenty independent lays[2]. Unfortunately for the analogy, later researches have made this view of the *Nibelungenlied* improbable.

The arbitrary character of such a theory as Lachmann's is shown by the plurality of such theories. Köchly, too, has dissected the *Iliad* into sixteen lays besides books 9 and 10[3]. But Köchly's lays are not Lachmann's. The two operators take different views of the anatomy. A 'theory of small songs' (*Klein-Lieder-Theorie*), whatever special form it may assume, necessarily excludes the view that any one poet had a dominant influence on the general plan of the poems.

15. Hermann, on the other hand, developed Wolf's view more in Wolf's spirit[4]. Hermann clearly perceived one difficulty which Wolf had left unexplained. The weaving of the Homeric web was begun, said Wolf, by the first and chief poet, who carried it down 'to a certain point': then others continued it. But why should they have continued it only within such narrow limitations? Why did they confine themselves to a few days in the siege of Troy? Why did they sing the 'return' of no hero except Odysseus? Because, said Hermann, the great primitive poet ('Homer') had not simply carried a web down to a certain point. Rather, making large use of earlier materials, he had produced the original sketch of our *Iliad* and the original sketch of our *Odyssey* ('*Ur-Ilias*,' '*Ur-Odyssee*'). The task

[margin note: Hermann.]

---

[1] 'ihrem *Geiste* nach höchst verschiedene Lieder' (*Fernere Betrachtungen* etc., p. 18, § xxiii).

[2] *Ueber die ursprüngliche Gestalt des Gedichts von der Nibelungen Noth*, Berlin, 1816.

[3] *Iliadis Carmina XVI. Restituta edidit Arminius Köchly Turicensis*, 1861.

[4] *Dissertatio de Interpolationibus Homeri* in his *Opuscula*, vol. v. p. 52 (1834). *Ueber Homer und Sappho ib.* VI. pars I. p. 70 (1835). *De Iteratis apud Homerum, ib.* VIII. p. 11 (1840).

of after-comers was not to carry on a line of texture, but merely to complete a design within fixed outlines.

In accordance with the Wolfian view of a primitive poet, Hermann conceived each of these poems as short. But though 'of no great compass,' the two poems excelled all other productions of their age in 'spirit, vigour, and art.' The poets who came after Homer, down to the time of the 'Cyclic epics' (*i.e.* to about 800 B.C.), confined themselves to engrafting new work on the original *Iliad* and *Odyssey*. This work took chiefly three forms. (1) They added passages imitated from Homer, even repeating whole verses or groups of verses. The opening of *Iliad* 8 was in Hermann's view an instance of such imitation. (2) They expanded passages of the original poems: thus the fight of the gods in *Iliad* 21 was expanded from *Iliad* 20. 56—74. (3) Generally, they retouched or recast the original poems in such a way as to invest them with a new aspect. When Hermann spoke of '*interpolation*' in Homer, he did not mean *only* the insertion of verses. Writing in Latin, he used 'interpolation' in its Latin sense,—'furbishing up'[1]. These later poets would have had no audience, he argued, if they had stepped beyond the charmed circle traced by the primitive Homer. And lest the potency of the spell should seem too marvellous, he made a further supposition. Homer's work was not only supreme in merit, but new in kind. The bards before him had been wholly didactic. He was the first who sang the deeds of heroes. This assumption is improbable in itself; and, if granted, would not suffice to explain why two heroic themes should have monopolised the epic activity of centuries.

Re-
action.   16. Thus far we have seen Homer identified with the

[1] Hermann defined his own use of the term in a letter to Ilgen, prefixed to his ed. of the Hymns (1806) p. viii : 'Interpolationem autem dico non modo quam nunc plerique intelligunt, quae est *in adiectione novorum versuum*, sed quam antiqui appellabant, cuius est omnino *rem veterem nova specie induere*.' (Cp. Cic. *ad Q. Fr.* ii. 12 *togam...interpolet*, 'have his toga whitened anew.')

primitive epics of short unwritten lays.   That is the funda- The
mental idea common to Wolf and the genuine Wolfians, as epopee
Lachmann and Hermann.   We now turn to a radically view.
different conception, and one which is nearer to the
truth.   In this, Homer is no longer the primitive bard.
He is the great poetical artist who, coming after the age of
short lays, frames an epic on a larger plan.   He is the
founder of epopee.

    This view found an able exponent in G. W. Nitzsch, Nitzsch.
who represents the first effective reaction against the
Wolfian theory[1].   He pointed out that some of the 'Cyclic'
epics, dating from the seventh and eighth centuries B.C.,
presuppose our *Iliad* and *Odyssey* in something like their
present compass and form[2], being designed as supplements
or introductions to the Homeric poems[3].   He showed that
the Greek use of writing was presumably older than Wolf
had assumed, and might have been used to help the
memory long before there was a reading public.

    'By Homer,' says Nitzsch, 'I understand the man who
made a great advance from the various smaller songs by older

---

[1] *De Historia Homeri maximeque de scriptorum carminum aetate
meletemata* (Hanover, 1830—1837. Supplementary parts were published
at Kiel in 1837 and 1839).   His earliest contribution to the Homeric
question was his *Indagandae per Homeri Odysseum interpolationis
praeparatio* (1828).   Among his earlier Homeric writings may be
mentioned also the article 'Odyssee' in the 'Allgemeine Encyclopädie'
(1829).   His *Sagenpoesie der Griechen* appeared in 1852 : his *Beiträge
zur Geschichte der epischen Poesie*, in 1862.

[2] *De Hist. Hom.* p. 152.   He refers to (1) the *Aethiopis* and *Iliu
Persis* of Arctinus, (2) the *Cypria*, (3) the *Nosti* of Hagias, (4) the *Little
Iliad* of Lesches, (5) the *Telegonia* of Eugammon.   When these poems
were written, we must concede, he says, *Iliadem et Odysseam ambitu
ac forma in universum tales iam ac tantas extitisse, quantas hodie
habemus.*

[3] The first vol. of F. G. Welcker's 'Der Epische Cyclus oder
die homerischen Dichter'—the book which first threw a clear light
on the 'Cyclic' epics—appeared at Bonn in 1835 (2nd ed., 1865):
the second vol. in 1849.   Nitzsch's position was much strengthened by
Welcker's results.

bards which treated of the Trojan war, and shaped the
'*Iliad*'—which previously had dealt only with the 'counsel
of Zeus'—into our *Iliad* on 'the wrath of Achilles.'...In
this poem, I fancy that much from older songs was retained.
The *Odyssey* was the work, perhaps, of the same poet, older
sources being used in a similar way.' But in the *Odyssey*,
Nitzsch adds, we see the poet's originality more fully than
in the *Iliad*. The *Odyssey* was the first great epic of its
kind,—*i.e.* dealing with a complex series of romantic
adventures. And the details of embellishment in the
Odyssey were almost all due to the author himself.

Thus Nitzsch conceives Homer as a very ancient poet,
and as one with whom an epoch begins. He found a number
of *short* lays about Troy. He achieved a work of a new
kind by building up, partly from these, a large epic on
the wrath of Achilles. Minor interpolations and changes
were made afterwards. But our *Iliad*, mainly the work
of one man, and our *Odyssey*, perhaps by the same
author, had taken substantially their present shape considerably earlier than 800 B.C.

Grote. 17. Grote accepts the essential part of Nitzsch's view[1].
He conceives Homer as belonging to the second, not the
first, stage in the development of epos,—as the composer of
the large epic, not as the primitive bard of the short lays.
But he thinks that our *Iliad* has outgrown the plan of the
large poem as originally composed. That poem was on the
wrath of Achilles: it was an *Achilleid*. Another poet, or
poets, aimed at converting it into a poem on the war of
Troy generally,—an *Iliad*. Whole rhapsodies were added
which have no strict relation with the *Achilleid* proper, and
interrupt or unduly prolong it.

---

[1] *Hist. Gr.* c. xxi. vol. II. p. 234: 'The age of the epos is followed
by that of the epopee—short spontaneous effusions preparing the way,
and furnishing materials, for the architectonic genius of the poet...
Such, in my judgement, is the right conception of the Homeric epoch—
an organising poetical mind, still preserving that freshness of observation
and vivacity of details which constitutes the charm of the ballad.'

The original *Achilleid* consisted only of books 1, 8, and 11 to 22 inclusive, ending with the slaying of Hector by Achilles. Books 2 to 7 inclusive, 9, 10, 23 and 24 were added with the view of making this *Achilleid* into an *Iliad*. In book 1 Zeus promises to punish the Greeks for the affront to Achilles : why does he do nothing to fulfil his promise till book 8 ? Books 2—7 are simply 'a splendid picture of the war generally.' Then in book 9 (the embassy) the Greeks humble themselves before Achilles, and he spurns them; this is unseemly,—nay, shocking to the 'sentiment of Nemesis'; and in book 16. 52—87 Achilles speaks as if no such supplication had been made to him. Book 10, though fitted to its place, is a detached episode, with no bearing on the sequel. Book 23 (the funeral games for Patroclus) and book 24 (the ransoming of Hector's corpse) 'may have formed part of the original Iliad,' but are more probably later additions.

18. Grote's arguments against the several 'non-Achillean' books have very different degrees of force. Book 10, though composed for its present place, is unquestionably later than any other large part of the *Iliad*. The language gives many indications of this[1]; and the characteristic nobleness of the *Iliad* here sinks to a lower style and tone. As to book 9, Grote's objection to its general fitness is over-strained. Achilles is possessed by a burning resentment : it is not enough for him that the Greeks should confess their fault; they must smart for it. But Grote is right in saying that book 9 cannot have been known to the composer of book 16. 52—87. Book 9 certainly

'Achilleid'.

Estimate of Grote's theory.

---

[1] See Monro, *Il.* I.—XII., p. 354. Among them are, some perfects in κα from derivative verbs, as βεβληκεν : μιγήσεσθαι (365), the only 2nd fut. pass. in Homer, except δαήσομαι (in *Od.* 3. 187, 19. 325): νῦν (v. 105) as='now': clear instances of the article used in a post-Homeric way: several words for armour and dress which occur nowhere else in Homer (as καταῖτυξ, σαυρωτήρ, ἐκταδίη, κτιδέη); and some words frequent in the Odyssey, but not elsewhere found in the *Iliad* (as δόσις, φῆμις, δόξα, ἀσάμινθος).

did not belong to the original form of the poem. It has traits of language and of matter which bring it nearer to parts of books 23, 24, and even 10, while they separate it from the body of the *Iliad*[1].

It is in regard to book 8 that Grote's theory is most decidedly at fault. He makes it part of his original *Achilleid*. But it stands in the most intimate poetical connection with book 9. The reverses of the Greeks in book 8 lead up to the embassy in 9, and the poet intended them to do so. And this fact agrees with the proofs in book 8 itself that its origin was later than that of the greater part of the *Iliad*. A large proportion of its verses has been borrowed or adapted from other parts of the *Iliad*, or from the *Odyssey*[2].

Books 2—7 delay the story, and almost certainly did not belong to the first form of the poem; but everything indicates that these books (excepting the 'Catalogue' in book 2) must have been among the earliest additions to it; and they are unquestionably older than book 8, whose poet has imitated them. Grote is right in regarding books 23 and 24 as additions to the original poem. But they stand on different levels. Book 24 is in the highest Homeric strain, and, if not contemplated in the first design of the poem, is at least entirely in unison with it. The games in book 23 are an addition by an inferior and probably later hand.

19. Few things in Homeric criticism are more interesting than to consider *how* Grote was led to form his theory, with book 8 for its pivot. He was looking for the earliest sign of Zeus fulfilling the promise made in book 1, and discomfiting the Greeks. He found this in book 8, and thence inferred that, in the original 'Achilleid,' book 8 immediately

[1] Examples are—ὥστε with infin. (42); the impers. δεῖ (337) : the mention of Apollo's shrine at Pytho (Delphi, 405): the mention of Egypt (382): the use of Ἑλλάς in a large sense, as at least = Northern Thessaly (447)—all unique in the *Iliad*.

[2] On book 8 see Christ's *Prolegomena* to the *Iliad*, pp. 69 f.

followed book 1. Now, there are two distinct moments in the *Iliad* at which the tide of war turns against the Greeks. One is book 8. The other is book 11. Grote saw that books 9 and 10 were later than the original form of the poem. But he omitted to observe that the poet who abased the Greeks before Achilles in book 9 would have felt the necessity of first discomfiting them in war; that, therefore, book 9 would account for book 8; and that the primary form of the poem becomes both simpler and more intelligible if we suppose that, in it, book 1 was once closely followed by book 11. That such was the case, the results of more recent studies strongly tend to show.

Grote recognised that the books which he rejected from the original Achilleid were, in large part, of high intrinsic excellence. 'Amongst them are comprehended some of the noblest efforts of the Grecian epic.' He also held that they were of practically the same date as the Achilleid itself :—'they belong to the same generation.' The *Odyssey*, in his belief, was the work of one author, who was distinct from the author of the Achilleid, but coeval with him,—their age being 'a very early one, anterior to the first Olympiad' (776 B.C.)[1]. *Source and age of the non-Achillean books.*

20. Accepting Grote's definition of the Achilleid, Geddes[2] has maintained that the non-Achillean books of the *Iliad* were composed by a later poet, the author of the *Odyssey*. He 'engrafted on a more ancient poem, the Achilleid, splendid and vigorous saplings of his own, transforming and enlarging it into an Iliad, but an Iliad in which the engrafting is not absolutely complete, where the 'sutures' are still visible.' The kinship between the *Odyssey* and the 'non-Achillean' books of the *Iliad* (*i.e.* 2—7, 9, 10, 23, 24) is recognised especially (1) in the mode *Geddes.*

---

[1] Grote *Hist. Gr.* vol. II. pp. 236, 262, 273.

[2] *The Problem of the Homeric Poems.* By William D. Geddes, LL.D., Professor of Greek in [now Principal of] the University of Aberdeen. (Macmillan, 1878.)

of presenting Odysseus, Hector, Helen, and some other persons; (2) in the aspects of the gods and their worship, (3) in ethical purpose; (4) in local marks of origin,—the traces of an Ionian origin being common to the *Odyssey* with the non-Achillean books of the *Iliad*, and with those alone.

It can scarcely be questioned that the *Odyssey*, while bearing the general impress of the same early age as the *Iliad*, belongs to a somewhat later part of that age. We have seen some tokens of this in Chapter II. Nor can it be doubted that many real affinities exist between the *Odyssey* and the later books of the *Iliad*. But it is less easy to decide how far these traits are due to a single mind, to the influence of a school, or to the traditional form of epic material. On any view, the work of Geddes will always rank as a very able and original contribution to the question[1].

W. Christ.   21. A view of the *Iliad* which is in some measure conservative, and which aims at reconciling divergent theories, has been fully expounded by Christ, in the *Prolegomena* to his edition of the text (1884). The following is an outline of it.

A great poet, Homer, composed a number of epic lays, intended to be recited separately, and therefore to some extent independent, but also connected by an organic plan which was definitely before his mind. The 'old,' or original, *Iliad* consisted of these lays, and formed a whole complete in itself. It contained the quarrel of Agamemnon and Achilles (bk. I. 1—305); the resolve of Zeus to avenge Achilles (bk. I. 306—end); the exploits of Agamemnon, his wounding, and the rout of the Greeks (bk. II. 1—595); the sally of Patroclus to help the Greeks, and his slaying by Hector (bks. 16 and 17); the return of Achilles to the war,

---

[1] Of especial interest are the chapters on the 'Local Mint-marks (XVIII.—XXI.), showing how the traits which indicate personal knowledge of European and Asiatic Hellas respectively are distributed in the poems.

his routing of the Trojans, and his slaying of Hector (bks. 18—22, excepting some large interpolations).

This 'old' *Iliad* was, however, amplified in many ways; partly by its author, Homer; partly by poets to whom he had entrusted 'the keeping, reciting, and publishing' of his poem.   Christ calls these poets 'Homeridae,' and conceives Homer as 'the founder of their clan' ('conditor gentis').

22.   To distinguish between the additions made to the 'old' *Iliad* by Homer himself, and those made by the 'Homeridae,' is, he thinks, as difficult as to distinguish 'between the genuine and the spurious elements in Mozart's *Requiem.*'   However, he can discern at least four main groups of additions.

(1)   The earliest additions consisted, roughly, of bks. 2, 3, 4, 5, *minus* the 'Catalogue' in bk. 2.   The object was to gratify the 'Aeolian and Ionian fellow-citizens of Homer' by praises of ancestral chiefs.

(2)   Then those parts of bks. 5 and 6 which relate to Sarpedon and Glaucus were added from a similar motive. Christ dwells on the fact that in the *Iliad* we have two sets of Lycians; the northern, neighbours to Troy, and led by Pandarus; and the southern, under Sarpedon and Glaucus. The latter, with their chiefs, were brought in to please Ionians claiming descent from Glaucus.

The building of the wall at the Greek camp was now invented, in order to give occasion for the splendid scenes of assault and repulse.   Books 12, 13, 14 (part), and 15 were added.

(3)   Another poet now sought to perfect the *Iliad* by connecting its parts more closely; by adding the embassy to Achilles; and by closing the poem with the ransoming of Hector's corpse.   He added books 7, 8, 9, the latter part of 11 (from 596), 19 (to 356), 23 (to 256), and 24.   Such a book as 24 had, indeed, been part of the original Homer's design.

The *Iliad* was now complete in its enlarged form.   All

this had been done 'some time before' *circ.* 800 B.C.: Christ
is dubious as to the number of poets, but thinks that, including the original Homer, there were not more than four.

(4) The 'Homerid rhapsodes' further added some
passages, which were composed while the epic art still
flourished. Such are the part assigned to Phoenix in bk. 9;
bk. 10 (the Doloneia); the making of the armour in bk. 18;
the fight of Achilles and Aeneas in bk. 20 (75—352). Lastly,
some tasteless rhapsodes made minor additions, and, among
other things, thrust the 'Catalogue' into bk. 2. The additions of this fourth group were made in the 8th and
7th centuries B.C.

23. Dr Christ divides the *Iliad* into 40 lays, which follow
each other in the order of our text, and were meant to be recited in that order, though composed (as we have seen) at
various times. The *Iliad* had been committed to writing, he
thinks, before the time of Peisistratus, but only in these
separate lays, with separate titles. Peisistratus first caused the
series to be committed to writing as a single ordered whole.
It will be seen that Christ somewhat resembles Hermann
(whose work on 'interpolation' he admires) in his way of
conceiving the relation between Homer and post-Homeric
additions. His reasoning is strict, yet not rigid. Much
of it deals with points on which it is hopeless to expect
general agreement[1]. But he has greatly strengthened
the general conclusion that the *Iliad* is an *enlargement* of an
epic by a great poet, who worked on a great but comparatively simple plan, leaving room for others to complete or to
complicate it[2]

Texture
of the
Odyssey.

24. The closer unity of plan in the *Odyssey*, as compared
with the *Iliad*, has been recognised by every modern critic
from Wolf onwards. In some degree, this greater unity is a

[1] As, indeed, he feels; *Proleg.* p. 95: 'Sed haec sunt altioris
indaginis, quae vereor ut umquam omnibus plane persuaderi possint.'

[2] A feature of peculiar value in Christ's edition is the analysis of his
40 lays in what he regards as the chronological order of their composition,—showing in detail how each was related to the rest, whether
as model or as imitation (*Proleg.* pp. 57—78).

necessary result of the generic difference between the two poems. The person of Odysseus knits together all the parts of the *Odyssey* more strictly than the wrath of Achilles could knit together all the parts of an *Iliad*. But, over and above this, it is clear that in the dove-tailing of the *Odyssey* we see the work of one mind. The question is whether we can discern different bodies of original material which the single constructor used.

With regard to the composition of the *Odyssey*, the most Kirchelaborate and ingenious view which has yet been put forward hoff. is that of Kirchhoff. It is as follows. There was a very old poem on the 'Return of Odysseus' (Νόστος 'Οδυσσέως). It contained the adventures of the hero on his homeward voyage down to his landing in Ithaca, and answered roughly to our books 5, 6, 7 (greater part), 9, 11 (greater part), and 13 (to v. 184). The 'Return' was not a mere folk-song. It was an epic poem, composed, probably, long after the epic art had been matured.

Later, but still before 800 B.C., another poet composed a sequel to the 'Return,' telling the adventures of Odysseus *after* his arrival in Ithaca. This sequel consisted of bks. 13 (from v. 185) to 23 (v. 296) inclusive, excepting bk. 15. (Book 23. v. 296 is the point at which Aristarchus thought that the genuine *Odyssey* ended.) The author of the sequel used a number of popular epic lays, but lacked the skill to blend them into a perfect unity. Hence many contradictions and inequalities remain. But he carried the fusion at least so far that we can no longer clearly separate the original lays.

The sequel never existed apart from the old 'Return.' The 'Return' and the sequel together formed a single poem. Kirchhoff calls this poem 'the older redaction' of the *Odyssey*,—older than *circ.* 800 B.C.

About 660 B.C. a third poet took up the work. The framework of the *Odyssey* was already complete. But this new poet wished to incorporate with it some other lays of the same group. He wished also to give it a better ending.

He added the adventures of Telemachus (bks. 1—4)[1]; bks.
8, 10, 12[2], 15, 23 (from v. 297), and 24. In doing this, he
freely altered or mutilated the text of the 'older redaction.'
Thus arose the 'later redaction,' which is our *Odyssey*, save
for some small interpolations by later hands.

25. Kirchhoff's arguments are given partly in a continuous
commentary on the text, partly in short essays. A brief
summary would be unjust. The strength of his case depends
essentially on the cumulative force of a great number of
subtle observations[3]. Even those who cannot accept his

[1] Kirchhoff regards the first 87 verses of bk. 1 as having formed
the exordium of the original Νόστος. The Telemachy begins at
bk. 1. 88. A curious discrepancy of time between the Telemachy
and the rest of the poem had long ago been noticed. Telemachus
leaves Ithaca on the evening of the 2nd day after the *Odyssey*
opens, intending to be absent not more than 12 days (2. 374 ff.:
cp. 4. 632). He reaches Sparta on the evening of the 5th day of the
poem, and is left there by the poet on the morning of the 6th, purposing
to return at once, as his companions at Pylos are awaiting him (4.
595 ff.). Then book 5 turns to Odysseus : who at last reaches Ithaca on
the 36th day of the poem (13. 119). But Telemachus returns to Ithaca
one day later than his father : *i.e.* on the 37th of the poem, and the
36th of his own absence. (Mure, *Hist. Gk. Lit.* I. 440 ff.) Geddes
(p. 32) suggests an interesting possibility—viz., that the poet may
originally have intended to send Telemachus on from Sparta to the
court of Idomeneus in Crete,—a visit which would account for the
superfluous days. In *Od.* I, after v. 93, in which Athene says that she
will send Telemachus to Pylos and Sparta, some ancient copies read,—
κεῖθεν δ' ἐς Κρήτην τε (κεῖθεν δὲ Κρήτηνδε?) παρ' Ἰδομενῆα ἄνακτα· | ὃς
γὰρ δεύτατος ἦλθεν Ἀχαιῶν χαλκοχιτώνων.

[2] Books 10 and 12—now part of the narrative given by Odysseus to
Alcinous—were adapted (Kirchhoff thinks) from lays in which the poet
told the story in the third person. Book 9 and the old part of book 11
had always been in the first person ; and the third poet had to suit the
new books to their place.

[3] In estimating Kirchhoff's view, undue prominence has sometimes
been given to one of his particular arguments, which is easily answered
—that in the Νόστος Odysseus is in his prime, and in the 'sequel' is an
old man. The transformation is due to Athene's magic (13. 429);
and her wand cannot well be explained as a device for harmonising the
two poems.—It has been noticed that in *Od.* 13. 399 the hero's hair is

theory in detail must (I think) allow that he has proved two general propositions, or at least has shown them to be in the highest degree probable. (1) The *Odyssey* contains distinct strata of poetical material, from different sources and periods. (2) The poem owes its present unity of form to one man; but, under this unity of form, there are perceptible traces of a process by which different compositions were adapted to each other.

Against Kirchhoff's theory, Niese[1] has re-asserted the view which had previously been general,—that the *Odyssey*, nearly in its present form, had been completed before 776 B.C. But the influence of Kirchhoff's work, especially in Germany, has been deeply felt, and is not likely to diminish. It is in the *Iliad*, however, that the main interest of the Homeric question must always be centred. The *Odyssey* problem is not only different, but less importunate. In the *Odyssey* we have a poem which owes at least its existing shape to a single hand, and which, notwithstanding the patent or latent discrepancies, can be read without the question of a complex origin being forced upon the mind. Further analysis is less interesting than in the case of the *Iliad*, while it is also necessarily more difficult.

26. The history of early epics in other languages is a source from which illustration of the Homeric question has been sought. But the history of such epics is often itself more or less obscure. And, from the nature of the case, the only illustration which can be expected is of the most general kind. Before any definite solution of the Homeric problem could derive scientific support from such analogies, it would be necessary to show that the particular conditions under which the Homeric poems

auburn (ξανθός), in 16. 176 it is *dark* (κυάνεος),—as also in 6. 231, unless the ὑακίνθινον ἄνθος is an image merely for curliness, not for colour. Note that, on Kirchhoff's view, this would be a case of the author of the 'sequel' contradicting *himself*; for both 13. 399 and 16. 176 are his.

[1] *Entwickelung der homerischen Poesie* (Berlin, 1882), pp. 222 ff.

appear in early Greece had been reproduced with sufficient
closeness elsewhere.   Still, it is necessary for the student of
Homer to know the general scope of such comparisons,
if only in order to control the arguments drawn from them.
Among the early epics which offer some general resemblance
to the Homeric poems, the following are the principal.

27. (1) The *Mahābhārata* and the *Rāmāyana*.   Of
these two great Sanscrit epics, the latter has been compared to the *Odyssey*, because (a) the interest is concentrated upon a single hero, Rama; and (b) the structure
has greater unity[1].   The *Mahābhārata*, on the other hand,
so far resembles the *Iliad* that (a) the heroic interest
is more divided, and (b) there are stronger traces of
its having been put together, at least to some extent,
from parts originally distinct, and of different dates[2].
As the *Odyssey* is now generally believed to be, as à whole,
later than the *Iliad*, so, according to one view, the *Rāmāyana* is later than the greater part of the *Mahābhārata*.

28. (2) The early French romances of chivalry, or 'Chansons de Geste.'   These, which are traced back to the eleventh
century, represent 'the earliest form which finished literature took in France[3],' just as the Homeric poems stand at
the beginning of Greek literature.   Like Homer, they were
a native growth.   Like Homer, they were recited.   The
composer, or 'trouvère,' was usually a distinct person from
the reciter, or 'jongleur,' who corresponded to the Greek
rhapsode.   As a type of the 'Chansons de Geste' may be
taken the *Chanson de Roland*, of the eleventh century,
which is a sort of French Achilleid.   It opens when
Charlemagne has been warring for seven years against the
Saracens in Spain , and after its hero, the French Roland,

[1] As Grote says that the *Odyssey* was 'moulded at one projection,'
so Lassen (*Indisch. Alth.* i. 584) says that the Rāmāyana is 'from
a single mould' (*aus einem Gusse*).

[2] 'Es kann keine Frage seyn, dass wir im Mahābhārata Stücke aus
sehr verschiedenen Zeiten, wie sehr verschieden an Inhalt und Farbe
vor uns haben' (Lassen *l.c.*).

[3] Saintsbury, *Short History of French Literature*, ch. 11. p. 10.

has been slain in the Pyrenees, the poem relates the doom
of a false knight who had betrayed him to death. The
'Chansons de Geste,' it has been supposed, had been preceded by short historical ballads called 'cantilenae,' which
were worked up in the 'Chansons.' But the 'cantilenae'
are lost; and the theory lacks good evidence[1]. Were it
otherwise, then the 'cantilenae' would have been analo-
gous to the short heroic lays ($\kappa\lambda\acute{\epsilon}a$ $\mathring{a}\nu\delta\rho\mathring{\omega}\nu$) which appear
to have preceded the Homeric epics.

29. (3) The poetic *Edda* of Iceland[2]. This is a
collection of poems, most of which date probably from
the 8th or 9th century, some of them being merely
fragments of longer heroic lays which are not extant.
They deal with the myths and religious legends of
early Scandinavian civilisation. But they do not form
a single epic. Gathered, probably, from oral tradition,
long after they were composed, they were thrown together,
in a body which has no poetical unity, about 1100 A.D.
Thus, if any inference could properly be drawn from the
Edda, it would be that short separate poems on cognate
subjects can long exist as a collection, *without* coalescing
into such an artistic whole as the *Iliad* or the *Odyssey*.

30. (4) The *Nibelungenlied* (or *Der Nibelunge Nôt*[3]).
As the Homeric poems give an artistic form to older legends,
so the German romantic epic is only the final shape of a

---

[1] The Homeric theories of Wolf and his followers suggested similar
theories in regard to the Chansons de Geste, as M. Paul remarks
(*Recherches sur l'Épopée française*, p. 65).

[2] The name *Edda* is borne by two entirely distinct bodies of ancient
Icelandic writings. One is the poetic *Edda* noticed above. The other,
to which the name is more anciently and properly given, is the prose
Edda, a miscellaneous collection of writings, ascribed to Snorri
Sturluson, the most eminent of early Scandinavian writers, and probably
completed about 1222. See Mr F. W. Gosse in the *Encycl. Brit.*
(9th ed.) vol. VII. p. 649.

[3] The Nibelungen are a race of mysterious and supernatural beings.
Siegfried, the hero of the poem, has carried off a great treasure of gold
and gems from two princes of the Nibelungen-land, to whom it had
been bequeathed by their father, the king Nibelung. The subject

Teutonic saga which had appeared in many earlier forms. So far, Lachmann's view (1816) was plausible, that it had been put together about 1210 A.D. from twenty old ballads. But the view now generally received is that of Prof. K. Bartsch. The *Nibelungenlied* was written, by one man, about 1140,— the lines ending in assonances, not in rhymes. About 1170 another poet partially introduced rhyme instead of assonance: and between 1190 and 1200 this process was completed, in two distinct recensions, by two different hands. One of these has preserved the original form more closely than the other[1]. Thus, if we could argue at all from the case of the *Nibelungenlied*, the argument would tell against the Wolfians, and in favour of such a view as that of Nitzsch, described above.

31. (5) The *Kalewala* of Finland. This is a kind of epic poem, called from 'Kaleva,' a happy land, three heroes of which struggle against foes from the land of cold and the land of death. It was the *Kalewala* that suggested Longfellow's *Hiawatha*. It embodies the old folk-lore of the Finns, and existed only in scattered songs, preserved by memory alone, until they were collected and written down early in this century. Dr E. Lönnrot, the chief collector, published 12,000 verses in 1835, and in 1849 a new edition of 22,793[2]. Here, then, is a case seemingly in favour of Lachmann—Dr Lönnrot answering to Peisistratus or his commission. But, on the other hand, the texture of the *Kalewala* is said to be of a very loose kind: it has not unity of plot in at all the same sense as the *Iliad* and the *Odyssey* have it[3] The *Kalewala* could not,

of the epic is the 'doom' or curse which this enchanted hoard brings on its possessor, as exemplified in the ill-starred loves of Siegfried and the heroine Kriemhild, and in the sequel thereof.

[1] See Mr. James Sime in *Encycl. Brit.* (9th ed.) vol. XVII. p. 476.

[2] See Mr. J. S. Keltie, in *Encycl. Brit.* (9th ed.) vol. IX. p. 219.

[3] 'It has none of the unity of structure which we find in Homer, but ranges over the whole life of the hero, from his birth to his disappearance in extreme old age': Mr. Monro in *Journal of Philology*, vol. XI. p. 59.

of course, be cited as an instance of an epic arising from a fortuitous or spontaneous aggregation of songs: the editor would naturally seek to give them such unity as he could. And it further fails to prove that mere combining and editing can form an artistic whole out of originally distinct songs, even though concerned with closely-related themes.

32.   (6)   The Persian epic, the *Shahnamah*, or 'Book of Kings,' is a history of Persia in 60,000 verses, based on old popular legends[1]. It is wholly the work of Firdousí (a name assumed by Abu 'l Cásim Mansúr), who completed it in 1009 A.D.   It claims notice here as supplying perhaps the fairest illustration for the ancient view of the Homeric epics as wholly the work of one man, in this respect—that the *Shahnamah* became the popular national epic of Persia almost as the Homeric poems became the national epics of Greece.

33.   (7)   The early war-poetry of England.   In such pieces as the '*Battle Song of Brunanburh*' (937 A.D.) and the '*Song of the Fight at Maldon*' (991 A.D.) there are several traits which might remind us of Homer[2].   The Maldon song is about as long as one book of the *Iliad*.   If twenty-four such songs had grown into one English epic, taking unity from a central theme, that would have been an English *Iliad*.   According to the primary relation of the songs to each other, it would have offered an analogy favourable to the view of Wolf, of Hermann, or of Lachmann.   But in our country, as in others, we fail to find any true parallel to the case of the Homeric poems.   These poems must be studied in themselves, without looking for aid, in this sense, to the comparative method.

[1] See the article on Firdousí, by the late Prof. E. H. Palmer, in the *Encycl. Brit.* (9th ed.) vol. IX. p. 225.

[2] Referring to the Song of Maldon, Mr. Stopford Brooke says:— 'In the speeches of heralds and warriors before the fight, in the speeches and single combats of the chiefs, in the loud laugh and mock which follow a good death-stroke, in the rapid rush of the verse when the battle is joined, the poem, though broken,—as Homer's verse is not,—is Homeric.' (*Primer of English Literature*, p. 15.)

There are only two sources from which we can hope for any real light on their origin. One is their subject-matter, of which an outline has been given in Chapter II. The other is their language.

Homeric language. 34. The general character of Homeric language—that which is common to *Iliad* and *Odyssey*—attests the high anti-quity of the poems. The dialect of Homer is Ionic. In the fifth century B.C. there is the Ionic of Herodotus, while a kindred, though distinct, dialect has taken a mature form in the Attic literature. A comparison of Homer's Ionic with the fifth-century Ionic and Attic shows differences of two classes. One class is concerned with the forms of words: the other, with their arrangement in sentences. And these differences are not merely matters of detail or of caprice. They are such as to show that Homer's Ionic belongs to an earlier stage in the development of the language [1]. In order to give time for such changes, it is necessary to allow an interval of at least two or three centuries. That is, the stamp of Homeric language, as a whole, indicates that we should place the Homeric poems not later than about 800—700 B.C.

Traditional epic element. 35. But the Ionic of Homer cannot have been the spoken dialect of one time. It comprises too great a number of alternative forms for even the commonest words [2]. The Homeric poet used the spoken Ionic of his own day; but, besides this, he used also an element of earlier Ionic as it came to him in the traditional diction of poetry. At a very early date—how early, we do not know—Ionic became the accepted dialect of epic poetry for all Greeks, as Tuscan became the literary dialect for all Italians. Some forms occur in Homer which are Aeolic. It is possible that these forms may have been adopted into Ionic, as the national

---

[1] See Note at the end of the book.

[2] *e.g.* εἶναι, ἔμεν, ἔμμεν, ἔμεναι, ἔμμεναι: νηυσί, νήεσσι, ναῦφι: πόλεις, πόλιες, πόληες: πολύν, πουλύν, πολλόν: πολέες, πολεῖς, πολλοί: Πηληϊάδεω, Πηληϊάδαο, Πηλείδεω, Πηλείδαο: Ἀχιλῆι, Ἀχιλλῆι, Ἀχιλλεῖ: πᾶσι, πάντεσσι: κυσί, κύνεσσι: υἱέες, υἷες: etc.

dialect for epic poetry, from old Aeolian lays. But it is also possible that they originally belonged to the old Ionic itself, as well as to the old Aeolic. The only thing certain about such forms is that they are very old[1]. They were part of an epic style which the Ionic poets inherited.

36. And the presence of this traditional element might easily have a further result. A poet using words or phrases which lived only in epic convention would be apt to coin similar forms by analogy. In doing this, he would not be controlled by the instinct of *living* speech; and in those days there was no scientific philology to keep him right. Analogy, then, might prove a misleading guide. The forms which he devised,—believing them to be warranted by similar old forms,—might happen to be incorrect. This would be the origin of 'false archaisms.' There are undoubtedly some 'false archaisms' in Homer[2], though probably not so many as some critics have assumed[3]. But it is well to mark the

False archaisms.

---

[1] Such Homeric forms as ἐγών, πίσυρες, ἄμμες, ὔμμες or ὔμμες, are Aeolic; τεΐν, τύνη, etc., Doric. See, on this subject, Mr Monro's papers, 'Traces of different Dialects in the language of Homer' (*Journ. of Philology*, IX. p. 252), and 'Further Notes on Homeric Subjects' (*ib.* vol. XI. p. 56).

[2] Thus ὑπὸ κράτεσφι (*Il.* 10. 156) = 'under his head,' κράτεσφι being formed on the analogy of στήθεσφι (from the stem στήθες of στῆθος), and meant for the dat. sing. (κρατί): but this is incorrect, since the stem is not κρατες, but κρατ. So (*ib.* 361) ἐπείγετον, if meant for the 3rd pers. dual *subjunctive* (as προθέῃσι in 362 suggests) is wrong, since Homer has η in the subjunct. where the indic. has ε. Again (*ib.* 346) παραφθαίῃσι is meant for the optat. παραφθαίη, but is wrongly formed on the analogy of *subjunctives* in -ῃσι. These false archaisms in *Il.* 10. confirm the *relative* lateness of the book, but only with the reserve indicated above. In *Il.* 15. 415, ἐείσατο, 'he went,' may, as Curtius thought (*Princ.* ii. 207), be a false archaism, suggested by the analogy of ἐϝείσατο, 'seemed' (*Od.* 2. 320): but this is doubtful. Wackernagel's view is that it is merely an error for ἐήσατο, which he would identify with Sanscr. *ayâsat* (Monro *Gr.* § 401 n.).

[3] False archaisms have a large place in Prof. Paley's theory,—that 'our *Iliad* and *Odyssey* were put together only in the latter part of the 5th century B.C., from the large mass of ballad literature which Pindar and the Tragics know of in their entirety' (Pref. to *Iliad*, vol. II. p. xxi).

limit of the inference which can be drawn from such instances. It has sometimes been argued that a 'false
archaism' proves the passage in which it occurs to be
altogether later than the age of Ionian epos,—as late (say)
as 450—400 B. C. This inference is unsound. The possibility of false archaisms began as soon as there were
genuine archaisms. False archaisms might have been made
in 800 or 900 B. C., as easily as in 450 B. C., by an Ionian
poet who found in the traditional epic diction certain
forms or phrases which no longer existed in the living
idiom of his day.

Dif-
ferences
between
Iliad
and
Odyssey.

37. So far, we have been considering the general stamp
of Homeric language, as seen in both the great epics. But
the language of the *Odyssey* has certain traits of its own,
which indicate that, as a whole, it is later than that of the
Iliad. It is not safe to lay much stress on mere differences
of vocabulary in the two poems. The *Iliad* deals chiefly
with war-scenes, the *Odyssey* with adventurous travel or
domestic life. We should naturally expect a corresponding
difference in the classes of words used. Further, many
differences might be due to local or personal causes rather
than to separation in time. Perhaps the only argument
from vocabulary that has any force is the greater frequency
in the *Odyssey* of words which interpret the religious or
moral sense[1]. But the evidence of syntax is more significant. The *Odyssey* has a number of constructions
and usages which distinguish it from the *Iliad*. They

[1] As to these, see p. 55, n. 1. It is not strange that in the *Odyssey*
alone should be found ἱστίη, λέσχη (a place where men meet to talk, in
Mod. Greek='club'), χέρνιψ (water for washing the hands), δημιοεργός
(one who plies a peaceful calling). Nor is it strange that φόβος ('flight')
and ῥήγνυμι ('to break'),—so frequent in the *Iliad* battle-scenes, should
occur only once each in the *Odyssey*. Words afterwards so common
as ἐσθής, χρήματα ('property') occur only in the *Odyssey*, and this is
perhaps more significant. ἐλπίς and δόξα occur only in the *Odyssey*,
except that δόξης occurs once in *Il.* 10. 324, a book which has other
non-Iliadic words in common with the *Odyssey*, as δόσις, φῆμις, δαίτη,
ἀωτέω, ἀδηκότες, εἶσθα, τοῖσδεσσι.

fall chiefly under the following heads[1]. (1) Uses of prepositions. (2) Uses of the article, of pronouns, conjunctions,
particles, and adverbs. (3) Dependent clauses. In regard
to metre, again some distinctive points may be noticed[2].

38. These characteristics of the *Odyssey* are either
wholly absent from the *Iliad*, or occur only in a limited area
of it, which is almost always confined to books 9, 10, 23,
24; books which, as we saw, have been held, on other
grounds, to be later than most of the others. The lateness which these particular traits argue is, however, only
relative. There is nothing in them which is not consistent with the earliest date which could, on other grounds,
be claimed for the *Odyssey* as a whole. They do not affect
the generally ancient stamp which its language shares with
that of the *Iliad*. Their effect is only to draw certain
limited parts of the *Iliad* nearer to the *Odyssey*. They
strengthen the probability that some interval of time must
be supposed between the bulk of the *Iliad* and those parts
of it which here exhibit a marked affinity with the *Odyssey*.

39. Homeric metre exhibits traces of certain sounds or Lost
letters which were unknown to the Ionic of the historical sounds.
age. In one very common word (ὡς) we see the metrical
influence of a lost initial *y*[3]. A few instances, though these

---

[1] See Note at the end of the book.

[2] (1) A pause in the verse sometimes excuses the non-elision of a
vowel (hiatus), and one case of this is when the beginning of the 5th
foot coincides with the beginning of a word : as *Od.* 2. 57 εἰλαπινάζουσιν
πίνουσί τε | αἴθοπα οἶνον. This division of the verse is called the
'bucolic diaeresis,' because especially characteristic of the hexameter in
pastoral poetry. Hiatus in this bucolic diaeresis is about twice as
frequent in the *Od.* as in the *Il.* So also is hiatus after the vowel ε.
In both these metrical points, however, books 23 and 24 of the *Iliad*
show an affinity with the *Odyssey*. Monro *Gr.* § 382.

[3] By the lengthening of a short syllable before it, as *Il.* 11. 58
Αἰνείαν θ', ὃς Τρωσὶ θεὸς ὣς τίετο δήμῳ (as though it were *y*ὣς). This
occurs in some 36 places, but the exceptions are scarcely less numerous:
as *Il.* 3. 196, αὐτὸς δὲ κτίλος ὣς (where Bentley proposed αὐτὰρ ψιλὸς
ἐών). Monro *Hom. Gr.* § 397. Cp. Peile, *Greek and Latin Etymology*,
pp. 76, 229.

are more doubtful, suggest the similar influence of a lost initial σ[1]. But the most important case is that of the letter *vau*, answering in sound to our V or W. The character for this was like F, or one Greek Γ placed on top of another: hence its name, 'double gamma', 'digamma[2].' This was one of the ordinary letters of the earliest Greek alphabet. It occurs in Doric inscriptions, and in the Aeolic inscriptions of Greece Proper (Boeotia, Elis, etc.), though not in those of the Asiatic Aeolis. For the existence of the letter in the Ionic alphabet, the evidence is very slender; in any case, it ceased to be used in Ionic as early, at least, as 500 B.C.[3] Nor is there any evidence that the letter F was ever *written* in the ancient texts of Homer. But in

---

[1] As ἐπι-άλμενος (*salio*), ἀμφί-αλος (*sal*), ἀμφί-επον (*sequor*), καταῖσχεται (for -σίσχεται), σύνεχές (as if for συσσεχές, *Od.* 5. 257), and occasional hiatus before ὕλη, ὕπνος, ἑός (*silva, somnus, suus*).

[2] Bentley was the first modern scholar who recognised the presence of the digamma in Homeric metre. The earliest hint of his discovery occurs in a note written by him, in 1713, on a blank leaf in his copy of the 'Discourse of Free-Thinking' 'by Anthony Collins' (in the Library of Trin. Coll., Cambridge) :—'Homer's δίγαμμα Aeolicum to be added. οἶνος, Ϝοῖνος, vinū: a Demonstration of this, because Ϝοῖνος has always preceding it a vowel : so οἰνοποτάζων.' The digamma was first printed in a quotation from Homer in Bentley's edition of *Paradise Lost* (1732), a capital F being used : whence Pope's lines in the *Dunciad* : 'While tow'ring o'er your alphabet, like Saul, | Stands our digamma, and o'ertops them all.' The substance of Bentley's ms. notes on the digamma was published in Dr. J. W. Donaldson's *New Cratylus*. Cp. 'Bentley,' in 'English Men of Letters,' pp. 149—154.

[3] In the Dorian inscriptions of the 6th and 5th centuries B.C. Ϝ is usually retained as an *initial* letter, even where it is neglected in the body of a word. The *Tabulae Heracleenses* of the Dorian Heraclea in Magna Graecia (4th cent. B.C.) show the Ϝ retained in some words, and omitted in others. For Ϝ in the Ionic alphabet the chief evidence is (1) one word in a Naxian inscription of *circ.* 510 B.C. : (2) three names on vases found in Magna Graecia, and said to have come from Chalcis in Euboea : (3) the name of the town *Velia*, founded by Ionians of Phocaea. The earliest Ionic inscriptions of Euboea itself (6th cent. B.C.) show no trace of Ϝ. Tudeer, *De digammo* pp. 5 ff., thinks that the loss of Ϝ in Ionic happened between 800—500 B.C. (Monro, *Hom. Gr.* §§ 404 f.)

Homeric verse the presence of the *sound* is often indicated. This occurs in two ways. (1) It warrants '*hiatus:*' i.e. prevents the elision of a vowel before another vowel: as *Il.* 9. 128 ἀμύμονα ἔργα ἰδυίας. Here ἔργα and ἰδυίας are treated, for metrical purposes, as if they were written *werga widuias*. (2) It makes '*position:*' i.e. it lengthens a preceding syllable which would otherwise have been short: as *Il.* 4. 182 ὥς ποτέ τις ἐρέει, where τις is lengthened as if followed by *wereei*.

40.   Now, if these effects were constant, there would be less difficulty. We should then have to suppose that a fixed epic tradition compelled the poet to assume the sound *w* before certain words, whether that sound or letter was generally used in his day, or not. But we find that the Homeric use fluctuates, even in regard to the same words. The digamma does not *always* prevent elision, or lengthen a short syllable. It does so in upwards of 3300 places. It fails to do so in upwards of 600 places[1]. How are we to explain the failures? No conclusive answer has yet been given to this question[2].

Inconstant use of it in Homer.

---

[1] This is the reckoning of Prof. W. Hartel (*Homerische Studien* III.), whose results are given by Mr Monro, *Hom. Gr.* § 398. Prof. Hartel's precise figures are 3354 against 617. (1) Of the 3354 cases in which F is *operative*, it prevents the elision of a short vowel in 2324; in 507 it follows a long vowel or diphthong in arsis; in 164 it prevents the shortening of a diphthong in thesis; and in 359 it lengthens a short syllable ending in a consonant. (2) Of the 617 cases in which F is *inoperative*, it fails to prevent elision in 324: it permits a preceding long vowel or diphthong to be shortened in 78; and it fails to lengthen a short syllable ending in a consonant in 215.

[2] The principal theories which have been broached are briefly these. (1) Bentley's:—All places where F is ignored are corrupt. This theory is too sweeping. But it is true that initial F can be restored, without violence, to a very large proportion of places in those parts of the *Iliad* which are indisputably old. Medial F, too, can often be restored to some words by resolving a diphthong, as by writing κόϊλος for κοῖλος (cp. Curt. *Etym.* § 79), Ἀτρεΐδης for Ἀτρείδης. (2) F was going out of use, and so words which originally had F could be used by the poet either with or without F. There were alternative forms. In the case, however, of such words as ἄναξ, ἄστυ, ἔργον, οἶκος, ἰδεῖν, the

One thing, at least, is certain. The sound of the digamma was known as a living sound in the language by the
first Greeks who made epic verse, whether these were
Ionians or not. As regards the use in Homer, the following points appear probable. (1) The tradition of the
digamma in epic verse had come down to Ionian poets in
whose own day the sound had either disappeared from
Ionic, or was tending to disappear. (2) The tradition
was felt as decidedly more binding in regard to some
words and phrases than to others, perhaps because their
association with the digamma was traditionally more familiar. (3) Within certain limits, and without absolutely
rigid exception of any word, the Ionian poet was free to
treat the digamma as a trait of epic style, observing or
ignoring it as metrical convenience prompted. (4) The
tendency to observe it slightly decreased with increasing
distance from the time in which the digamma was a living
sound in daily speech[1].

Sup-
posed
errors of
translit-
eration.

41. It has been supposed that some of the Homeric
forms which present difficulties are mere blunders of
ancient transcribers, made in transliterating Homer from
the older Attic alphabet into the Ionic alphabet, after

observance of Ϝ is more frequent than the neglect in the ratio of about
14 : 1. (3) The Ϝ was confined to certain fixed epic phrases. But
it is found also in words which occur more rarely (ἴτυς, ἰτέη, ἄρνες
etc.). And there are no false instances, such as imitation might
generate. (4) Hiatus before any word which once had Ϝ was an
epic survival. But this does not explain why Ϝ should also make
position.' (5) Prof. W. Hartel's theory. Ϝ was neither a full consonant nor a full vowel, but something between the two. Used as
a semi-consonant, it could prevent elision or shortening. Used as a
semi-vowel, it was compatible with either. Hence the Homeric
inconstancy of use would be only apparent: the observance of Ϝ would
be really universal.

[1] As applied to different parts of the *Iliad* and the *Odyssey*,
this test hardly yields any results on which stress can be laid.
But in the Homeric 'hymns,' which belong chiefly to *circ.* 750—
500 B.C., the neglect of Ϝ is decidedly more frequent than in the *Iliad*
or the *Odyssey*.

it had been formally adopted at Athens in 403 B.C.[1]　But it is very doubtful whether any errors have really been due to this cause[2].

Whatever disturbing causes may have affected Homeric tradition, at least they have not affected the general complexion of Homeric language.　Its essential characteristics can still be recognised with certainty.　It shows that the *Iliad* and the *Odyssey*, viewed as a whole, belong to an early age.　This conclusion would remain unshaken, even if assent were given to the theory lately put forward with much ingenuity by Prof. Fick.

42.　He believes that the Homeric poems existed in a purely Aeolic dialect down to about 530—500 B.C., when they were translated into Ionic[3].　The author of 'the Ionic redaction' was Cynaethus, a rhapsode of Chios, the reputed author of the hymn to the Delian Apollo.　According to the scholiast on Pindar, *Nem.* 2. 1, Cynaethus was the first who recited 'Homer's poems' at Syracuse, about the 69th olympiad (504 B. C.).　At the time when the Aeolic Homer was thus turned into Ionic, or shortly afterwards, Ionic

Fick's theory.

---

[1] Thus Curtius thinks that such Homeric infinitives as φυγέειν, ἰδέειν, should be φυγέεν, ἰδέεν, and that the error arose from the Attic transliterators (οἱ μεταχαρακτηρίζοντες) supposing that the second E in ΦΥΓΕΕΝ, etc., was Ionic for EI.　Similarly he suspects that ἔην should be ἔεν, from EEN.　*Greek Verb* II. 111 (p. 348 Eng. tr.).

[2] As a fact limiting the possible range of such errors, it should be noted that in the Ionic alphabet E represented ει only when the latter was 'spurious,' *i.e.* came from ε + ε, or ε + a compensatory lengthening (as in ΕΝΑΙ for εἶναι).　'Genuine' ει, from ε + ι, was written EI (except sometimes before vowels).　Hence (*e.g.*) ἐείσατο would have been written ΕΕΙΣΑΤΟ, not ΕΕΣΑΤΟ.　So O represented ου only when due to ο + ο, or ο + compensatory lengthening: not when due to ο + υ.　Cp. Meisterhans, *Grammatik der Attischen Inschriften* p. 11 (1885).

[3] Fick (*Ilias*, p. XXXIII, 1885) quotes Ritschl as expressing a similar view so long ago as 1834.　Ritschl's view, however,—as the quotation shows,—was essentially different.　He thought that Homer went over from Greece with the Aeolian emigrants, and composed short Aeolic lays at Smyrna.　Then a series of Ionian poets enlarged and Ionicised them.　But this process was complete before 776 B.C.

additions were made to both epics. Fick dwells on the
fact that in the undoubtedly old parts of Homer we find
Aeolic forms which could not have been metrically replaced
by the corresponding Ionic forms, and which were therefore
retained by the Ionic translator. Conversely, in the later
parts, which were Ionic from the first, we find forms which
metrically resist Aeolicising. His theory suggests the
following remarks.

Estimate
of it.

43. (1) The first question which has to be decided is,
'What is Aeolic, or Ionic?' In regard to alleged 'Aeolisms' in Homer, Fick has to prove, not only that they
were Aeolic, but also that they were not old Ionic. We
have no sufficient evidence as to the state of the Greek
dialects *circ.* 900—600 B.C. The Aeolic inscriptions are all
later than the fifth century B.C. The Ionic evidence,
though less scanty, is not less inadequate for this purpose.
It was the habit of the ancient grammarians to set down
any Homeric archaism as an 'Aeolism,' if it happened to
exist in Aeolic also, and sometimes even when it did not.
The digamma itself was long called 'Aeolic,' and regarded
as peculiarly belonging to that dialect,—an error, as we
now know. Hinrichs[1] has greatly reduced the number of
Aeolisms in Homer. Further scrutiny may perhaps reduce
it still more[2].

[1] *De Homericae elocutionis vestigiis Aeolicis* (Jena, 1875).

[2] In the *Philologus* (XLIII. 1. 1—31) Karl Sittl has examined the
residuum of Homeric 'Aeolisms' left by Hinrichs. His results are
epitomized by M. W. Humphreys in *Amer. Journ. Phil.* v. 521.
Thus : (1) He eliminates from the 'Aeolisms' those which do not even
occur in Aeolic. *E.g.*, the 'Aeolic' υ (for ο) has been unduly extended.
It occurred only in the Aeolic υι = οι of the locative (also Doric). (2)
Fick assumes an Aeolic ϝείκοσι as parent of the Homeric ἐείκοσι.
When ϝ preceded by a consonant began a word, all Greeks sometimes
prefixed ε (as if we had ἐδϝείκοσι). But, ϝείκοσι, having lost its initial
δ, was no longer entitled to an initial ε. The Homeric ἐϝείκοσι was a
false formation on the analogy of words which had *not* lost the consonant before ϝ. The Aeolians never vocalised initial ϝ. The apparent
examples are all aspirated, and not Aeolic. (3) As to long ᾱ, the
non-Ionic uses of it in Homer are almost confined to proper names

44. (2) Fick's view implies that the Ionic version, made about 530—500 B. C., at once and for ever superseded in general favour the original Aeolic Homer, though the latter had been familiar throughout Hellas for generations. This is incomprehensible. And, supposing that this happened, can we further suppose that ancient literature would have preserved no reference to the fact of the transcription which, at a blow, had robbed the Aeolian race of its most glorious inheritance,—one which, for so long a period, all Greeks had publicly recognised as belonging to it? There were flourishing Aeolian states then, and Aeolian writers. To take a rough parallel, suppose that at the present day an Englishman should clothe the poems of Robert Burns in an English dress: would the transcription be likely to supersede the Scottish original as the standard form of the poems throughout the English-speaking world? Yet this is what Fick supposes the Ionic Cynaethus to have accomplished in the case of the Aeolic Homer.[1] The unexampled success of Cynaethus becomes still more astounding when we observe how limited his poetical skill is assumed to have been. He left a great many Aeolisms in his Homer. Why? Because their direct Ionic equivalents would not scan.

But the fact is that the Pindaric scholium is an utterly

taken from old lays. Many seeming examples can be explained : thus ἄριστον (*Il.* 24. 124) should be ἀϝέριστον (like ἀϝέκοντε) : δαλός (*Il.* 13. 320) should be δαϝελός. (4) Pronouns. τοι, τείν, τύνη, τεός, ἀμμός, are admittedly archaisms. This may be true also of the 'Aeolic' ἄμμες, ὔμμες (etc.), if once written ἀμμές (or ἀμμές), ὑμμές (=jυσμές), whence, by suppression and compensation ἡμές, ὑμές, and by analogy ἡμέες (ἡμεῖς), ὑμέες (ὑμεῖς). These are only specimens of Sittl's analysis. It may be added that Hinrichs was not slow to make a vigorous reply.

[1] Prof. Fick appeals to instances of inscriptions, or other short pieces, presumably composed in a dialect different from that in which they have come down to us. For example, he thinks that the couplet of Simonides on the Peloponnesians slain at Thermopylae (Her. 7. 228) was originally in the Laconian dialect, thus: μυριάσιν ποκὰ τῇδε τριακατίαις ἐμάχοντο | ἐκ Πελοποννάσω χηλιάδες τέτορες. Between such cases, and the Ionicising of Homer by Cynaethus, the difference, he says, is only 'one of degree' (*Ilias* p. 1X). But surely it is also a difference of kind.

insufficient basis on which to build the hypothesis about
Cynaethus.   And it would be easy to show that Homer had
been known in Ionic from an earlier date.   Simonides of
Ceos was born 556 B.C., and was therefore already of mature
age at the time when the supposed 'Ionic redaction' was
made.   The Homer known to his boyhood and youth must
then, according to Fick, have been Aeolic.   But he quotes
Il. 6. 148 (one of the certainly older parts of the epic), in
Ionic, as by 'the man of Chios,' meaning Homer ; whom he
therefore regarded as an Ionian poet.   It will hardly be
maintained that by 'the man of Chios' he meant his contemporary Cynaethus[1].

45.   (3)   The pre-Homeric epic lays were doubtless
Achaean.   Those Homeric forms which can be proved to have
existed in post-Homeric Aeolic admit of two different explan-
ations, which do not, however, necessarily exclude each other.
One of them may apply to some instances, and the other to
others.   (i) These forms, or some of them, may have
belonged also to an older Ionic.   Those who deny this
have to prove the negative.   (ii) If originally peculiar to
Achaean (or old Aeolic), such forms may have been
adopted by old Ionian poetry because they were associated, through Achaean lays, with epic composition.   Fick's
theory of the late and wholesale transcription is altogether
incredible[2].   But, whether the original Homeric dialect
was Achaean or old Ionic, it may be granted that it had
undergone modifying influences at the hands of Ionian poets
and rhapsodes, tending to bring it somewhat nearer to the
later Ionic, and so increasing that appearance of a 'mixed
dialect' which it now presents.   A modernising process, in

[1] If the Simonides is he of Amorgos (p. 88 n. 2), we are taken
back to 660 B.C.

[2] Apart from that hypothesis, however, he has done good service
in promoting a closer study of the Homeric dialect.   The question as to
how far the Aeolic in which he has clothed the epic is, or is not, possible
Aeolic, matters little : his version is given mainly for the purpose of
illustration.   His Aeolic *Odyssey* has been reviewed by Christ in the
Philol. Anzeiger (XIV. 90—98), by Cauer in the *Zeitschr. f. d. österr.
Gymnas.* (X. 290—311), and by Hinrichs in the *Deutsch. Litteratur-
zeitung* (1885 pp. 6——) who are all opposed to the theory

this limited sense, was entirely compatible with the pre-
servation, in all main features, of its essentially ancient
character.

46. The evidence of Homeric language has thus been
found to agree with the evidence furnished by the subject-
matter of the poems. Their claim to a high antiquity is confirmed. In connection with their age, there is a further ques- *The tale
tion which must now be briefly noticed. We saw that, as a *of Troy,
how far*
general picture of an early civilisation, the Homeric poetry *histori-*
has the value of history. But how much of historical fact *cal.*
can be supposed to reside in the story of the Trojan War?

The tale of Troy, as we have it in Homer, is essentially
a poetic creation; and the poet is the sole witness. The *Analogy
from*
romance of Charlemagne embodies the historical fact *from
romance.*
that an Emperor once ruled Western Europe from the
Eider to the Ebro. It also departs from history in send-
ing Charlemagne on a crusade to Jerusalem, because,
when the romance arose, a crusade belonged to the ideal of
chivalry. Analogy might suggest that an Achaean prince *Limit of
safe in-
ference.*
had once really held a position like that of Agamemnon; *safe inference.*
also, that some Achaean expedition to the Troad had
occurred, whether this Achaean prince had himself borne
part in it or not. Both inferences are probable on other
grounds. Some memorable capture of a town in the Troad
had probably been made by Greek warriors; beyond this
we cannot safely go. It is fantastic to treat the siege of
Troy as merely a solar myth,—to explain the abduction of
Helen by Paris as the extinction of the sunlight in the
West, and Troy as the region of the dawn beset and
possessed by the sunrise. It is equally fantastic, and more
illogical, to follow the 'rationalising' method—to deduct
the supernatural element, and claim the whole residuum as
historical fact. Homer says that Achilles slew Hector with
the aid of Athene. We are not entitled to omit Athene,
and still to affirm that Achilles slew Hector[1].

[1] See the article in the *Edinburgh Review* on Schliemann's *Ilios*,
No. CCCXIV., pp. 517 ff. (1881). Freeman's essay on 'The Mythical and

47. After the recent excavations in the Troad, an impression appeared to exist in some minds that the Homeric narrative of the Trojan War had been proved historical, because remains had been found which (it was alleged) might be those of Troy. It is well, then, briefly to state the relation between the evidence of the Homeric text and the evidence of those excavations.

Site of Homeric Troy. The *Iliad* shows a personal acquaintance with the plain of Troy, and with the dominant features of the surrounding landscape[1]. In the site of Troy, as described by Homer, the capital feature is the acropolis,—'lofty', 'windy', 'beetling',—with those precipitous crags over which it was proposed to hurl the wooden horse[2]. This suits one site *Bunár-* only in the Trojan plain,—that above the village of *bashi.* Bunárbashi, on the lower slopes of the hills which fringe the plain to the south. Here the hill called the Bali Dagh rises some 400 feet above the plain, with sheer sides descending on S. and S.W. to the valley of the Mendere (Scamander). A little N.W. of Homeric Troy two natural *The springs.* springs rose. A little N.W. of Bunárbashi these springs still exist, and no others like them exist anywhere else in the plain. As Prof. Ernst Curtius well says,—'This pair

Romantic Elements in Early English History' is a lucid and excellent statement of the critical principles applicable to such cases.

[1] Cp. 'A Tour in the Troad' (*Fortnightly Review*, April, 1883, p. 514 f.). Perhaps the thing which most surprises a reader of Homer is the absence of high mountains from the neighbourhood of the Trojan plain. Ida (5700 feet) is only a pale blue form on the S.E. horizon, some 30 miles away. The island peak of Samothrace (5,200 feet, 45 miles off to the N.W.)—Poseidon's watching-place, as Ida is that of Zeus—is a more impressive feature of the view. In the plain can still be found 'wheat-bearing' tracts (*Il.* 21. 602),—the 'reedy marsh' (*Od.* 14. 474)—'elms, willows and tamarisks' (*Il.* 21. 350); the cry of the heron (*Il.* 10. 274) may still be heard; an eagle 'of dark plumage' (*Il.* 24. 316) may still be seen there,—or cranes, leaving the Troad for northern climes, 'when they have escaped the winter' (*Il.* 3. 4).

[2] *Od.* 8. 508, ἣ κατὰ πετράων βαλέειν ἐρύσαντας ἐπ' ἄκρης. In *Troy*, p. 18, Dr Schliemann 'most positively' asserted that Troy had no acropolis.

of rivulets is the immutable mark of nature, by which the height towering above is recognised as the citadel of Ilium[1].' Though the site at Bunárbashi has not yet been thoroughly explored[2], pottery has been found there which is referred to 1000—900 B.C.[3] Since Le Chevalier's visit in 1785, the striking features of agreement between Bunárbashi and the Homeric picture of Troy—features unique in the Trojan plain—have been emphatically recognised by a series of the most competent observers, including Leake, Moltke, Forchhammer, Kiepert, Ernst Curtius, and Tozer[4]. Leake remarked that any person at all accustomed to observe the sites of ancient Greek towns must fix on Bunárbashi 'for the site of the chief place of the surrounding country.' The same opinion was expressed to Prof. E. Curtius by Count Moltke,—that 'he knew no other site in the Trojan plain for a chief town of ancient time.'

48. The low mound of Hissarlik stands in the open plain, about three miles from the Hellespont. It measures some 325 yards by 235, and stands only some 112 feet above the plain. This mound marks the site of a historical Greek town, to which the first settlers gave the name of 'Ilium' (perhaps about 700 B.C.), and which existed here down to Roman times. In the mound have been discovered (1) remains of this Greek town, (2) some prehistoric remains. Dr Schliemann asserts that the prehistoric remains are those of Homeric Troy. If this means that they represent a prehistoric town *which gave rise to the legend of Troy*, the assertion is one which can no longer be either proved or disproved. No objects found at Hissarlik tend in the slightest degree to prove it. On the other hand, one important fact is certain. The low site at Hissarlik is in the strongest con-

His-sarli [margin note]

---

[1] *History of Greece*, vol. 1. ch. iii. p. 79 (transl. Ward).

[2] 'Eine *genaue* Untersuchung hat noch nicht stattgefunden, so viel ich weiss' (Prof. E. Curtius, in a letter of Feb. 9, 1884).

[3] This is admitted by Dr Schliemann; *Troja*, p. 268.

[4] See their testimonies in my article, 'Homeric Troy,' *Fortnightly Review*, April, 1884, p. 447.

trast with the site of spacious and 'lofty' Troy as described
by Homer, while the site at Bunárbashi is as strikingly in
harmony with that description. The solitary phrase in the
Iliad which favours Hissarlik,—*Il.* 20. 216 f., where Ilios is
'in the plain,'—belongs to a passage which, as Dr Christ
has proved, is not only later than the bulk of the *Iliad*, but
is one of the latest additions of all,—having been added
by some dweller in the Troad, desirous of glorifying the
Aeneadae, after the Greek Ilium had been built in the plain[1].
The Homeric hymn to Aphrodite, which also celebrates the
Aeneadae, is probably of the same age (the seventh century
B.C.), and from a kindred source. The Greek settlers at
Hissarlik naturally affirmed that their 'Ilium' stood on the
site of Troy ; in proof of it, they showed the stone on which
Palamedes had played draughts. Their paradox, a mere
birth of local vanity, was as decisively rejected by sound
criticism in ancient as in modern times[2].

Origin
of the
Homeric
picture
of Troy.
49. The Homeric poet who created the Troy of the
Iliad probably knew—personally, or by description—a strong
town at Bunárbashi as the ruling city of the surrounding
district. The legend of a siege, on which the *Iliad* is
founded, may, or may not, have arisen from the actual
siege of an older town at Hissarlik, which, in the poet's
day, had already perished. He would easily be led to
place the Troy of his poem in a position like that of the
existing city on the Bali Dagh. He would give it a 'lofty'
and 'beetling' acropolis. He would endow it with handsome

---

[1] *Il.* 20. 216 κτίσσε δὲ Δαρδανίην, ἐπεὶ οὔπω Ἴλιος ἱρὴ | ἐν πεδίῳ πε-
πόλιστο. As Prof. Michaelis said early in 1884 (see *Fortn. Review*,
April, 1884, p. 452), 'it would not be difficult to show that the whole
part in Υ in which Ilios ἐν πεδίῳ πεπόλιστο belongs to an ἐμβόλιμον
which is not in good accord with the main part of the book.' Later in
the same year Christ's *Iliad* appeared. He shows (*Proleg.* p. 76) that
Il. 20. 75—353 is one of the latest interpolations, due to a rhapsode 'qui
in agro Troiano magis quam in Musarum nemoribus versatus esse vide-
tur.' Its author has imitated various passages in bks. 5, 6, 12, 17, 21,
and even 8.

[2] See the *Journal of Hellenic Studies*, Vol. III. pp. 203—217.

buildings. His epic would reproduce the general course of the rivers, and that striking feature, the natural springs at the foot of the hill, just outside the city gates. Impressed by the strength of the acropolis,—with its sheer precipices descending to the narrow valley of the Scamander, and its command of the plain stretching towards the Hellespont,— he would see in this natural strength a confirmation of the legend that the resistance of Troy to the united force of the Achaeans had been prolonged and stubborn.

But, while the site at Bunárbashi thus supplied the dominant features of his conception, he might also modify the picture by traits taken from other scenes known to him, or from imagination. His topography might be in some measure eclectic, or even freely poetical[1]. With regard to the tactical data—those furnished by the incidents of warfare in the *Iliad*—they cannot be treated with the rigour applicable to a military history. It has been shown[2], however, that, if so treated, they are conclusive against the notion that the poet imagined his Troy at Hissarlik, while on the other hand they can be brought into general accord with the site at Bunárbashi.[3]

We find, then, that the essentially poetical story of the Trojan War, as presented by Homer, contains nothing incompatible with the other evidence for the age of the poems, but nothing, on the other hand, which can help to fix that age by any definite relationships to historical fact.

50. The lost poems of the Epic Cycle require notice The here, as they help to fix the lower limit for the age of the Epic Cycle

---

[1] See my paper on 'The Ruins at Hissarlik,' *Journ. Hellen. Stud.* III. pp. 192 ff.

[2] By Mr George Nikolaïdes, in his Ἰλιάδος Στρατηγικὴ Διασκευή (1883),—a development of his earlier work, 'Topographie et plan stratégique de l'Iliade.'

[3] On the question of Bunárbashi *versus* Hissarlik, Prof. Michaelis wrote to me in 1884 ;—'Certainly, ἔσσεται ἦμαρ ὅταν ποτέ the full truth will come to light; and I have little doubt that it will not be far from what you have exposed in your articles in the *Journal of Hellenic Studies.*'

Homeric poems.¹   The Epic Cycle² was a body of epic poems by various hands, arranged in the chronological order of the subjects, so as to form a continuous history of the mythical world.   It began with the marriage of Heaven and Earth––whence sprang the Giants and the Cyclopes––and went down to the slaying of Odysseus by his son Telegonus.

When this body of epics was first put together, we do not know.   The earliest notice of it is due to a grammarian named Proclus,³ who lived probably about 140 A.D., and wrote a 'Manual of Literature' (Χρηστομάθεια γραμματική).⁴   In this manual he gave short prose summaries, or 'arguments,' of the poems which formed the Epic Cycle. Extant fragments of the manual give what he said about the poems in *one part* of the Epic Cycle,––viz., the part concerning the war of Troy.

¹ See, on this subject, the papers by Mr Monro in the *Journal of Hellenic Studies*, vol. IV. pp. 305 ff., vol. V. pp. 1 ff.

² Ἐπικὸς κύκλος. The word κύκλος meant:––(1) a routine, generally: esp. in the language of the Homeric scholiasts, the *conventional epic manner:* thus, a stock phrase, like Ἀχαιῶν χαλκοχιτώνων, is said to be τοῦ κύκλου: see Monro *l. c.* p. 329. (2) An epigram so made that the first and last lines could change places,––as in the epitaph on the tomb of Midas, Plat. *Phaedr.* 264 D. Aristotle has κύκλος in this sense (referring to some epigram ascribed to Homer in *Soph. Elench.* 10. 6). (3) A comprehensive summary, whether in verse or prose;––as the ἱστορικὸς κύκλος (a prose outline of mythology) ascribed by Suidas to Dionysius of Miletus. Ἐγκύκλιος παιδεία, ἐγκ. μαθήματα=simply 'usual' course of instruction, studies, &c. But κυκλικός commonly had a *bad* sense, 'conventional, trite.' Esp. as epithet of poet or poem, it implied (1) trite epic material, (2) epic mannerism, (3) a merely chronological order of treatment: thus Callimachus tauntingly applied it to Apollonius Rhodius (τὸ ποίημα τὸ κυκλικόν *Anthol.* 12, 43), and Horace speaks of a *scriptor cyclicus* who begins the Trojan war from the double egg (*Ars Poet.* 135).

³ Conjecturally identified by Welcker with Eutychius Proclus of Sicca, who taught the Emperor M. Antoninus.

The patriarch Photius (9th cent.), in his *Bibliotheca*, gives some extracts from the Χρηστομάθεια of Proclus, with an account of that work, and of the Epic Cycle as epitomised therein.

⁴ The fragments are included in Gaisford's Hephaestion (new ed., Oxford, 1855).

51. The Trojan chapter of the Cycle contained eight Analysis epics, Homer's *Iliad* standing second, and Homer's *Odyssey* of the Trojan seventh. The chief facts about the other epics may be Cycle. most briefly and clearly shown in a tabular form.

1. *Cypria* (Κύπρια): 11 books. Author doubtful (Stasīnus of Cyprus?). Date, *circ*. 776 B.C.

Subject:—Zeus resolves to reduce the burdens of the teeming earth by a great war, and sends Discord to the wedding of Peleus and Thetis. 'Judgment of Paris,' giving the prize to Aphrodite. Paris carries off Helen. War of Troy down to the point at which Zeus resolves to help the Trojans by withdrawing Achilles. Hero of the epic—Paris. The *Cypria* seems to have been a sort of chronicle, beginning from the first cause of the Trojan War, and going down to the point at which the *Iliad* opens.

Non-Homeric traits:—Apotheosis of the Dioscuri who in Homer (*Il.* 3. 243) are merely dead men.—Story of Iphigenia (whom the *Cypria* distinguished from Homer's Iphianassa, *Il.* 9. 145). Story of Palamedes. Helen is now the daughter of Nemesis—who, pursued by Zeus, changes into many shapes to elude him. Cassandra has the gift of prophecy, which Homer does not give to her.

2. Homer's *Iliad*.

3. *Aethiopis* (Αἰθιοπίς): 5 books. Author, Arctinus of Miletus, *circ.* 776 B.C.

Subject:—After the funeral of Hector (*Iliad* 24), the Amazon queen, Penthesileia, comes to the aid of Troy. Her death. Exploits and death of Memnon. Death of Achilles. Ajax and Odysseus contend for his arms: the latter obtains them. Hero of the epic—Achilles.

Non-Homeric traits:—The worship of men after their death as 'heroes' (Achilles and Memnon being made immortal). A ritual of purification from the guilt of homicide, under the favour of Apollo καθάρσιος.

4. *Little Iliad* ('Ιλιὰς Μικρά): 4 books. Author doubtful (Lesches of Mitylene?). Date, *circ.* 700 B.C.

Subject:—Trojan war, from the award of the Achillean arms to Odysseus, down to the capture of Troy: including the return and healing of Philoctetes, and the episode of the wooden horse. Hero of the epic—Odysseus.—The poem seems to have been directly inspired by the tone of the *Odyssey*, and to have had more material in common with Homer than any other of the Cyclic epics.

Non-Homeric traits:—The magic Palladium (image of Pallas), on which the fate of Troy depends. Story of Sinon (Virg. *Aeneid* 11). Story of Aethra, mother of Theseus, carried off from Attica by the Dioscuri.

5. *Iliupersis* ('Ιλίου πέρσις): 2 books. Author, Arctinus of Miletus, *circ.* 776 B.C.

Subject:—The Trojans resolve to dedicate the wooden horse on their acropolis. Laocoon and one of his sons are killed by serpents. Aeneas and some followers, warned by this portent, retire from Troy to Mount Ida. Fall of Troy. Departure of the Greeks. Hero of the epic—Neoptolemus, the son of Achilles.

Non-Homeric traits:—Episode of Laocoon and flight of Aeneas. Sacrifice of Priam's daughter, Polyxena, at the tomb of Achilles—indicating hero-worship. Other points (as the stories of Sinon and Aethra) are common to this poem and the *Little Iliad*.

6. *Nostoi* (Νόστοι): 5 books. Author, Agias of Troezen, *circ.* 750 B.C.

Subject:—The adventures of some heroes on their return from Troy,—chiefly those of Menelaus, who visits Egypt, and of Agamemnon, who is slain by Clytaemnestra. The poem was a sort of tragic *Odyssey*, bridging the passage from Homer to Aeschylus.

Non-Homeric traits:—Death of Calchas, on meeting a greater seer than himself (Mopsus, at Colophon). Journey of Neoptolemus to Epeirus—where the Molossi are first named. The shade of Achilles warns Agamemnon of his doom. The enchantress Medea.

7. Homer's *Odyssey.*

8. *Telegonia* (Τηλεγονία): 2 books. Author, Eugammon of Cyrene, *circ.* 566 B.C.

Subject:—Telegonus, son of the enchantress Circe by Odysseus, unwittingly slays his father in Ithaca. Made aware of his sin, he takes his sire's corpse, with Telemachus and Penelope, to his mother. She makes the living immortal: Telegonus is wedded to Penelope, and Telemachus to Circe. In the earlier part, Odysseus was made to marry a Thesprotian queen, Callidice. Here is seen the wish to work in genealogies of families claiming descent from Odysseus.

Summary.

52. The foregoing sketch shows that some of the earliest Cyclic epics, dating from *circ.* 776 B.C., presuppose the *Iliad*, being planned to introduce or to continue it. In some copies the Cyclic *Aethiopis* was actually pieced on to the twenty-fourth book of the *Iliad*[1]. But that book was certainly one of the later additions to the epic. It would

[1] The last verse of the *Iliad* (24. 804) is ὣς οἵ γ᾽ ἀμφίεπον τάφον Ἕκτορος ἱπποδάμοιο. The *Aethiopis* was linked to it by reading, ὣς οἵ γ᾽ ἀμφίεπον τάφον Ἕκτορος· ἦλθε δ᾽ Ἀμαζών, | Ἄρηος θυγάτηρ μεγαλήτορος ἀνδροφόνοιο. This is mentioned in the Victorian scholia on the *Iliad* (p. 101, n. 1). Cp. Welcker, *Epic Cycle*, II. 170.

appear, then, that the *Iliad* must have existed, in something like its present compass, as early as 800 B.C.; indeed, a considerably earlier date will seem probable, if due time is allowed for the poem to have grown into such fame as would incite the effort to continue it. As compared with the *Iliad* and *Odyssey*, the Cyclic epics show the stamp of a later age (*a*) in certain ideas,—as hero-worship, purifying rituals, etc.: (*b*) in a larger circle of geographical knowledge, and a wider range of mythical material.

The external evidence of the Epic Cycle thus confirms the twofold internal evidence of Homeric matter and Homeric language. The bulk of the Homeric poems must be older than 800 B.C., although some particular additions to them are later.

53. We may now collect the results of the preceding inquiry, and consider how far they warrant any definite conclusions respecting the origin of the Homeric poems. The *Iliad* must be taken separately from the *Odyssey*. *General survey o results.*

At the outset, the ground may be partly cleared by setting aside two extreme views, which few persons, acquainted with the results of recent criticism, would now maintain. One of these is the theory with which Lachmann's name is especially associated,—that the *Iliad* has been pieced together out of short lays which were not originally connected by any common design (§ 14). The other is the theory which was generally prevalent down to Wolf's time, —that the *Iliad* is the work of one poet, Homer, as the *Aeneid* is the work of Virgil. In England, if nowhere else, this view is still cherished, though more often, perhaps, as a sentiment than as an opinion. Most Englishmen have been accustomed to read the *Iliad* with delight in the spirit of the whole, rather than with attention to the characteristics of different parts. This, too, is the way in which modern poets have usually read Homer; and as, consequently, the poets have mostly believed in Homeric unity, an impression has gained ground, especially in England, that throughout *Views which may be rejected.*

the Homeric poems there exists a personal unity of genius, which men of poetical genius can feel, and which is infinitely more significant than those discrepancies of detail with which critics occupy themselves. This popular impression has been strengthened by a special cause.

Deceptive unity of the epic style.

54. The traditional style of Ionian epos—developed in the course of generations—gives a general uniformity of effect which is delusive. The old Ionic, with its wealth of liquid sounds, with its union of softness and strength, was naturally fitted to render the epic hexameter musical, rapid, and majestic   Epic usage had gradually shaped a large number of phrases and formulas which constantly recur in like situations, without close regard to circumstances which distinguish one occasion from another[1]. An Ionian poet who wished to insert an episode in the *Iliad* had this epic language at command.   Even if his natural gifts were somewhat inferior to those of the poet whose work he was enlarging, the style would go far to veil the inequality.   Mr Matthew Arnold says :—'The insurmountable obstacle to believing the *Iliad* a consolidated work of several poets is this—that the work of great masters is unique ; and the *Iliad* has a great master's genuine stamp, and that stamp is *the grand style.*'   Now, 'the grand style' spoken of here, in so far as it can be claimed for the whole epic, is simply the Ionian style of heroic epos.   If we look closer, we see that the manner of the tenth book, for instance, is unlike that of the rest ; the twenty-fourth book, and some other books or passages, have traits of style which are their own ; the 'Catalogue' is distinct in style from its setting.   Suppose that the poems of the Epic Cycle had been extant as one work under Homer's name, with no record of their several authors. The 'grand style' could doubtless have been claimed for that work ; not, perhaps, in an equal degree with the *Iliad*, but still in a sense which could have furnished an argument like the above for unity of authorship.   On the other hand,

[1] According to Carl Eduard Schmidt, the sum of the repeated verses in the two epics amounts to sixteen thousand.

this traditional epic style imposes a special caution on all *precise* theories of composite authorship. It makes it harder to say exactly where one hand ceases and another begins.

55. Yet the defenders of Homeric unity may find comfort in the thought that, if the old form of their faith has become untenable, much of its essence has been preserved and reinvigorated. In the doctrine of Wolf himself, as we have seen, the analytic element was tempered by a strongly conservative element; he conceded to Homer 'the greater part of the songs,' and an influence which guided the composition of the rest. The analytic element in his theory was that which arrested attention, because, when it was published, it was sharply contrasted with the old belief in one Homer; and hence his work has often been associated with a purely destructive tendency which was quite foreign to its spirit. The great result of recent criticism has been to develope the conservative element in Wolf's doctrine; not, however, exactly in Hermann's way, but by adjusting it to the more correct point of view taken by Nitzsch,— that the original *Iliad* was already an epic poem, and not merely the lay of a primitive bard. *Conservative tendency of recent studies.*

56. Everything tends to show that the *Iliad* was planned by one great poet, who also executed the most essential parts of it. By the 'primary' *Iliad* we shall here denote the first form which the poet probably gave to his work, as distinguished from the enlarged form afterwards given to it, partly (perhaps) by himself, partly by others. *The primary poem.*

There is no doubt that the first book of the existing *Iliad* formed the beginning of the primary *Iliad*. The probable compass of the primary poem may best be judged by the nature of the theme from which it sets out,—a quarrel between Achilles and Agamemnon. Such a feud between two prominent heroes is found elsewhere as a popular *motif* of epic song. The minstrel Demodocus (*Od.* 8. 75) sang 'a lay whereof the fame had then reached the wide heaven; namely the quarrel between Odysseus and Achilles, son of Peleus, how once on a time they contended

in fierce words at a rich festival of the gods ; but Agamemnon, king of men, was inly glad, when the noblest of the
Achaeans fell at variance.' Such a subject would give
scope for brilliant speeches, exhibiting the general characteristics of the disputants. The poet who planned the *Iliad*,
—whether he had, or had not, poetical precedent for taking
a quarrel between heroes as his subject,—was presumably
original in his perception of the peculiar advantage which
belonged to his choice of persons. A grievance against a
subordinate chief would not have warranted Achilles in
withdrawing his aid from the whole Greek army. But
Agamemnon, as supreme leader, represented the Greek
army : when wronged by Agamemnon, Achilles had excuse
for making the quarrel a public one. And the retirement
of the most brilliant Greek hero, Achilles, left the Greeks
at a disadvantage, thus creating an opportunity for the
efforts of minor Greek heroes, and also for the pictures of a
doubtful warfare.

Special advantages of the subject.

57. Unless, then, we are prepared to assume that the
poet who sang 'the wrath of Achilles' was insensible to the
special capabilities of his theme, we can scarcely refuse to
believe that his epic was more than an 'Achilleid,' cele-
brating a merely personal episode. It must have been,
from the first, an 'Iliad,' including some general description of that struggle between Greeks and Trojans in which
a new crisis was occasioned by the temporary withdrawal of
Achilles. Precisely the distinction of the poet's invention
(I conceive) was the choice of a moment which could
combine the personal interest of a feud between two heroes
with the variety and splendour of large battle-scenes.

The poem was an 'Iliad' from the first.

And the plot of this primary *Iliad*, as foreshadowed in
the first book, must have comprised the following series of
events. Agamemnon wrongs Achilles, who retires from the
war. Zeus promises Thetis that he will avenge her son by
causing the Greeks to be discomfited. The tide of fortune
presently turns in favour of the Trojans ; the Greeks are
hard pressed, and, in attempting to succour them, Patroclus

Its compass.

is slain. The death of his friend rouses Achilles; he is reconciled to Agamemnon, and, after doing great deeds against the Trojans, slays their foremost champion, Hector.

These events are contained in books 1, 11, and 16 to 22 inclusive, which probably represent the substance of the primary *Iliad*,—allowance being made for later interpolations, large or small, in books 16—22. In this primary *Iliad*, the turning-point is book 11, which relates the discomfiture of the Greeks, in accordance with the promise of Zeus.

58. We may now ask how this primary *Iliad* would have been viewed by a poet—whether the first, or another— who desired to enlarge it without materially altering the plot. Two places in it would naturally recommend themselves, in preference to others, for the insertion of new matter; viz., the place between books 1 and 11, and that between books 11 and 16. But it is also evident that, of these two places, the former would be a poet's first choice. The purpose of Zeus to humiliate the Greeks might well be represented as effecting itself only gradually, and by a process consistent with vicissitudes of fortune. Thus there was no poetical necessity that book 1 should be closely followed by book 11. *Enlargement of the primary Iliad.*

The general contents of books 2 to 7 inclusive agree with the supposition that this group represents the earliest series of additions made (not all at one time or by one hand) to the primary *Iliad*. From book 2 we except the 'Catalogue,' which was a much later interpolation. The older part of book 2 contains the deceptive dream sent by Zeus, which fills Agamemnon with hopes of victory, and beguiles him into preparing for battle; the Council of the chiefs; and the Assembly of the army. Books 3 and 4 are closely connected, the main subjects being the truce between Greeks and Trojans, and the single combat of Menelaus and Paris, which has no decisive issue, Paris being saved by Aphrodite. Books 5 and 6, again, hang together, the prowess of Diomede being the central theme. *Books 2 to 7.*

In book 7 we have a second duel,—this time between Ajax and Hector,—which, like the former, is indecisive,— the combatants making gifts to each other at the end of it. Then the Greeks bury their dead, and build the wall at their camp.

The general characteristic of these six books (2—7) is that we have a series of detached episodes, while 'the purpose of Zeus,' announced in book 1, remains in suspense.

Books 12 to 15.   59.   Different and more difficult conditions had to be satisfied by any new work which should be inserted in the other manifestly available place,—viz., between book 11 and book 16. Zeus having utterly discomfited the Greeks in book 11, poetical fitness set a limit to the interval which could be allowed to elapse before Patroclus, the precursor of Achilles, should come to the rescue in book 16. And as the end of book 11 already forms a climax—the distress of the Greeks being extreme—in adding anything between that point and book 16 it was necessary to avoid an anti-climax. These requirements are fulfilled by the Battle at the Camp, told in books 12, 13, 14 and 15. It is the last desperate defence of the Greeks. The Trojans are rushing on to burn the ships. Ajax can barely keep the foes at bay. Then, at the supreme crisis, Patroclus arrives, in the armour of Achilles.

These four books (12—15), apart from some interpolations, possess all the intrinsic qualities of great poetry. The best proof of it is that, though the struggle is thus drawn out, our interest in it does not flag. When, however, the *Iliad* is read continuously, it is difficult to resist the belief that book 11 was originally designed to be followed more closely by book 16. Books 12 to 15, thus read, impress the mind rather as a skilful and brilliant expansion.

60.   Our primary *Iliad*, consisting of books 1, 11, and 16 to 22, has now been enlarged by the accession of these two groups; books 2—7 before book 11, and books 12—15 after it. The original plot preserves its simplicity. The

only difference is that the purpose of Zeus is now delayed, and the agony of the Greeks is prolonged.

Let us next suppose that a poet, conscious especially of rhetorical gifts, found the *Iliad* in this enlarged form. If he wished to insert some large piece of his own work, how could he best proceed, without injury to the epic framework? The part between books 11 and 16 would no longer tolerate any considerable amplification. If, again, the series of episodes between books 1 and 11 should be merely extended, the effect would be tedious, and the delay in 'the purpose of Zeus' would appear excessive. *Books 8 and 9.*

But another resource remained. Without fundamentally changing the plot, it was possible to duplicate it. The Greeks might be twice discomfited. After the first reverse, they might sue for help to Achilles—and be rejected;—an episode full of splendid opportunities for poetical eloquence and pathos. If such an episode were to be added, the right place for it evidently was immediately before the original (now to be the *second*) discomfiture of the Greeks in book 11.

The poet who conceived this idea added books 8 and 9 to the *Iliad*. Book 10 did not yet exist.

61.   Books 23 and 24 form a sequel. They are concerned with a subject always of extreme interest to Greek hearers—as, at a later period, the Attic dramatists so often remind us—the rendering of due burial rites to the chief hero slain on either side, Patroclus and Hector. The episode of the funeral games in book 23 (from v. 257 to the end) was certainly a separate addition, and is probably much later than the preceding part of that book, which relates the burial of Patroclus. The case of books 23 and 24 differs in one material respect from that of the other books which we have been considering in the light of additions to the primary *Iliad*. If books 23 and 24 are viewed simply in relation to the plot, there is no reason why they should not have belonged to the primary *Iliad* itself. It is the internal evidence of language and style which makes this improbable. Book 24 is in many ways so *Books 23 and 24.*

fine, and forms so fitting a conclusion to the *Iliad*, that
Dr Christ would ascribe it either to the first poet himself,
or to a successor executing his design.   A hint of that
design may (it is suggested) be found in book 23, where
the gods protect the corpse of Hector from disfigurement
(184—191).   On this view, books 23 and 24 would at least
be decidedly older than book 9.

These three books, however, have several traits in
common with each other, and with the *Odyssey*, which
distinguish them from the undoubtedly older parts of the
Relation *Iliad.*   And I am disposed to think that book 24, at least,
of book was mainly composed by the author of book 9.   This view
24 to
book 9. is confirmed by a comparison of the speeches in the two
books, especially in regard to a particular trait—the
rhetorical enumeration of names of places in passages
marked by strong feeling[1].   A certain emotional character,
more easily felt than defined, pervades both books; and in
both the conception of Achilles has distinctive features.
The love of contrast as a source of effect, which can be
traced in book 9, is equally present in book 24, where the
helpless old king supplicates the young warrior.   And book
24 is itself a brilliant antithesis to book 9.   The great
rhetorical poet who had shown Achilles inexorable to the
Achaean chiefs may have wished to paint a companion
picture, and to show him relenting at the prayer of the aged
Priam[2].

Book 10.   62.   All those parts of the *Iliad* which have thus far
been considered must be older than *circ.* 850—800 B.C.
Book 10 remains.   As we have already seen (§ 18), it has a
stamp of its own, which clearly marks it as a later work,

[1] *E.g.*, with 9. 149 ff. and 381 f. I would compare 24. 544 ff.
[2] Space precludes me from here developing in detail the resemblances between the two books.   But I may refer to the five verses
which describe Achilles in his tent, as he is found by the Greek envoys,
(9. 186—191).   Compare these with the five verses which describe him
in his tent as he is found by Priam (24. 471—476).   While neither
passage imitates the other, the same mind can be felt in both.

referable, perhaps, to *circ.* 750—600 B.C. A similar age
may be assigned to 'the greater interpolations.' This name
will conveniently describe a class of passages which differ
much in style and merit,—some of them containing parts of
great intrinsic brilliancy,—but which have one general
characteristic in common. Each of them presents the
appearance of a separate effort by a poet who elaborated a
single episode in a vein suited to his own resources, and
then inserted it in the *Iliad*, without much regard to the
interests of the epic as a whole. In this general character
we may recognise the mark of a period when the higher epic
art was declining, while poetical rhetoric and ingenuity
found their favourite occupation in giving an elaborate finish
to shorter pieces.

The following passages come under this class. (1) In
book 9, the episode of Phoenix, vv. 432—619—where the
desire to tell the story of Meleager was one of the motives.
(2) In book 11, the interview between Nestor and Patroclus,
vv. 596—848, or at least so much of it as is comprised in
665—762. (3) In book 18, the making of the armour of the
Achilles, vv. 369—end. (4) The Theomachia, in book 20,
vv. 4—380, (including the combat of Aeneas and Achilles,
vv. 75—352, in which Aeneas is saved by Poseidon,) and
in book 21, 383—end. (5) In book 23, the funeral games,
vv. 257—end. (6) The case of the 'Catalogue' in book 2
is peculiar. The list of the Greek forces (484—779) was
mainly the work of a Boeotian poet of the Hesiodic school,
and was probably composed long before it was inserted in
the *Iliad*. The list of the Trojan forces (816—877) seems
to have been a later adjunct to it by a different hand.

The above list might be enlarged if we included all the
passages, of any considerable extent, which have with more
or less reason been regarded as interpolations. But here
we must be content to indicate some of the more important
and more certain examples. Interpolations of the smaller
kind, which have been numerous throughout the *Iliad*, do
not fall within the scope of the present survey.

63. Thus, when the several parts of the *Iliad* are considered in relation to each other and to the whole, the result is such as to suggest that the primary *Iliad* has been enlarged by a series of additions, made at successive periods. To the earliest period belong those additions which are represented by books 2 to 7 and 12 to 15. To the next period belong, probably, books 8, 9, 23 (to v. 256), and 24. To the last period belong book 10 and the greater interpolations.

It may now be asked how far it is possible to conjecture the approximate age of the primary *Iliad*, and what relations of age and authorship probably subsist between it and the additions of the earliest period.

Achilles is a Thessalian hero, of the time when Achaean princes ruled in Peloponnesus and over a great part of northern Greece. The saga which the *Iliad* embodies undoubtedly belongs to Greece Proper, and to the Achaean age. The Dorian conquest of Peloponnesus caused a displacement of Achaean population, and impelled that tide of emigration from Greece Proper which resulted in the settlement of Greek colonies on the western coasts of Asia Minor. The eleventh century B.C. is the period traditionally assigned to this movement.

The Ionian emigrants certainly carried with them the Achaean legend of the *Iliad*. But in what shape did they carry it? As a legend not yet expressed in song? Or as a legend which the Achaean bards of Greece Proper had already embodied in comparatively rude and short lays? Or, lastly, as a poem of matured epic form—our *Iliad*, or the more essential parts of it?

64. It is the last answer which is usually intended when 'the European origin' of the *Iliad* is affirmed. Arguments in favour of the European origin have recently been advanced by Mr Monro, to the following effect[1].

---

[1] 'Homer and the Early History of Greece,' in the *English Historical Review*, No. 1, Jan., 1886.

Two strata of mythical, or mythico-historical, narrative can be distinguished in the *Iliad*. First, there are the heroes of the Trojan war. Secondly, there are heroes whom local traditions in Greece connect with an age before the Trojan war. Thus, in the time of the war, Corinth and Sicyon are under the rule of Agamemnon. But there are also notices of an earlier time, when Corinth had been subject to the dynasty represented by Sisyphus, and Sicyon to the dynasty represented by Adrastus. Now, if the *Iliad* arose in Greece Proper, it is natural that the poet who knew the legends of Agamemnon's empire should also know the older local legends, and should be able to use both sets of legends without confusing them. But, if the *Iliad* arose in Asia Minor, it is improbable that the Ionian colonists, who carried the Achaean legends over with them, should also have preserved a distinct memory of the older local legends.

65. In estimating this argument, I would suggest that the intellectual feat performed by the Ionian colonists, on the hypothesis of an Asiatic origin for the *Iliad*, seems scarcely so difficult as the argument implies. The legends of the Trojan war were presumably not the only legends which Ionian emigrants would carry with them from Greece to Asia. They would know also the more famous local legends of Greece, such as those concerning Sisyphus of Corinth, Adrastus of Sicyon, or the Perseid kings of Argos. The references in the *Iliad* to such local legends are extremely slight, being almost limited, indeed, as a rule, to the mention of names. Such knowledge might very easily have been preserved by tradition through several generations of colonists. But suppose that the knowledge shown were much fuller and more precise than it actually is: still the particular difficulty in question—that of keeping two sets of legends distinct—would exist only if the legends of the Trojan war conflicted with the local legends in such a manner that the latter would have been likely to be obscured by the greater popularity of the former, unless

kept fresh by actual residence in or near the places concerned.   In the *Iliad*, however, there is no conflict of this
nature between two sets of legends.   At the most, there is a
distinction between Achaean and pre-Achaean dynasties.
And, further, the clear evidence for this distinction is
confined to the Catalogue of the Greek forces.   It is only
the Catalogue, for example, that represents Agamemnon as
ruling *directly* over Corinth, and over Sicyon, 'where
Adrastus formerly reigned[1].'   From the rest of the *Iliad* it
appears only that Agamemnon has the seat of his empire at
Mycenae, and exercises the authority of a suzerain over a
number of subordinate kings and chiefs.   Apart from the
Catalogue, nothing in the *Iliad* is incompatible with the
supposition that the immediate ruler of Corinth, under the
emperor Agamemnon, was a king claiming descent from
Sisyphus, or of Sicyon, a king claiming descent from
Adrastus.   But the Catalogue of the Greek forces was
unquestionably composed in Boeotia, long before it was
inserted in the *Iliad*.   So far, then, as a distinction between
Achaean and pre-Achaean dynasties is clearly marked, it is
due to a poet who was certainly composing in Greece Proper.

The ar-   66.   More force belongs (in my opinion) to another
gument
from   head of argument used by Mr Monro, which concerns
Homeric   inferences that may be drawn from Homeric silence, es-
silence.

[1] *Il.* 2. 572.   The mention of Sisyphus is in *Il.* 6. 153.—Other
instances are the following.   (1) Diomede is king of Argos in the
Catalogue (2. 563).   The reign of Proetus at Argos is alluded to in
6. 157.   Sthenelus, son of Perseus, and Eurystheus, son of Sthenelus,
are referred to as kings of Argos in 19. 116 ff.   (Dr Christ regards 19.
90—356 as a later interpolation.)   (2) The Catalogue makes Thoas
leader of the Aetolians,—remarking that Oeneus and his sons were now
dead: 2. 638 ff.   (3) The Catalogue mentions Eurytus as a former
king of Oechalia (2. 596), but represents the contingent from Oechalia
as led by the sons of Asclepius,—Podaleirius and Machaon (2. 732).—As
to Castor and Polydeuces, the *Iliad* simply notices the fact of their
having died (3. 237).   Neither in it nor in the *Odyssey* (11. 299) do they
appear as representing a dynasty of kings, anterior to the Pelopid
dynasty which began with Menelaus.

pecially on three points. (i) Several of the Ionian colonies in Asia Minor claimed to have been founded by Neleidae, descendants of the Homeric Nestor. These Neleidae, the Ionians said, had removed from Pylus to Athens. But the Homeric poems nowhere connect Nestor's family with Athens. If the *Iliad* had been shaped in the Ionian colonies, the link between Pylus and Athens would probably have been supplied. (ii) The name 'Ionian' occurs once (in the *Iliad*), and 'Dorian' once (in the *Odyssey*); the name 'Aeolian' is unknown to Homer. These tribal names could hardly have failed to be more prominent if the poems had arisen in Asia Minor. (iii) The Greek colonies in Asia Minor are ignored by the Homeric poems. Even the sequel of the Trojan war concerns European Greece alone. No Homeric hero returns to Aeolis or Ionia. In one of the Cyclic poems (the Νόστοι), on the other hand, Calchas goes to Colophon.

67. What all this tends to show is, that the events, persons and names of the Trojan legend had been fixed, from a time before the Ionian emigration, in such a manner that poets could no longer venture to innovate in any essential matter. Suppose, for instance, that a poet living in Asia Minor wished to create Homeric honours for his city or its founders. He could not do so, because every one knew that the authentic Homer did not recognise that city or those persons.

Inference— early fixity of form in the Iliad.

The question is, then,—Would this degree of fixity have been already secured, if the Achaean legends had come to Asia Minor, not yet in a matured epic form, but only in the shape of comparatively rude Aeolian lays, which the Ionian poets afterwards used as material?

This is difficult to believe. It seems to me hardly possible to explain the sustained resistance of the Homeric legend to the intrusion of patriotic anachronisms except on the supposition that its form had already been fixed, in the greater lines, before it arrived in Ionia. And Dr Geddes has shown very fully how strong are the marks of a Thessalian origin in certain parts of the *Iliad*. The area over which he traces them is that of Grote's 'Achilleid',—books 1, 8, and 11 to 22. But it will be found, I think, that the area within which such marks are clearest is the more limited one of our 'primary *Iliad*,'—books 1, 11, and 16 to 22.

68. These conditions of the problem would be satisfied by a hypothesis which, if it cannot claim to be more, has at least a considerable degree of probability in its favour. A poet living in Northern Greece may have composed the substance of the primary *Iliad*,—books 1, 11, and those parts of books 16 to 22 which are essential to the plan of the epic. His work may have been done in the eleventh century B.C. The epic would then be brought by emigrants from Greece to Asia Minor with its form already fixed to an extent which would exercise a general control over subsequent enlargements. The silence of the *Iliad* on the points noticed above would be explained.

It is impossible to say with any exactness what would have been the complexion of the dialect used by a Thessalian poet *circ.* 1100—1000 B.C. But it is at least certain that it would have had a large number of word-forms in common with the Aeolic of the historical age, since Aeolic was the most conservative of the dialects in regard to the oldest forms of the language. The original, or Achaean, dialect of the *Iliad* would in Ionia be gradually modified under Ionicising influences, through Ionian poets who enlarged the epic, and rhapsodes who recited it. It would thus by degrees assume that aspect of a 'mixed dialect'—Ionic, but with an Aeolic tinge—which it now presents, and which suggested Fick's theory of a translation from Aeolic into Ionic.

69. Such a modification of dialect would not, however, suffice to explain the belief, practically universal in ancient Greece, which associated 'Homer' with the western coasts of Asia Minor. This is a fact with which we have to reckon; and it is one which the advocates of a European Homer

have often esteemed too lightly. The general belief of ancient Greece, has a significance which remains unimpaired by the rejection of local legends connecting Homer with particular cities. The case is not that of a chain which can be no stronger than its weakest link. The general belief did not rest on the aggregate of local legends. Rather, the several local claimants were emboldened to display their usually slender credentials, because, while no one knew the precise birth-place of Homer, most people were agreed that he belonged to Asia Minor. We know, too, that, from about 800 B.C., at least, Ionia was pre-eminently fertile in epic poetry. It was also the mother-country of that poetry which came next after the epic in order of development, the elegiac and iambic.

70. The Asiatic claim to Homer seems, however, entirely compatible with the European origin of the *Iliad*. The earliest additions are probably represented, as we have seen, by the older parts of books 2 to 7. In these books we can trace a personal knowledge of Asia Minor. It is in them, too, that we meet with Sarpedon and Glaucus, the leaders of the southern Lycians (cp. § 22), whose prominence is probably due to the reputed lineage of some Ionian houses. Book 12, again, shows local knowledge of Asia Minor; Sarpedon and Glaucus figure in it; and it coheres closely with books 13, 14, and 15. The older parts of books 2 to 7, and 12 to 15, may have been added in Ionia at a very early date. Books 8, 9, 23 (to v. 256), and 24— in parts of which Ionian traits occur—were also of Ionian authorship, and can hardly be later than 850—800 B.C. *The European claim can be reconciled with the Asiatic.*

Thus, while the primary *Iliad* was Thessalian, the enlarged *Iliad* would have been known, from a high antiquity, as Ionian.

71. In books 2 to 7 (excluding the Catalogue) at least two poets have wrought. In book 3 it is proposed to decide the war by a combat of two heroes, which takes place, but is indecisive: book 7 repeats the incident, only with different *Authorship of the earlier enlargements.*

persons. Both episodes cannot be due to the same hand, and that in book 7 is probably the original. Can the earlier poet of these books be the original poet of the primary *Iliad*, working under the influences of a new home in Ionia? It is possible; and the possibility must be estimated from an ancient point of view: the ancient epic poet composed with a view to recitation; only limited portions of his work could be heard at a time; and he would feel free to add new episodes, so long as they did not mar his general design. But, though possible, it seems very improbable, if the primary *Iliad* was indeed a product of Northern Greece. A poet who had migrated thence would have been unlikely to show such sympathy with Ionian life and tradition as can be traced in the allusions and persons of these books.

With regard to books 12 to 15, many features of their economy, as well as the pervading style and spirit, seem to warrant the opinion that their author, or authors, though highly gifted, had no hand in the primary *Iliad*. Whether he, or they, bore any part in the composition of books 2 to 7, there is nothing to show. Judging by the evidence of style and tone, I should say, probably not. We have seen that books 8 and 9 may be assigned to a distinct author, who probably composed also the older parts of 24, and perhaps of 23.

Predo-
minant
signifi-
cance of
the first
poet.

72. If, however, the primary *Iliad* is rightly ascribed to one poet, the attempt to define the partnership of different hands in the enlargement has only a diminished interest; as it can have, at best, only a very indecisive result. However eminent were the gifts of the enlargers, it is to the poet of the primary *Iliad*, if to any one, that the name of Homer belongs, so far as that epic is concerned. It seems vain to conjecture what relations existed between this first poet and the enlargers of his work. There is no real evidence for a clan or guild of 'Homeridae,' whom many critics (including Dr Christ) have conceived as poets standing in some peculiarly near relationship to Homer, and as, in a manner,

the direct inheritors of his art, in contradistinction to later and alien poets or rhapsodes who also contributed to the *Iliad*. As to the original 'rhapsodies' or cantos in which the poem was composed, every attempt to determine their precise limits is (in my belief) foredoomed to failure. In some particular instances the result may be accurate, or nearly so. But a complete dissection of the *Iliad* into cantos must always be largely guess-work.

73. The argument noticed above, derived from Homeric silence regarding the Asiatic colonies and the tribal names, applies to the *Odyssey* no less than to the *Iliad*. From a date prior to the settlement of the Asiatic colonies the form of the story was probably so far fixed as to preclude such references. *Origin of the Odyssey.*

It appears probable that the original 'Return of Odysseus' was a poem of small compass, composed, before the Ionian migration, in Greece Proper, though not with any close knowledge of Ithaca and the western coasts (cp. p. 44). Having been brought to Ionia by the colonists, it was there greatly enlarged.

74. The broad difference between the case of the *Iliad* and that of the *Odyssey* may be expressed by saying that the latter, in its present form, is far more thoroughly and characteristically Ionian. One cause of this may be that the original 'Return of Odysseus'—native to Greece Proper —bore a much less important relation to the final Ionian form of the poem than the primary Thessalian *Iliad* bore to the Ionian enlargement. This, indeed, would almost follow from the respective natures of the two themes, if the compass of the primary *Iliad* was rightly indicated above (§ 57). The original 'Return of Odysseus' secured fixity of general conception sufficiently to exclude allusions to the Ionian colonies, and the like. But it left a much larger scope for expansion, under specially Ionian influences, than the primary *Iliad* had left. The subject of the *Odyssey* was essentially congenial to Ionians, with their love of maritime *Ionian development of the poem.*

adventure, and their peculiar sympathy with the qualities
personified in the hero. The poem shows a familiar knowledge of Delos—the sacred island to which Ionians annually
repaired for the festival of Apollo—and of the Asiatic coast
adjacent to Chios. Still more significant is the Ionian
impress which the *Odyssey* bears as a whole,—in the tone of
thought and feeling, in the glimpses of distant voyages,
and in the gentle graces of domestic life.

Author-
ship.

75. While few careful readers can doubt that the *Odyssey*,
as it stands, has been put together by one man, there are
parts which more or less clearly reveal themselves as additions
to an earlier form of the poem: especially the 'Telemachy'
(books 1—4), the latter part of book 23 (from v. 297), and
book 24. I believe, with Kirchhoff, that the original
'Return' existed in an enlarged Ionian form, before the
present, or finally enlarged, form was given to it by another
and later Ionian hand. But I much doubt whether the
original limits of the 'Return', and of the first enlargement,
can now be determined.

Rela-
tions
with the
Iliad.

76. If any reliance can be placed on internal evidence, it
may be taken as certain that the poet of the primary *Iliad*
had no share in the authorship of the *Odyssey*. The differences of style, versification, and spirit are not merely of a
nature which could be explained by difference of subject;
the more these differences are considered, the more con-
vincingly do they attest the workings of a different mind.
It is, however, quite possible, and not improbable, that
the Ionian poet (or poets) who enlarged the *Odyssey* had
a hand in the enlargement of the *Iliad*. But, though un-
mistakeable affinities of language and manner can be traced
between the *Odyssey* and later parts of the *Iliad* (especially
books 9 and 24), we still seem to be left without adequate
evidence on which to found a presumption of personal
identity.

Age of
the
Odyssey.

With regard to the age of the *Odyssey*, we may suppose that the original 'Return' was composed in Greece

Proper as early as the eleventh century B.C., and that the
first enlargement had been made before 850 B.C. The
Cyclic *Little Iliad* (*circ.* 700 B.C.) showed the influence of
the *Odyssey*; but the only Cyclic poem which implies an
Odyssey complete in its present compass is the *Telegonia*,
which dated only from the earlier half of the sixth century
B.C. It cannot be shown, then, that Kirchhoff has gone too
low in assigning *circ.* 660 B.C. as the date of the second
enlargement.

77. In the foregoing pages the endeavour has been to Conclu-
present a connected view of the probabilities concerning sion
the Homeric question, as they now appear to me. That
view differs, as a whole, from any which (so far as I know)
has yet been stated, but harmonises several elements which
have been regarded as essential by others. Care has been
taken to distinguish at each step (as far as possible) between
what is reasonably certain, and what is only matter of
conjecture, recommended by a greater or less degree of
likelihood. The limits within which any definite solution
of the Homeric problem is possible have been more clearly
marked—as we have seen—by the labours of successive
scholars; and, with regard to these general limits, there
is now comparatively little divergence of opinion. But
the details of a question in which the individual literary
sense has so large a scope must continue to wear different
aspects for different minds. There is little prospect of
any general agreement as to what is exactly the best
mode of co-ordinating the generally accepted facts or
probabilities. Where certainty is unattainable, caution
might prescribe a merely negative attitude; but an ex-
plicit hypothesis, duly guarded, has at least the advantage of providing a basis for discussion. The reader
is induced to consider how far he agrees, or dissents, and
so to think for himself. It is possible that the progress
of Homeric study may yet throw some further light on

matters which are now obscure. The best hope of such
a gain depends on the continued examination of the
Homeric text itself, in regard to contents, language, and
style.

APPENDIX.

NOTE 1, p. 61.

THE HOUSE AT TIRYNS.

THE ancient fortress of Tiryns stood in the S. E. corner of the plain of Argos, about ¾ of a mile from the shores of the Gulf. It was built on a limestone rock, which forms a ridge measuring about 328 yards from N. to S., with an average breadth of about 109 yards. The upper part of the citadel was at the southern end, where the rock is highest. The lower citadel was at the northern end. The upper and lower citadels were separated by a section of the rocky plateau to which stairs led down from the upper citadel, and which has been designated as the middle citadel.

The excavations of Dr Schliemann have been confined to the upper and the middle citadel. The exploration of the site thus remains in-complete. The lower citadel still awaits an explorer. In the opinion of some who can judge, an excavation of the lower citadel would probably reveal the existence of chambers at a greater depth than has yet been reached. Every one must share the hope expressed by the correspondent of the *Times* (April 24, 1886), that this task may some day be undertaken. It is in the lower citadel, as the same writer observes, that the true key to the archaic history of the site may possibly be found.

The only Homeric mention of Tiryns is in the Catalogue of the Greek forces, which, as we have seen (p. 42), was mainly the work of a Boeotian poet. He is enumerating the cities whose men were led by Diomede and Sthenelus (*Il.* 2. 559):—

οἱ δ' Ἄργος τ' εἶχον Τίρυνθά τε τειχιόεσσαν.

The whole citadel of Tiryns is still encompassed by those massive walls to which the epithet refers. They are formed of huge irregular blocks of limestone, piled on one another, the interstices being filled with small stones. It had always been supposed that, in such 'Cyclopean' walls the stones were unhewn, and were not bound by mortar, being kept in position simply by their great weight. In both particulars the general belief has been corrected by the recent examination of the walls at Tiryns. It now appears that almost all the stones, before being used, had been wrought with a pick-hammer on one or several faces, and thus roughly dressed; also that, as Dr F. Adler had surmised, a clay mortar had been used for bonding.

The remains of a Byzantine Church, and of some Byzantine tombs, exist at the S. end of the plateau of the upper citadel. At his earlier visit to Tiryns, Dr Schliemann was disposed to think, from indications on the surface, that the other remains, which he has since laid bare, must be also Byzantine. These consist of house-walls, which now stand nowhere more than about a yard above the ground, while in some parts the destruction has been complete. From these remains, Dr Dörpfeld, the architect employed by Dr Schliemann, has restored the ground-plan of the original house, as shown in the accompanying sketch. Dr Dörpfeld supposes the house to have been built by

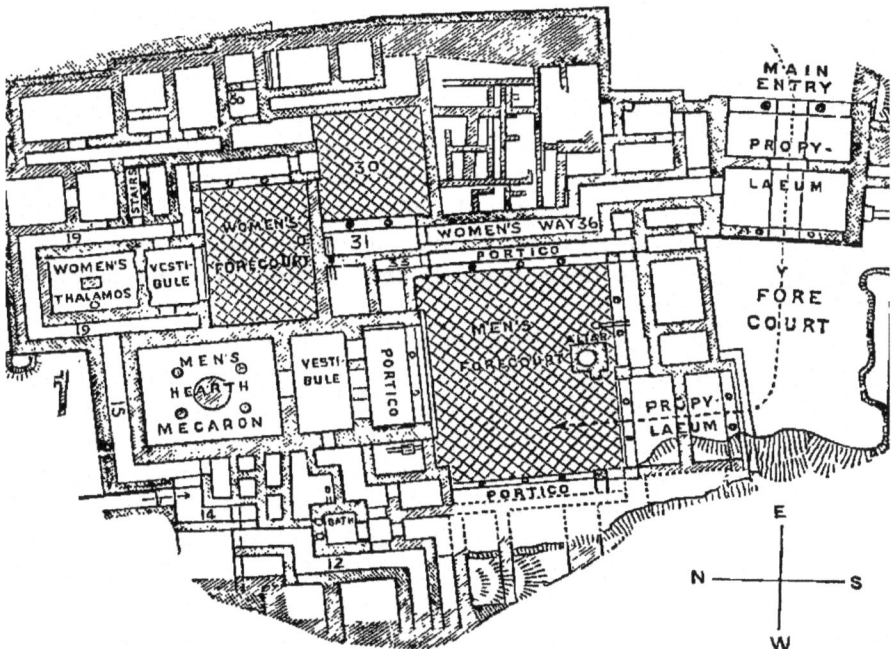

THE HOUSE AT TIRYNS.

Phoenicians, about 1100 B.C., or earlier. Mr J. C. Penrose formerly urged several objections to so early a date. The substance of his argument was reported in the *Times* of July 2, 1886, from which extracts were here cited in the previous editions of this book. The points on which he dwelt were chiefly three :—(1) 'A fundamental difference in character of work' between the 'so-called palace at Tiryns' and the really prehistoric work at Mycenae, such as the 'Treasury of Athens' and the Gate of Lions. (2) Traces of the stone-saw 'all over the newly-discovered remains.' (3) The presence of baked bricks, which, 'in the opinion of an experienced brickmaker,' could not have been brought into that state simply by a fire in which the house was burned down, if they had originally been raw bricks—as they ought to have been, on the prehistoric hypothesis. But Mr Penrose has since revisited the remains, under the guidance of Dr Dörpfeld, and has waived these objections (*Athenaeum*, Nov. 12, 1887). The advocates of a 'prehistoric' date are fully entitled to all the benefit of such a recantation. If the question as to the age of the remains is ever to be settled, it can only be settled by persons specially versed in ancient wall-building. But the impression left on most minds by the discussion, so far as it has yet gone, will be that there is ample room for disagreement, even among the most skilful. The architectural evidence is not only scanty, but is disastrously confused by the presence of 'some walls' (to quote Mr Penrose's most recent opinion) 'clearly of later date, which interfere with the proper ground-plan.' The latest utterance of an expert is Mr Stillman's (*Times*, Jan. 9, 1888), who refers to the arguments for a Byzantine date.

It is perhaps hardly necessary for the present writer to observe that he has never advanced any opinion whatever on this architectural question, as to the age of the remains at Tiryns. For the purpose of this Note, it is immaterial whether the older house-walls at Tiryns are Phoenician, of 1100 B.C., or Greek, of any period. The question with which this Note deals is solely the relation of the remains at Tiryns to Homeric evidence.

It is affirmed by Dr Schliemann and Dr Dörpfeld that the houses of the Homeric age, so far as they are known from Homer, were on the same general plan as the house at Tiryns. Now, the house of Odysseus in the *Odyssey* is the only Homeric house concerning which we have data of a kind which enables us to form a tolerably complete idea of the interior arrangements. Confirmatory evidence on some points, and additional light on others, may be gathered from the houses of Menelaus and Alcinous. These houses appear to represent the same general ground-plan. But the house of Odysseus is not merely described in more detail than the others. It happens also to be the scene of an elaborate domestic drama, occupying several books of the *Odyssey*. We have thus a searching test by which to try the correctness of any notions which we may have formed as to the plan of that house. The true plan must be such as to make the house a possible theatre for that drama.

Let the matter at issue be distinctly understood, since some confusion about it is traceable in Dr Schliemann's book *Tiryns*, as well as in the utterances of those who maintain his theory.   If the Homeric indications do not agree with the house at Tiryns, that fact does not, of itself, prove that the house is not of the Homeric (or pre-Homeric) age. No one would contend that all the houses of that age must have been built on exactly the same plan.   But in *Tiryns* (p. 227) appeal is made specifically to the house of Odysseus.   It is argued that the plan of *that* house was in general agreement with the plan found at Tiryns, and that the drama enacted in it could have been enacted at Tiryns.

Now, the evidence of the *Odyssey* proves that the poet had in his mind a house of an entirely different kind from the house at Tiryns. The difference is not merely a variation of detail.   It is a difference of type.

Dr Dörpfeld speaks with acknowledged weight when he speaks as an architect on a question of ancient architecture.   But the attempt to dispose of the literary evidence of the *Odyssey* to which he devotes a few lines at p. 227 of *Tiryns* is grotesquely superficial.   It could not have been offered, or accepted, by any one who had even a rudimentary idea of what is meant by an adequate examination of literary evidence. He notices only five verses in the whole epic.   Of these five verses, four (1. 333, 16. 415, 18. 209, 21. 64) are simply the oft-repeated

$$\sigma\tau\hat{\eta} \ \rho\alpha \ \pi\alpha\rho\grave{\alpha} \ \sigma\tau\alpha\theta\mu\grave{o}\nu \ \tau\acute{e}\gamma\epsilon os \ \pi\acute{\nu}\kappa\alpha \ \pi o\iota\eta\tau o\hat{\iota}o.$$

On this, he merely asserts, without attempting to prove, that the door at the *lower* end of the hall is intended.   The other verse (since he thus has really only two) is 21. 236, where, before the slaying of the suitors, Eurycleia is commanded

$$\kappa\lambda\eta\hat{\iota}\sigma\alpha\iota \ \mu\epsilon\gamma\acute{\alpha}\rho o\iota o \ \theta\acute{\nu}\rho\alpha s \ \pi\nu\kappa\iota\nu\hat{\omega}s \ \acute{\alpha}\rho\alpha\rho\upsilon\acute{\iota}\alpha s.$$

On this, he remarks that there is nothing to show that these doors opened on the hall; and that the object of closing them was, ' not to keep the suitors from escaping, but to keep the women undisturbed within.'

In a foot-note on the same page (227) another passage is adduced from *Od.* 6. 50 ff., where it is said that Nausicaa, after finding her mother at the hearth, met with ($\xi\acute{\nu}\mu\beta\lambda\eta\tau o$) her father as he was going forth to the council.   This argument assumes that the hearth at which Nausicaa found her mother was in the women's apartments, and that, as Nausicaa, coming thence, 'met' her father leaving the house, she entered the hall by the door from the court.   The answer is furnished by *Od.* 7. 139 ff.   We find Aretè and Alcinous sitting together in the *men's* hall near the $\dot{\epsilon}\sigma\chi\acute{\alpha}\rho\alpha$ at its upper end,—where Penelope also sits in 20. 55, and where Helen joins Menelaus (4. 121).   Nausicaa, on awaking, wishes to tell her dream to her parents.   She goes $\delta\iota\grave{\alpha}$ $\delta\acute{\omega}\mu\alpha\tau\alpha$, 'through the house,' from her own bed-chamber in the women's apartments, to the men's hall,—the door between them being open.   In the hall she finds her mother.   Her father she found, we may suppose, in the prodomus or in the aulè, 'about to go forth.' We cannot press ξύμβλητο as if it necessarily implied that the two persons were moving in exactly contrary directions. It means simply 'fell in with,' 'chanced to find.'

The evidence of the *Odyssey* on this question is not to be gauged by three phrases isolated from their context, and interpreted in a fashion at once dogmatic and unsound. It must be tested by a close and consecutive examination of the whole story, so far as it can illustrate the plan of the house. Such an examination I have attempted to make in the *Journal of Hellenic Studies*, vol. VII. p. 170 ('The Homeric House in relation to the Remains at Tiryns').

Reference to the accompanying plan will show that the house at Tiryns has certain general features in common with the Homeric house. The Homeric πρόθυρον, or front gateway of the court, is represented at Tiryns by a propylaeum,—a kind of gateway formed by placing two porticoes back to back,—which in Greece had not hitherto been found before the 5th century B.C. At Tiryns we have also a court-yard (αὐλή)— called the 'Men's Fore-Court' in the plan—with porticoes (αἴθουσαι). The *prodomus*, however, is not, at Tiryns, the space covered by the αἴθουσα, or portico, but a distinct room beyond it (called 'Vestibule' in the plan). Then there is the great hall,—the 'Men's Megaron' in the plan. So far there is a resemblance, though only of the most general kind.

But we now come to a difference much more striking and essential than the points of likeness. At Tiryns the men's hall has no outlet except the door by which it is entered from the 'Vestibule.' The women's apartments are identified with a second and smaller hall, completely isolated from the other, which has its own vestibule, its own court, and its own egress.

There is nothing whatever to show that this smaller hall and court really belonged to women. The more reasonable supposition would be that they belonged to a second and smaller house, distinct from the larger house. The arbitrary manner in which such theories can be formed or changed is curiously illustrated at p. 224 of *Tiryns*. At Hissarlik in the Troad, as at Tiryns, there are the remains of two buildings, a larger and a smaller, side by side. After propounding other views about them, Dr Schliemann had decided in *Troja* that they were to be temples. But, because the smaller court at Tiryns is to be the women's court, Dr Dörpfeld now says that the larger building at Hissarlik was a dwelling for men, and the smaller building beside it a dwelling for women. He doubts, however, whether the smaller building at Hissarlik was not 'a smaller men's house' (p. 224). Why, then, should not the smaller court at Tiryns be a smaller men's court?

From the men's hall at Tiryns to the so-called women's hall the only modes of access were by very circuitous and intricate routes. They are thus described by Dr Dörpfeld (*Tiryns*, p. 236):—'In the north-west part of the palace lies a small court, with colonnades and adjoining rooms, which has no direct connection with the main court; it is the court of the women's dwelling. You must pass many doors and corridors to reach this inner part of the palace. There appear to have been three ways of reaching it. First, from the back-hall of the great Propylaeum, through the long passage XXXVI., to the colonnade XXXI.; and from this, through the outer court XXX., to the east colonnade of the women's court. Secondly, you could go from the great court or from the megaron, past the bath-room, into corridor XII., and then through passages XIV., XV., and XIX., to reach the vestibule of the women's apartments. A third way probably went from the east colonnade of the great court, through room XXXIII., into the colonnade XXI., and then along the first way into the court of the women's apartments. All these three approaches are stopped in several places by doors, and the women's apartment was therefore quite separated from the great hall of the men's court.'

The above three routes can readily be traced on our plan by means of the Arabic numerals which I have placed to represent Dr Dörpfeld's Roman numerals:—(1) for the first route,—36, 31, 30: (2) for the second, 12, 14, 15, 19: (3) for the third, 33, 31, 30.

In the house of Odysseus, on the contrary, the women's apartments were immediately behind the men's hall, and directly communicated with it by a door. This is proved by many passages, among which are the following.

1. In book 17 Odysseus comes to his house in the guise of an aged beggar. Telemachus, to whom alone the secret is known, is in the great hall with the suitors. Odysseus, with the humility proper to his supposed quality, sits down 'on the threshold of ash, within the doors' (17. 339):

ἷζε δ' ἐπὶ μελίνου οὐδοῦ ἔντοσθε θυρίων,

i.e. at the lower end of the hall, on the threshold of the doorway leading into it from the prodomus. The suitors who, with their retinue, numbered about a hundred and twenty, were feasting at a series of small tables, which may be imagined as arranged in two rows from end to end of the hall, leaving in the middle a free space in which the twelve axes were afterwards set up. Telemachus sends food to Odysseus, with a message that he should advance into the hall, and beg alms from table to table among the suitors. Odysseus does so; and, while he is thus engaged, one of the suitors, Antinous, strikes him. Odysseus then returns to his place on the ashen threshold. Meanwhile Penelope is sitting among her handmaids in the women's apartments (17. 505). She hears—doubtless through one of the women-servants—of the blow dealt by Antinous to the humble stranger; and she sends to the hall for Eumaeus. When he comes, she desires him to go and bring the mendicant into her presence. He delivers her message to Odysseus, who is still seated on the ashen threshold. Odysseus replies that he would gladly go to Penelope; 'but,' he adds, 'I somewhat fear the throng of the froward wooers. . . . . . For even now, as I was going through the hall, when yon man struck me, and pained me sore,—though I had done no wrong,—neither Telemachus nor anyone else came to my aid.' That is, he declines to go to Penelope, because, in order to reach her apartments, he would have *to pass up the hall*, among the suitors, one of whom had already insulted him.

2. The supposed mendicant is then accommodated for the night with a rough 'shake-down' in the prodomus—the fore-hall or vestibule of the megaron. As he lies awake there, he observes some of the handmaids pass forth from the men's hall (20. 6) :—

$$\kappa\epsilon\hat{\iota}\tau' \,\,\dot{\epsilon}\gamma\rho\eta\gamma\rho\acute{o}\omega\nu\cdot\,\,\tau\alpha\hat{\iota}\,\,\delta'\,\,\dot{\epsilon}\kappa\,\,\mu\epsilon\gamma\acute{a}\rho\omega\iota\,\,\gamma\upsilon\nu\alpha\hat{\iota}\kappa\epsilon\varsigma$$
$$\ddot{\eta}\ddot{\iota}\sigma\alpha\nu.$$

But, after escorting Penelope to the interview with the stranger in the hall, they had returned to the women's apartments (19. 60). Thus again it appears that the direct way from the women's apartments to the court lay through the men's hall.

3. The next day, while the suitors are revelling in the hall, and taunting Telemachus, Penelope is sitting, as before, in the women's apartments. She is not in her own room on the upper storey, to which she presently ascends (21. 5), but on the ground-floor, level with the hall. She places her chair 'over against' the hall ($\kappa\alpha\tau'$ $\dot{\alpha}\nu\tau\eta\sigma\tau\iota\nu$, 20. 387), *i.e.* close to the wall dividing the hall from the women's apartments; and thus 'she heard the words of each one of the men in the hall' (20. 389). Similarly in 17. 541, being in the women's apartments, she heard Telemachus sneeze in the hall. Such incidents would be impossible in a house of the type supposed at Tiryns.

4. In preparation for the slaying of the suitors, Odysseus and his son decide to remove the arms from the hall, and to carry them to a room in the inner part of the house. That such was the position of the armoury is made certain by the phrases used with regard to it,—$\epsilon\ddot{\iota}\sigma\omega$ (19. 4), $\dot{\epsilon}\sigma\phi\acute{o}\rho\epsilon\omicron\nu$ (19. 32), $\ddot{\epsilon}\nu\delta\omicron\nu$ (22. 140). But, before doing this, Telemachus, in the hall, 'called forth' the nurse Eurycleia (19. 15), and said to her: 'Shut up the women in their chambers, till I shall have laid by in the armoury the goodly weapons of my father.' Thereupon 'she closed the doors of the chambers' (19. 30), and the removal of the arms was effected. Whence was Eurycleia 'called forth' into the

hall? Evidently from the women's apartments immediately behind it, as in the similar case at 21. 378. The doors which she closed were those leading from the women's apartments into the hall. The arms were then taken from the hall to the armoury by a side-passage (to be noticed presently), which ran along the wall on the outside.

5. The threshold on which Odysseus first sat is called, as we have seen, the threshold of ash (μέλινος), and was at the lower end of the hall (17. 339). Next day, Telemachus makes him sit down 'by the *stone* threshold' (παρὰ λάϊνον οὐδόν, 20. 258), which was clearly at the upper end of the hall. The stone threshold is that which Penelope crosses in passing from the women's apartments to the hall (23. 88). Odysseus is still sitting by the stone threshold, when Eumaeus comes to his side, and calls forth Eurycleia from the women's apartments,— another indication that the door opening upon those apartments was at the upper end of the hall.

It has been suggested that we can obviate the difficulty of supposing the women's apartments at Tiryns to have had no communication with the men's except by circuitous routes, if we imagine that, in a side-wall of the men's hall, on the right hand of a person entering it, there once existed a side-door, raised some feet above the level of the floor, and no longer traceable in the existing remains of the house-walls, which are nowhere more than about a yard in height. Such a side-door is mentioned in *Od.* 22. 126: ὀρσοθύρη δέ τις ἔσκεν ἐϋδμήτῳ ἐνὶ τοίχῳ, This ὀρσοθύρη, or 'raised postern,' opened upon a passage (λαύρη), which ran along the outside of the hall. (See the plan at p. 58.)

Let us suppose, then, that such an ὀρσοθύρη once existed at Tiryns, though no trace of it is now visible. It would have necessarily been the usual mode of access from the women's to the men's hall, as being, at Tiryns, the only one which was not extremely circuitous. To it, therefore, we should have to refer the often-repeated phrase concerning Penelope as she enters the men's hall from the women's apartments: στῆ ῥα παρὰ σταθμὸν τέγεος πύκα ποιητοῖο (1. 333, etc.). But this phrase, 'she stood by the door-post of the hall,' must refer to one of the principal entrances to the hall. It is manifestly quite inapplicable to a small raised postern in a side-wall.

Moreover, the hypothesis of an ὀρσοθύρη at Tiryns leaves a whole series of difficulties untouched. The following are some of them,— the first three turning on passages noticed above.

(1) Odysseus, being at the *lower* end of the hall, refuses to go to the women's rooms because he would have to pass up the hall among the suitors. At Tiryns he would only have had to turn his back upon the suitors, and to leave the hall.

(2) The women, coming from their own sleeping-rooms at night, issue from the men's hall, and pass by Odysseus sleeping in the pro-

domus. At Tiryns they would have gone out by the separate approach to their own court. They could not have passed through the men's hall, or its prodomus.

(3) Eumaeus, when at the *upper* end of the hall, is in the right position to call forth Eurycleia from the women's apartments, and to charge her privily to close them. At Tiryns, even with the hypothetical ὀρσοθύρη, this could not have so happened.

(4) After the slaying of the suitors, Telemachůs, being in the men's hall, calls forth Eurycleia by striking a closed door (22. 394). Now, the ὀρσοθύρη was at this time open (22. 333); so, also, was the door at the lower end of the hall (22. 399). The door, leading to the women's apartments, which Telemachus struck, must therefore be a third door, distinct from both of these. It was the door at the upper end of the hall, as the whole evidence of the *Odyssey* shows. In the house at Tiryns it has no existence.

(5) In the house at Tiryns the armoury (θάλαμος ὅπλων) has to be identified with one of the small rooms on the side of the women's hall furthest from the men's hall. Such a position,—accessible from the men's hall only by long and intricate routes,—is wholly irreconcileable with that easy and swift access to the armoury which is required by the narrative of the μνηστηροφονία in book 22 of the *Odyssey* : see especially vv. 106—112.

‘A suggested restoration of the Great Hall in the Palace of Tiryns’ has been published by Prof. J. H. Middleton in the *Journ. Hellen. Studies*, VII. 161. Some points in this call for notice. (1) In *Od.* 22. 142,—where the suitors, shut into the hall, are being shot down by Odysseus from the threshold at its lower end,—the goat-herd Melanthius, an ally of the suitors, contrives to escape from the hall, and to bring armour for them from the armoury. The way in which Melanthius left the hall is thus described :—‘he went up by the ῥῶγες of the hall’:—

> ὡς εἰπὼν ἀνέβαινε Μελάνθιος, αἰπόλος αἰγῶν,
> ἐς θαλάμους Ὀδυσῆος ἀνὰ ῥῶγας μεγάροιο.

What the ῥῶγες were, is doubtful: to me it seems most probable that they were the narrow passages, reached from the hall by the ὀρσοθύρη, by which one could pass round, outside the hall, into the back part of the house, where the armoury was. This was the view of Eustathius, and it has recently been supported by Mr J. Protodikos, in his essay *De Aedibus Homericis* (Leipsic, 1877). The Modern Greek ῥοῦγα, ‘narrow passage,’ is probably the Homeric ῥώξ, ῥωγός,—ω having become ου as in the Modern σκουλίκι from σκώληξ, etc.; and the old noun of the 3rd decl. having given the stem for a new noun of the 1st, as in the Modern νύχτα from νύξ, etc. Another suggested etymology for ῥοῦγα,—from the low Latin *ruga* as = 'path', whence O. It. *ruga* and Fr. *rue* (see Brachet *s. v.*),—fails to carry ῥοῦγα far enough back ; and the way in which the ῥῶγες are mentioned (*Od.* 22. 143) proves that the word was in familiar use. Prof. Constantinides has given me an illustration of the modern use which is curiously apposite. It is in a folk-song from the country near Cyzicus. A monster is chasing a princess :—

στοὺς δρόμους τὴν κυνήγαγε,
μὲς τὴν αὐλὴ τὴν διώχνει,
καὶ μὲς ταῖς ῥούγαις ταῖς στεναῖς
τοῦ παλατιοῦ τὴν φθάνει:

'he hunts her to the streets, he pursues her into the court, and *in the narrow passages of the palace* he overtakes her.'

Prof. Middleton favours a different view. Dr Dörpfeld had suggested that over the four pillars of the hall at Tiryns there may have been a lantern, serving for the escape of smoke from the hearth, as well as for light. [The late Mr James Fergusson, who had suggested such an arrangement in the case of the Parthenon, thought it improbable, on account of the dimensions, at Tiryns; where he rather believed that the hall had been lighted by vertical openings in the upper parts of the side-walls: *Tiryns*, p. 218, n.] Prof. Middleton suggests that the ῥῶγες may have been windows in this lantern. He supposes that Melanthius swarmed up one of the pillars in the hall, escaped by the windows on to the roof, and thence descended by a stair to the armoury. But he has overlooked some points in the Homeric story which appear conclusive against this theory. The first exit of Melanthius—who goes twice to the armoury—is not observed by Odysseus, or by any one of his three supporters. This is an absurdity, if Melanthius had performed the feat of climbing from the floor to the roof of the hall up one of the central pillars, in full view of his alert adversaries. Further, Melanthius returns from the armoury with twelve shields, twelve spears, and twelve helmets (22. 144). His return is as unnoticed as his exit. But to climb down the pillar, with the load just described, and yet entirely to elude the observation of watchful enemies, would be a feat even more remarkable than the furtive ascent. If the ῥῶγες are to be lantern-windows, some way, other than a pillar, must be shown by which they could have been reached. (2) Prof. Middleton puts the 'stone threshold' at the *lower* end of the hall (since he assumes that the hall had no door at the upper end). He puts the threshold of ash in the prodomus. But, on his view, the ὀρσοθύρη in the side-wall was the 'direct communication between the Megaron of the men and the women's apartments' (p. 167). Yet, in passing from the women's apartments to the men's hall, Penelope crosses the stone threshold (*Od.* 23. 88).

All the Homeric evidence tends to show that the Homeric house is the prototype of the later Greek house of the historical age. A dwelling on the supposed Tirynthian plan differs from this Greek type in a vital respect. By placing the women in a practically separate house, with a separate egress, it fails to provide for their seclusion in the sense which ancient Greek feeling required.

The space which has here been given to this subject is amply justified by its importance in two general aspects. First,—the interpretation of the *Odyssey* is reduced to chaos, if these fragmentary house-walls at Tiryns,—of doubtful age and origin,—are accepted as at once sufficing to upset all the plainest evidence of the Homeric text. Secondly,—this case is typical of a tendency which, in the interests alike of archaeology and of scholarship, is to be deprecated. No one questions the intrinsic interest and value of the Tiryns remains, whatever may be their date or source. Nor is the classical scholarship of the present day at all disposed to neglect the invaluable light derived from classical archaeology. But when, as at Tiryns, it is sought to bring monuments into relation with texts, then the difficulties which those texts present should be either fairly answered or frankly allowed.

NOTE 2, p. 136.

DIFFERENCES BETWEEN HOMERIC AND LATER CLASSICAL GREEK.

The following synopsis exhibits the principal points of difference. On the subject of this Note, as on those of Notes 3 and 4, students may be referred for further illustrations to Mr Monro's *Grammar of the Homeric Dialect* (Clarendon Press, 1882).

I. *Forms of words.*

1. The number of *strong aorists* in Homer is much larger than in later Greek. (A 'strong' aorist is one formed directly from the verbal stem, as ἔλαβον from λαβ: a 'weak' aorist is one formed with a suffix: as ἔλυ-σα. So in English 'took' is a strong tense : 'loos-ed' is a weak tense.) 'Strong' tenses are mostly formed in the vigorous youth of a language : then it ceases to add to their number, or even drops some of them out of use, and tends to multiply 'weak' tenses. Further, certain *kinds* of strong aorist occur in Homer which afterwards became extinct : viz., (i) the 2nd aor. midd. formed from the stem without a connecting (or 'thematic') vowel (like the o in ἔλαβ-ο-ν, the ε in ἔλαβ-ε-s), as ἆλ-το, 'leaped.' (ii) The reduplicated aor. act. and midd., as δέδαεν, λελάβεσθαι, of which ἤγαγον is the only Attic example.

2. In post-Homeric Greek the vowels ω and η *regularly* mark the subjunctive in all tenses. In Homer they mark it (chiefly in the pres. subjunct.) *only when the indicative has* o *or* ε. Thus Homer has subj. ἔλωμεν, the indic. being εἴλομεν : but subj. ἴομεν ('let us go'), the indic. being ἴμεν.

3. In Homer, the perfect-stem (formed by reduplicating the verbal stem) varies from long to short in different parts of the same perfect (or pluperf.) tense : as ἀρήρει, ἀρηρώς, but ἀρἄρυῖα : τεθήλει, but τεθἄλυῖα. Here, as in the subjunct. with short vowel, Homer agrees with Vedic Sanscrit. In Attic this variation is a rare exception, as in οἶδ-α, ἴσ-μεν.

II. *Syntax.*

1. In Homer the Definite Article ὁ, ἡ, τό most often occurs in the *substantival* use, *i.e.*, as an independent pronoun. Attic (except in a few special usages, such as ὁ μέν...ὁ δέ) has the *attributive* use, *i.e.*, the art. is joined to a noun.

2. Besides the particle ἄν, Homer has also κεν, of which the meaning is almost identical, the main differences being these : (*a*) κεν is commoner than ἄν, the ratio in the *Iliad* being about four to one. (*b*) ἄν is preferred in negative clauses. (*c*) ἄν is rarely used with the relative (ὅς, ὅττι, etc.), though often with temporal or final conjunctions (ὅτε, ὄφρα, etc.). (*d*) while κεν is frequent in two or more clauses of one sentence (as *Il.* 1. 324), ἄν is esp. used in the second clause (*Il.* 19. 228). Briefly, ἄν is preferred to κεν where the sense is *emphatic*, or *adversative*.

3. The *future indicative* is used with ἄν or κεν.

4. The *subjunctive* is used with ἄν or κεν in simple sentences (*Il.* 3. 54 οὐκ ἄν τοι χραίσμῃ, 'shall not avail thee').

5. The subjunctive is used after εἰ, not only with ἄν or κεν, but also without it.

6. The subjunctive = an emphatic future in *negative* clauses (*Il.* 1. 262, οὐδὲ ἴδωμαι, nor *shall* I see) : and also in the phrase καί ποτέ τις εἴπῃσι (*shall* say), *Il.* 6. 459 etc.

7. The *optative* in a simple sentence, without ἄν or κεν, can express *possibility*, usu. in a negative sentence (*Il.* 19. 321), but sometimes in an affirmative (*Od.* 3. 231).

8. Homer uses *prepositions* with the freedom of *adverbs :* separating them (*a*) from the verb which they qualify ('tmesis'), or (*b*) from the case which they govern. In later Greek this usage has much narrower limits. This is another point of resemblance between Homeric language and Sanscrit, in which prepositions never reached the stage of governing nouns.

NOTE 3, p. 139.

DIFFERENCES BETWEEN THE LANGUAGE OF THE *ILIAD* AND OF THE *ODYSSEY.*

I. *Prepositions.*

The following uses are found in the *Odyssey*, while they are either absent from the *Iliad*, or occur only in certain later parts of it.

(1) ἀμφί='about', with dat., after a verb of *speaking* or *thinking*: 4. 151 ἀμφ᾽ Ὀδυσῆι | μυθεόμην.

(2) περί with gen., similarly: 1. 135 περὶ πατρὸς ἔροιτο.

(3) μετά with gen.='among' or 'with': 10. 320 μετ᾽ ἄλλων λέξο ἑταίρων. (So twice in later parts of *Iliad*, 21. 458, the θεῶν μάχη, and 24. 400.)

(4) ἐπί as='extending over': 1. 299 πάντας ἐπ᾽ ἀνθρώπους. (So in *Il.* 9, 10, 24.)

(5) πρός with dat.='besides': 10. 68 πρὸς τοῖσι.

(6) ἀνά with gen.: 2. 416 ἀνὰ νηὸς | βαίνω.

(7) κατά with acc. 'on' (business, etc.): 3. 72 κατὰ πρῆξιν.

(8) ἐνί='among', with persons or abstract words: 2. 194 ἐν πᾶσι. This occurs in *Il.*, but almost exclusively in 9, 10, 23, 24.

(9) ἐκ='in consequence of': 3. 135 μήνιος ἐξ ὀλοῆς. (So in *Il.* 9. 566.)

II. *Article.*

The *substantival* use of the art. is more frequent in Homer than the *attributive* (see Note 2). But certain special forms of the attributive use are clearly more frequent in *Il.* than in *Od.*, or *vice versa.* Thus:

(i) The *contrasting* use is more frequent in *Il.*, as 2. 217 φολκὸς ἔην, χωλὸς δ᾽ ἕτερον πόδα, τὼ δέ οἱ ὤμω, 'but then his shoulders'—where τώ *contrasts* them with the other members.

(ii) The *defining* use, often with a hostile or scornful tone (cp. *iste*), is more frequent in *Od.*: as 12. 113 τὴν ὀλοὴν...Χάρυβδιν, '*that* dire Charybdis': 18. 114 τοῦτον τὸν ἄναλτον, 'this man—insatiate that he is.'

III. *Pronouns.*

(1) The strictly reflexive use of ἕο is more frequent in *Il.* than in *Od.*, in a ratio of more than 2 : 1.

(2) τό as a relative pron., in the adverbial sense 'wherefore', often occurs in *Il.* (as 3. 176), but only once in *Od.* (8. 332).

(3) ὅς is sometimes demonstrative in *Il.*: never in *Od.*: unless in 4. 388, a doubtful example.

IV.   *Conjunctions, particles, adverbs, etc.*

(1)   ὅτι = 'that' is commoner in *Il.* than in *Od.*, which prefers ὡς or οὕνεκα.

(2)   οὕνεκα as = 'that' occurs several times after verbs of 'saying', ptc., in *Od.*, but only once in *Il.* (11. 21).

(3)   The combination μὲν οὖν, marking a transition, is characteristic of the *Odyssey* (with *Il.* 9. 550).

(4)   οὐδέν in *Il.* is usu. adv., 'not at all', or subst., 'nothing': in *Od.* it is also an adj. (οὐδὲν ἔπος, 4. 350 etc.), and so once in *Il.* 10. 216. (*Il.* 24. 370 is not a clear instance.)

V.   *Dependent clauses.*

(1)   Final relative clauses as *Od.* 10. 538 μάντις ἐλεύσεται ..ὅς κέν τοι εἴπῃσι.   Such clauses are decidedly more frequent in *Od.* than in *Il.* Of 24 examples brought by Delbrück (*Synt. Forsch.* 1. 130-2), 17 are from the *Odyssey*.

(2)   Object clauses with εἰ after verbs of telling, knowing, seeing, thinking etc. : as *Od.* 12. 112 ἐνίσπες | εἴπως...ὑπεκπροφύγοιμι.   This is frequent in *Od.*, but extremely rare in *Il.*

NOTE 4, p. 140.

HOMERIC WORDS WHICH SHOW TRACES OF THE DIGAMMA.

(1)   The following words, as used in Homeric verse, show traces of a lost initial *F*.   The effect of *F* appears either in warranting hiatus or in making position (see p. 141).   In almost all these words, however, the Homeric observance of *F* is more or less inconstant.   As regards most of them, the *F* is attested, independently of metre, by the corresponding forms in other languages.   But it will be seen that an asterisk is prefixed to a few words in the list.   This· means that, in their case, such confirmatory evidence is either wanting or doubtful, and that metre affords the principal (or the only) ground for supposing that they once began with *F*.

ἄγνυμι, *to break.*—ἅλις (rt. Fελ, *to press*), *enough.*—ἄναξ, *lord*, ἄνασσα, ἀνάσσειν.—*ἀραιός, *thin.*—ἄρνα, ἄρνες, etc., *lamb.* [In *Od.* 9. 444, however, ἀρνειός, *a young ram*, has no *F.*]—ἄστυ, *town.* Sanscr. *vāstu.*—ἔαρ, *spring.* Lat. *ver.*—εἴκοσι, *twenty.* Lat. *viginti.*—εἴλω (Fελ), *to press,* ἔλσαι, ἀλείς, ἐελμένος: with the cognate ἀλῶναι (cp. ἐ-άλων).—εἰλύω (Fελ, perh. distinct from the last), *to wrap round;* εἰλυφάζω, *to roll;* with the cognate ἑλίσσω, *to wind;* ἕλιξ, *spiral.*—εἴργω (Fεργ), *to keep off.* εἴρω (Fερ), *to say,* fut. ἐρέω. Cp. Lat. *ver-bum,* Eng. *word.*—ἕννυμι (Fεσ), *to clothe;* εἷμα, ἐσθής. Lat. *ves-tis.*—ἔπος (Fεπ), *word;* εἰπεῖν;

ὄψ, *voice.* Cp. Lat. *vox.*—ἔργον, *work;* ἔρδω. Cp. Eng. *work.*—ἐρύω,
to draw, ἔρρω, *to go away.* Cp. ἀπό-ερσε, *tore away,* and Lat. *verro.*—
ἕσπερος, *evening.* Lat. *vesper.*—ἔτος, *year.* Cp. Lat. *vetus.*—*ἤνοψ,*
gleaming.—ἦρα in ἐπὶ ἦρα φέρειν, *to gratify.* Cp. Sanscrit rt. *var,* 'to
choose'; Zend *vāra,* 'wish', 'gift': Curtius *Etym.* § 659.—*ἠρίον,* a
barrow. *Il.* 23. 126.—ἰάχω, *to cry aloud,* ἰαχή, ἠχή. (For αὔλαχος, see
Note on *Homeric Versification,* § VIII.)—ἰδεῖν, οἶδα, εἶδος. Lat. *video,*
Eng. *wit.*—*Ἴλιος. 50 instances make for Ϝίλιος, and 14 against it.—
ἴον, *violet,* ἴοεις, ἰοδνεφές. Lat. *viola.*—*Ἶρις and Ἶρος (connected with
εἴρω?).—ἴς, *sinew, strength,* ἶνες, ἶφι, ἴφια. Lat. *vis.*—ἶσος, *equal.*—
ἴτυς, *felloe of a wheel.*—ἰτέη, *willow.* Cp. Lat. *vimen, vitis:* Eng. *withe.*
—οἶκος, *house.* Lat. *vicus:* Eng. *-wick* in *Berwick,* etc.—οἶνος, *wine.*
Lat. *vinum.* Eng. *wine.*—οὐλαμός, *press of battle* (Ϝελ).

Words which once began with Ϝ sometimes have ε prefixed to them
in Homer: as ἐ-έλδωρ, *wish* (Ϝελδ): ἐ-είκοσι: ἐ-έργει: ἐ-έ. And the
syllabic augment or reduplication can be prefixed as if Ϝ remained: ἐ-άγη,
ἐ-έλπετο, ἔ-οικα, ἐ-ελμένος, etc.

(2) The following words originally began with σϜ. The rough
breathing represents the original σ. If, as is probable, the σ had
already been lost in Ionic at a time when the sound Ϝ was still used,
the initial sound of such words would then have been 'Ϝ, like Eng. *wh.*
For example, there would have been a period when the word originally
pronounced *swandano,* and afterwards *handano,* would have been
whandano ('Ϝανδάνω).

ἀνδάνω (σϜαδ), *to please,* Homeric aor. εὔαδον (=ἔϜαδον), perf. part.
ἐᾱδώς : ἡδύς. Lat. *suavis.*—ἔδνα, *a wooer's gifts,* is prob. from the same
rt.—ἑκυρός (σϜεκυρ), *father-in-law.* Lat. *socer* (where *so*=orig. *sva,* as
in *somnus,* =Sanscr. *svápnas*): cp. Germ. *Schwiegervater.*—ἕο, εὖ, οὗ,
οἷ, ἕ, pron. 3rd pers. sing., with possessive ἑός, ὅς. Sanscr. rt. *sva:* Lat.
sui, suus. This pron. is the only Homeric word in which Ϝ lengthens
a preceding short syllable *which has not ictus:* as *Il.* 9. 377 ἐρρέτω· |
ἐκ γάρ | εὖ φρένας εἵλετο κ.τ.λ. ἕξ, *six.* (Primitive form, *svaks:* Curt.
§ 584.)

The aspirate has been lost in ἤθεα, from rt. σϜεθ. Cp. Sanscr. *svadhā,*
'one's own doing': from *sva* comes also Lat. *sue-sco.*—ἔθων and εἴωθα
have no Ϝ in Hom.—ἔθνεα, which also takes Ϝ, is perh. akin to ἔθος,
ηθος.—A similar instance is prob. ἔτης, *companion* (σϜέ-της, 'one's own
man ').

(3) Initial δϜ.—δεῖσαι, *to fear,* δέος, δεινός, δειλός show the original
δϜ by often lengthening a short vowel before them. So also δήν, *for
a long while,* δηρόν, δηθά. Curtius, with Benfey and Leo Meyer, regards
δϜήν, δϜαν as shortened from διϜαν, accusative from stem διϜα 'day'.

(4) Initial Ϝρ.—While initial ῥ can represent an original σρ (as in
ῥέω), there are other instances in which t represents an original Ϝρ.

Such are ῥέξω, *to do*, ῥιγέω, *to shiver*, ῥεῖα, ῥέα, *easily;* before which a short vowel is sometimes, but not always, lengthened: ῥήγνυμι, *to break*, ῥίπτω, *to throw*, ῥάκος, *a rag;* before which a short vowel is always lengthened: ῥινός, *a hide*, ῥίζα, *u root;* before which it is usually lengthened.

(5) Medial *F.*—The loss of *F* from the middle of a word is sometimes shown (*a*) by contraction, as εἴρυσα, *I drew*, = ἐϝέρυσα : Λυκούργου = Λυκοϝργου : (*b*) by synizesis, as πολέας (a disyllable) from πολέϝας.— A lost *F* after a prep. in composition usually warrants hiatus, as διαειπέμεν : but there are exceptions, as ἀπειπέμεν (*Od.* 1. 91).

(6) Total disappearance of *F.* In some words, which certainly once had initial *F*, Homeric metre shows no trace of the fact. These words begin with ο, ου, or ω.

ὁράω, *to see;* οὖρος, οὐρεύς, *watcher;* ὄρεσθαι, *to watch.* Cp. Lat. *vereor:* Germ. *warten, wahren.*—ὄρος, *mountain.* Cp. Βορέας. Lat. *verr-uca,* 'a wart', has been compared.—Ὀρτυγίη, from ὄρτυξ, 'a quail', Sanscr. *vartakas.*—ὄχοι, ὄχεα, *chariot* (cp. Lat. *veho*); ὀχλίζω, *to heave up* (cp. Lat. *vectis*); ὀχθέω, *to be vexed* (cp. Lat. *vehemens, vexo*).—ὀμφή, *voice* (ϝεπ, *vox*).—οὐλαί, *barley-groats*, οὐλοχύται (ϝελ).—οὐρανός, *sky* (Sanscr. *várunas*, rt. *var*, 'to cover').—οὐτάω, *to wound;* ὠτειλή (cp. ἄ-ουτος = ἄϝουτος).—ὠθέω, *to push* (Sanscr. rt. *vadh*, to strike: cp. ἔ-ωσα = ἔϝωσα).—ὦνος, *price* (Sanscr. *vasnás*, Lat. *ven-um, ven-eo, ven-do*).

NOTE 5.

HOMERIC VERSIFICATION.

The best treatment of the subject, for English students, will be found in Prof. Seymour's *Homeric Language and Verse* (Boston, U. S. A., Ginn and Co., 1885). The scope of this Note is limited to giving a short view of the most essential matters, in a form convenient for reference.

I. *Dactyls and spondees.*

In the *Iliad* and *Odyssey* dactyls are about thrice as frequent as spondees. This is one of the causes to which the Homeric hexameter owes its rapidity, as the Virgilian hexameter often owes its peculiar majesty to the larger spondaic element—a condition which the Latin language imposed, and which Virgil treated with such consummate skill. Verses in which every foot except the sixth is a dactyl (τὸν δ' ἀπαμειβόμενος προσέφη πόδας ὠκὺς Ἀχιλλεύς) are far more frequent in Homer than in Virgil. On the other hand, verses in which every foot except the fifth is a spondee (*Ut belli signum Laurenti Turnus ab arce*) are much commoner in Virgil than in Homer.

Verses are technically called 'spondaic' (σπονδειάζοντες στίχοι, σπονδειακὰ ἔπη) when the fifth foot is a spondee, whether the first four feet are purely spondaic, or not. About 4 verses in every 100 of the *Iliad* are, in this limited sense, 'spondaic,'—a larger proportion than is found in Latin poetry. One or two apparent instances, however, break the rule that the hexameter must not end with two words, each of which is a spondee: thus in *Od.* 9. 306, ἠῶ δῖαν, we should write ἠόα; and in *Od.* 14. 239, δήμου φῆμις, δήμοο. Verses in which every foot is a spondee are extremely rare: our texts have only three in each epic (*Il.* 2. 544, 11. 130, 23. 221: *Od.* 15. 334, 21. 15, 22. 175, repeated 192); and most, if not all, of these would admit a dactyl by the restoration of uncontracted forms. In Latin, where the temptation was stronger, there was a similar reluctance to imitate Ennius in his *olli respondet rex Albai longai*.

II. *Caesura.*

'Caesura' is the 'cutting' (τομή) of a metrical foot by the break between two words; as in μῆνιν | ἄειδε the dactyl is cut. Such a break between words necessarily causes a slight pause of the voice; which may, or may not, coincide with a pause in the sense. Hence the phrase, 'caesural pause'; and the caesura itself is sometimes called simply a 'pause'.

In every metrical foot there is one syllable on which the chief strength of tone, or *ictus*, falls. This is called the 'ictus-syllable'. It is the first syllable in a dactyl ($\stackrel{\angle}{} \smile \smile$), and in a spondee ($\stackrel{\angle}{} -$). It is also called the *arsis* ('raising', as if the voice were raised on it); while the rest of the foot is called the *thesis* ('lowering'). This is the current use of the terms, derived from Roman writers. But the correct use—the old Greek one—is exactly opposite: in it, θέσις meant 'putting down the foot',—hence the syllable marked by the beat or *ictus:* ἄρσις meant the 'lifting of the foot',—hence the syllable, or syllables, not so marked.

When caesura follows the ictus-syllable, it is called *masculine*, because it gives a vigorous effect. When it comes between two syllables, neither of which has ictus (such as the second and third syllables of a dactyl), it is *feminine*.

The Homeric hexameter almost always has one or other of these two caesuras in the *third* foot: thus:—

(1) Masculine caesura. *Il.* 1. 1 μῆνιν ἄειδε, θε | ά, ∧ Πη | ληιάδεω Ἀχιλῆος. This is also called τομὴ πενθημιμερής, 'penthemimeral', as following the fifth half-foot of the verse.

(2) Feminine caesura. *Od.* 1. 1 ἄνδρα μοι ἔννεπε, | Μοῦσα, ∧ πολ | ύτροπον, ὃς μάλα πολλά. This is described by Greek writers as the τομὴ κατὰ τρίτον τροχαῖον. It is decidedly commoner in Homer than the masculine caesura of the third foot. The preference for it is shown

by the number of constant formulas, or 'tags,' which are adapted to it, such as πατὴρ ἀνδρῶν τε θεῶν τε, θεὰ γλαυκῶπις Ἀθήνη, etc. Those adapted to the masculine caesura, such as ἡγήτορες ἠδὲ μέδοντες, are fewer.

The principal pause of the verse must never come at the end of the third foot. Thus such a verse as this is impossible:—Λητοῦς καὶ Διὸς ἔκγονος· | ὡς βασιλῆι χολωθείς. This would cut the hexameter into two equal parts, and so destroy the rhythm. But, when the principal pause is not at the end of the third foot, a caesura in that foot is sometimes, though very rarely, dispensed with. (The number of verses with no caesura of the third foot is given by Seymour as 185 in the *Iliad*, and 71 in the *Odyssey*: p. 83, § 40 c.) It is less uncommon for the third foot to end with a word when the caesura saves the rhythm: as *Il.* 3. 185 ἔνθα ἴδον πλείστους Φρύγας | ἄνερας.

The masculine caesura of the fourth foot is somewhat more frequent in the *Iliad* than in the *Odyssey*, and often follows the feminine caesura of the third foot, as *Il.* 1. 5 οἰωνοῖσί τε πᾶσι· Διὸς δ᾽ ʌ ἐτελείετο βουλή. This is the τομὴ ἐφθημιμερής, as following the seventh half-foot of the verse.

The feminine caesura of the fourth foot is avoided. Thus such a verse as the following is very rare,—*Il.* 23. 760 ἄγχι μάλ᾽, ὡς ὅτε τίς τε γυναικὸς ʌ ἐϋζώνοιο. In *Il.* 9. 394, where the MSS. have Πηλεὺς θήν μοι ἔπειτα γυναῖκα ʌ γαμέσσεται αὐτός, Aristarchus amended γαμέσσεται into γε μάσσεται, which avoids this τομὴ κατὰ τέταρτον τροχαῖον, since the enclitic γε is considered as closely adhering to γυναῖκα.

III.   *The bucolic diaeresis.*

As a metrical term, διαίρεσις means that the end of a foot coincides with the end of a word. When the end of the fourth foot coincides with the end of a word, that is the διαίρεσις (or διποδία) βουκολική, as being a favourite rhythm with the bucolic, or pastoral, poets, such as Theocritus and Moschus. Thus in the *Lament for Bion* Moschus has this diaeresis in 102 out of 128 verses. Many Homeric formulas (chiefly designations of persons) are adapted to the bucolic diaeresis,—as Φοῖβος Ἀπόλλων, δῖα θεάων, ἰσόθεος φώς, etc. The fourth foot is in this case much oftener a dactyl than a spondee.

IV.   *Hiatus.*

Hiatus s the non-elision of a vowel or diphthong at the end of a word, when the next word begins with a vowel or diphthong. It is allowed in Homeric verse under the following conditions.

 1.   After the vowel ι, or υ: *Il.* 5. 50 ἔγχεϊ ὀξυόεντι: 6. 123 τίς δὲ σύ ἐσσι.

 2.   When a caesura comes between the words: *Il.* 1. 569 καὶ δ᾽

ἀκέουσα καθ | ἦστο Λ έ | πιγνάμψασα φίλον κῆρ. The feminine caesura of the third foot, as in this verse, is that which most frequently excuses hiatus.

3. After the first foot: *Il.* 1. 333 αὐτὰρ ὁ ἔγνω. This is rarer than the next case.

4. Before the bucolic diaeresis: *Il.* 5. 484 οἷόν κ' ἠὲ φέροιεν' Αχαιοὶ | ἢ κεν ἄγοιεν.

5. When the vowel at the end of the first word is long, and belongs to the ictus-syllable of a foot: *Il.* 1. 418 ἔπλεο· τῷ σε κακ | ῇ αἴσ | ῃ τέκον ἐν μεγάροισιν.

6. When a long vowel, or diphthong, is made short before the following vowel or diphthong: *Il.* 1. 29 τὴν δ' ἐγὼ οὐ λύσω: *ib.* 28 μή νύ τοι οὐ χραίσμῃ. In *Il.* 2. 87, ἔθνεα εἶσι could be brought under this head, if Hartel's doubtful view were accepted, that the final α of the Greek neuter plural was originally long.—Hiatus under this condition is sometimes called 'weak' (or 'improper') hiatus.

V. *Lengthening of a short syllable.*

A syllable which, according to ordinary rules, should be short is often lengthened in Homeric verse.

1. This is sometimes due to the influence of a lost consonant, viz.:—

(*a*) The digamma, Ϝ: *Il.* 11. 793 πάρειπών (παρϜειπών). *Il.* 1. 70 ὃς ἤδη (Ϝήδη). In *Il.* 24. 154 ὅς ἄξει, εἴως κεν ἄγων' Αχιλῆϊ πελάσσῃ, the pronoun Ϝε may have fallen out after ὅς. The occurrence of ἐπεί as the first word of the hexameter (*Il.* 22. 379, etc.) is perhaps traceable to an original ἐπϜεί (ἐπί + pron. stem *sva*). In *Il.* 19. 35 the ō in ἀπόειπών is perhaps due to a vocalisation of Ϝ (ἀπονειπών): see under VIII.

(*b*) The spirant jod (*j* sounded like our *y*): *Il.* 3. 230 Κρήτεσσι θεᾶς ὥς (*y*ὥς).

(*c*) Initial σ: *Il.* 1. 51 βέλος ἐχεπευκὲς ἐφείη (*quasi* σεχεπευκές, the stem of ἔχω being σεχ). So *Od.* 9. 74 συνεχὲς αἰεί (*quasi* συσσεχές).

(*d*) σϜ, in the pronoun of the 3rd person: *Il.* 20. 261 Πηλείδης δὲ σάκος μὲν ἀπὸ ἕο χειρὶ παχείῃ (*quasi* σϜέο): 17. 196 ὁ δ' ἀρᾶ ᾧ παιδὶ ὄπασσεν (*quasi* σϜῷ).

2. The metrical *ictus* is the most frequent cause for the Homeric lengthening of a short syllable. But this general cause is often aided by some further special cause. The instances in which ictus can be pleaded may therefore be distinguished into groups.

(i) Thus there are instances in which—unless ictus is assumed as the sole cause of the lengthening—the letter φ seems to be treated as a double consonant: *Il.* 12. 208 αἰόλον ὄφιν. If the first syllable of ὄφιν were really short here, the hexameter would be of the kind which Greek metrists called μείουρος,—of which specimens have been left in

J.   13

Greek by Lucian (in the Τραγῳδοποδάγρα), and in Latin by Terentianus
Maurus. (Cp. Hermann, *Epitome Doctr. Metr.*; 4th ed., 1869, p. 111.)
But, as the ancients saw, ὄφιν was here pronounced like ὄπφιν.
[Seymour, p. 93, § 41 n., remarks: 'ὄπφις is now written for ὄφις in
Hipponax Fıg. 49, and is justified etymologically; *cf.* Σάπφω from the
stem of σοφός, Ἴακχος from ἰάχω, ὀκχον (ὄχον) Pind. *Ol.* vi. 24, φαιό-
χίτωνες Aesch. *Choeph.* 1047.']—Cp. *Od.* 7. 119 Ζέφυρίη πνείουσα.—
In *Il.* 10. 502 ictus helps to account for πῖφαύσκων: but not so, *ib.* 478,
for πῖφαυσκε. It is possible, indeed, that the ι of the reduplication was
originally long.

(ii) The influence of ictus is sometimes reinforced by the natural
tendency of speech to avoid an uncomfortably long series of short
syllables. This conjunction of causes may probably be recognised
in *Od.* 12. 423 ἐπίτονος βέβλητο, as also in ἀγοράασθε ἀπονέοντο,
ἀθάνατος, θῡγατέρα (though θὑγάτηρ), Πρῑαμίδης (though Πρίαμος).

(iii) A pause in the sense can help ictus to lengthen a short
syllable: *Il.* 1. 19 ἐκπέμψαι Πριάμοιο πόλῑν, εὖ δ' οἴκαδ' ἱκέσθαι. *Od.*
10. 269 φεύγωμεν· ἔτι γάρ κεν ἀλύξαιμεν κακὸν ἦμαρ: 1. 326 εἴατ'
ἀκούοντες· ὁ δ' Ἀχαιῶν νόστον ἄειδεν.

(iv) A short vowel is sometimes lengthened before λ, μ, ν, ρ, or
σ. In such cases, the influence of ictus usually helps, as *Il.* 3. 222
ἔπεᾱ νιφάδεσσιν: 23. 198 ὕλη τε σεύαιτο: *Od.* 14. 434 διέμοιρᾱτο: 22. 46
ὅσᾱ ῥέζεσκον: but not always; thus in *Il.* 22. 91 πολλᾱ λισσομένω, the
α has no ictus.

(v) A short vowel is lengthened before δ in δέος, δεῖσαι, etc., of
which the stem was originally δϝι; and before δήν. In these cases
ictus is always a helping cause. *Il.* 1. 33 ἔδεισεν δ' ὁ γέρων. The
formula μάλᾱ δήν occurs only at the end of a verse; so, too, ἐτῑ δήν,
except in *Od.* 2. 36, and 6. 33.

3. The vowel ι.—In certain abstract nouns, the Homeric long ι is
still unexplained, and ictus, at least, has nothing to do with it: *Il.* 1.
205 ὑπεροπλίῃσι: 2. 588 προθυμίῃσι: *Od.* 13. 142 ἀτιμίῃσι.—In *Il.* 6.
81 πάντῃ ἐποιχόμενοι πρὶν αὖτ' ἐν χερσὶ γυναικῶν, the ι of πρίν merely
keeps its original length, the word being a contracted comparative.—
Final ι in the Homeric dat. of the 3rd declension is sometimes short;
sometimes (as regularly in Latin) it is long, as *Il.* 7. 142 κράτεῑ γε.
The ῑ of such an Ionic dat. as μήτι (*Il.* 23. 318) is separately justified
by the contraction from μήτι-ι.

4. Vocatival ε is sometimes lengthened, partly through ictus, but
partly also because the voice naturally dwells a little on it: *Il.* 4. 338
ὦ υἱὲ Πετεῶο.

5. Lastly, there are a few instances in which a short syllable at the
beginning of a verse cannot be explained on any of the special grounds
noticed above. If ictus is not the sole cause, it is uncertain what other
cause has helped.—*Il.* 3. 357 διὰ μὲν ἀσπίδος ἦλθε φαεινῆς ὄβριμον ἔγχος.

[Seymour suggests the influence of false analogy, through δῑ' Ἀφροδίτη, etc.]—*Il.* 4. 155 (etc.) φίλε κασίγνητε. The ῑ of φῖλαι (aor. imperat. midd., *Il.* 5. 117), and ἐφῖλατο (*ib.* 61), may be compared, but have analogies which make them less remarkable. [Leaf on *Il.*, *l. c.*, notes that, if φίλος is for (σ)φέ-ιλος, from stem σfε, *suus*, the contraction would justify the lengthening.]—*Il.* 9. 5 Βορέης καὶ Ζέφυρος (so again, but in dative, *Il.* 23. 193). It is simplest to regard Βορ as lengthened by ictus, and εης as one syllable by synizesis. (Curtius supposed a pronunciation Βορῆης.)

VI. *Shortening of a long syllable.*

1. In Homeric, as in Attic, verse, a diphthong can be shortened before a vowel following it in the same word: *Il.* 1. 489 διογενὴς Πηλῆος υἱός. *Od.* 7. 312 τοῖος ἐὼν οἷός ἐσσι. 20. 379 ἔμπαιον.

2. There are a few instances in which a vowel remains short before the double consonants ζ, σκ: *Il.* 2. 634 οἵ τε Ζάκυνθον ἔχον: *ib.* 824 οἳ δὲ Ζέλειαν ἔναιον: *ib.* 465 προχέοντο Σκαμάνδριον (and so ἄ before Σκάμανδρε, 21. 223): *Od.* 5. 237 ἔπειτα σκέπαρνον. Allowance must be made for the greater freedom in the metrical treatment of proper names which were indispensable to the poet; and σκέπαρνον might then be excused by the analogy of Σκάμανδρος. But it is also possible that there were older alternative forms with a single consonant, as Seymour suggests, comparing σκίδναμαι, κίδναμαι: σμικρός, μικρός. He illustrates a possible Δάκυνθος by Δεύξιππος for Ζεύξιππος in a Boeotian inscription. [Remark how well this agrees with the Boeotian origin of the 'Catalogue,' which furnishes both the examples of ἔ before ζ: see above, p. 41.] He also notes, however, that Ζάκυνθος was current as a Greek name for Saguntum, and that the Ζ, in this particular name, may have been sounded like Σ, when analogy might help to account for the ἔ before Ζέλειαν.

3. The short first syllable of ἀνδροτῆτα (*Il.* 16. 857, 22. 363, 24. 6) is unexplained. The word is probably a corruption of some older word equivalent to it in sense.

VII. *Vowels of variable quantity.—Alternative forms.*

Some vowels which, in later verse, were regularly short, are of variable quantity in Homeric verse. When they are long, they usually have ictus. But in many (at least) of these instances ictus cannot be assumed as the only cause. Rather, as Seymour observes, most of these vowels had originally been long, and were in process of becoming short; compare the Homeric ῑσος, κᾱλός, φᾱρος with the later ῐσος, κᾰλός, φᾰρος.—So ἄ in Ἀπόλλων, but ᾱ (with ictus) in Ἀπόλλωνος (*Il.* 1. 14): Ἄρες, Ἄρες (5. 31): ᾱ in ῑλαος: ῑ in ἱερός, ῑομεν, κονίη, in

several verbs in -ίω, and comparatives in -ίων : ῦ in ὕδωρ, and in verbs
in -ύω.   The *i* of the name *Sidon* is regularly long in later poetry, as in
Od. 4. 84 Σιδονίους: yet *Il.* 23. 743 has Σῐδόνες.

Alternative forms.—The number of such forms has been noticed
above (p. 136) as characteristic of the Homeric dialect.   They may be
roughly classified under two heads, as vocal and consonantal.   (*a*)   A
short vowel alternates with a long vowel or a diphthong : as ἐΰς, ἠΰς:
νεός, νηός: Διόνυσος (*Od.* 11. 325), Διώνυσος (*Il.* 6. 135): νέος, νείατος:
ἡμέων, ἡμείων: βαθέης, βαθείης: ὀλοός, ὀλοιός. So in verbal forms,
ἄγαμαι, ἀγαίομαι: τελέω, τελείω, etc.—A special cause of variety is
what is called 'metathesis (shifting) of quantity,' when, the first of two
vowels having been shortened, the second is lengthened.   Thus -āο, in
the genitive, passes (through -ηο) into -εω ('Ατρείδαο, 'Ατρείδεω).
Similarly such a form as στέωμεν (2nd aor. subj. ἵστημι) comes from
στήομεν.   (*b*) A single consonant alternates with a double consonant :
'Αχιλλεύς, 'Αχιλεύς: 'Οδυσσεύς, 'Οδυσεύς: Τρίκκη (*Il.* 2. 729), Τρῐκη (4.
202) : ἔμεναι, ἔμμεναι: μέσον, μέσσον: ὅπως, ὅππως, etc.

VIII.   *Synizesis.—Elision.—Apocope.*

συνίζησις (a 'settling down') means that two vowels collapse (as it
were) into one long sound, instead of either keeping their separate
metrical values, or coalescing into a diphthong.   So in *Il.* 3. 27, where
θεοειδέα is the last word of the verse, εα forms one syllable.   Cp. *Il.* 1.
15 χρυσέῳ ἀνὰ σκήπτρῳ: 2. 367 γνώσεαι δ': *Od.* 1. 298 ἦ οὐκ ἀίεις
(first words of verse).   In *Il.* 1. 340 εἴ ποτε δὴ αὖτε (not δ' αὖτε) is
thus justified.—Synizesis was probably less frequent in the original
Homeric text than it is in ours, owing to the use of some older forms
which were afterwards modified ; *e.g.*, Πηληιάδεω (*Il.* 1. 1) was doubtless Πηληιάδαʾ.

Elision.   The diphthong αι can be elided in the verbal endings
-μαι, -σαι (except in the infin.), -ται, -σθαι.—There is only one instance
in which the -αι of the nom. fem. plur. is elided, *Il.* 11. 272 ὡς ὀξεῖʾ
ὀδύναι, and the verse is doubtful.—οι can be elided in μοι, σοι [*Il.* 1. 170],
τοι.—Elision of datival *ι* occurs, though rarely : *Il.* 5. 5 ἀστέρʾ ὀπωρινῷ.
—ἀντί, περί, τί, ὅτι, τό, πρό, are not elided.

Apocope is the cutting off of a short final vowel before a consonant,
as *Il.* 1 8 τίς τʾ ἄρ σφωε (for ἄρα).   So ἄμ (ἀνὰ) πεδίον, κὰπ (κατὰ)
πεδίον, κασπορνῦσα (καταστορνῦσα, *Il.* 17. 32), πὰρ (παρὰ) νηῶν.   In *Il.*
1. 459 αὐέρυσαν probably comes from ἀναϝέρυσαν by apocope (ἀνϝέρυσαν),
assimilation (ἀϝϝέρυσαν), and, finally, vocalisation of ϝ into υ: as in *Il.*
13. 41 αὐίαχοι=ἀϝίαχοι, or α + ϝιαχή, (*i.e.* 'noiseless,' if the α be privative,
or 'with cries,' if it be copulative).   Cp. καυάξαις=καταϝάξαις (κατάγ-
νυμι), Hes. *Opp.* 666.—Besides the three prepositions just named, ἀπό

and ὑπό in composition can suffer apocope: *Od.* 15. 83 ἀππέμψει = ἀποπέμψει: *Il.* 19. 80 ὑββάλλειν = ὑποβάλλειν. Apocope was used in the ordinary speech of some dialects (*e.g.* Her. 1. 8, ἀμβώσας).

A LIST OF BOOKS ON HOMER.

The purpose of this list is not to give a full bibliography, even of recent work. Its aim is to help the student by indicating the more important books in each department, so that he may know, in outline, what has been done for Homer up to the present time, and what are the chief sources available for consultation.—Asterisks are prefixed to a few books, which may be especially recommended to English students, in sections I. III. IV. V.

I. *Editions and Commentaries.*

This list will include the more noteworthy of the old editions; because, even where they have been superseded in a critical sense, they retain their historical interest as land-marks in the modern study of Homer.

A line may conveniently be drawn between the editions before and after 1788, when Villoison, in his *Iliad*, based on Venetus A, first published the ancient scholia of that MS.

After a date. 'f.' denotes that the publication of the work was continued in the following year; 'ff.', in the following years.

1. Editions before 1788.—*Editio princeps:* Demetrius Chalcondylas, Florence, 1488.—First Aldine edition, Venice, 1504: second, 1517.—Juntine edition, Florence, 1519.—Francini, Venice, 1537.—Joachim Camerarius made the first modern essay in commenting on the *Iliad*, 1538 ff. His complete commentary appeared at Frankfort, 1584.—Turnebus, *Iliad*, Paris, 1554.—H. Stephanus, in *Poetae Graeci principes heroici*, Paris, 1566.—Barnes, with scholia and notes, Cambridge, 1711.—Samuel Clarke, with notes and Latin version, London 1729 ff.—Moor and Muirhead, Glasgow (Foulis Press), 1756 ff.—Ernesti, Leipsic, 1759 ff.

In connection with the earlier editions of Homer we should notice the *editio princeps* of the Commentary of Eustathius (see p. 100), published at Rome, 1542 ff. The latest ed. is that of G. Stallbaum, Leipsic, 1825 ff.

2. Editions in and after 1788.—Villoison, *Iliad*, 'ad veteris Cod. Veneti fidem recensita. Scholia in eam antiquissima ex eodem Cod. aliisque nunc primum ed. cum asteriscis, obeliscis, aliisque signis criticis.' Fol. Venice, 1788.—Wolf, *Iliad*, Halle, 1794. [The

Prolegomena appeared in a separate vol., in the spring of 1795.] His ed. of both *Il.* and *Od.*, in 4 vols., Leipsic, 1804 ff., embellished with 32 designs after Flaxman,—whose 64 plates had first appeared in 1795.—The Grenville Homer (edd. Randolph, Cleaver, Rogers) with Porson's collation of the Harleianus (see p. 101), Oxford, 1800.— Heyne, *Iliad*, Leipsic, 1802 ff.—W. Dindorf and F. Franke, Leipsic, 1826 ff.—Spitzner, *Iliad*, Gotha, 1832 ff.—Immanuel Bekker, *Iliad*, Berlin, 1843: both epics (2 vols.), Bonn, 1858. The first scientific attempt to attain a pre-Alexandrine text.—Kirchhoff, *Odyssey*, Berlin, 1859: 2nd ed., 1879. With notes and essays illustrating his views as to the origin of the epic.—La Roche, *Odyssey*, Leipsic, 1867 f.: *Iliad*, 1873 ff. The *apparatus criticus*, though full, is not always accurate: see D. B. Monro in *Trans. Oxf. Philol. Soc.*, 1886—7, p. 32. —Nauck, Berlin, 1874 ff.—Fick, the poems translated back into the supposed original Aeolic, *Odyssey* Göttingen, 1883: *Iliad*, 1885 f.— Hentze, text in Teubner's series, supplementing Dindorf, 1883.—Christ, *Iliad*, with Prolegomena and critical notes, Munich, 1884.—Rzach, text (with critical notes), Leipsic, 1886.

3. The interest of the editions above named is mainly (though not exclusively) critical. The following editions may be mentioned as valuable to students for the commentary which they supply, while at the same time they also deal more or less with criticism of the text.

Heyne, *Iliad* (see above).—Nitzsch, *Erklärende Anmerkungen zu Homer's Odyssee*, I—XII, Hanover, 1826 ff.—Nägelsbach, *Anmerkungen zur Ilias* (bks. I, II to 483, and III), 3rd ed. revised by Autenrieth, Nuremberg, 1864.—Hayman, *Odyssey*, 3 vols., London, 1866 ff. With marginal references, various readings, notes, and appendices.—Paley, *Iliad*, 2 vols., London, 1866 ff. [A 2nd ed. of vol. II has appeared.] With an Introduction to each vol., and commentary.—*Merry and Riddell, *Odyssey* I—XII, Oxford, 1876. With critical notes and commentary. Vol. II (bks. XIII—XXIV) is in preparation.—*Leaf, *Iliad* I—XII. With English notes [both critical and exegetical] and Introduction. London, 1886. Vol. II (bks. XIII—XXIV) is in preparation.

4. School editions, with commentary. — German. — *Iliad*.—La Roche, Berlin, 1870 ff.—Faesi and Franke, Berlin, 1871 ff.—Ameis and Hentze, Leipsic, 1872 ff.—Düntzer, Schöningh., 1873 f.—*Odyssey*. Faesi and Kayser, Berlin, 1871 ff. The latest ed. has been revised by Hinrichs.—Ameis and Hentze, Leipsic, new ed. 1874 ff.—Düntzer, Schöningh., new ed. 1875 f.—English.—*Iliad*.—Paley, London, 1867.— *Monro, bks. I—XII, Oxford, 1884.—*Pratt and Leaf (bks. I, IX, XI, XVI—XXIV), London, 1880.—*Odyssey*. *Merry, Oxford, new ed., 1884.—*J. E. B. Mayor, bks. IX—XII, London, 1873.

II. *Scholia, and Works bearing on the History of the Text.*

Scholia on the *Iliad.*—W. Dindorf, Oxford, 1875 ff. Four vols. have appeared.—Scholia on the *Odyssey.*—W. Dindorf, Oxford, 1855.

History of the text.—Lehrs, *De Aristarchi Studiis Homericis*, Leipsic, 3rd ed., 1882.—La Roche, *Die homerische Textkritik im Alterthum*, Leipsic, 1866 [not always accurate in citing Ven. A, as Monro shows: cp. above, p. 199, l. 13]: *Homerische Untersuchungen*, 1869.—Römer, *Die Werke der Aristarcheer im Cod. Venet. A.*, Munich, 1875.—Ludwich, *Aristarchs Homerische Textkritik nach den Fragmenten des Didymus*, Leipsic, 1884 f.

III. *Language.*

Buttmann, *Lexilogus*, 3rd Eng. ed., London, 1846. [Still valuable, especially as a model of critical discussion, though liable to correction, on some points, by later results in comparative philology.]—Bekker, *Homerische Blätter*, Bonn, 1863, 1872.—Ahrens, *Griechische Formenlehre des Homer. Dialektes*, Göttingen, 2nd ed., 1869.—Delbrück, *Syntaktische Forschungen*, Halle, 1871 ff.—Hartel, *Homerische Studien*, Vienna, 1871 ff.—Knös, *De Digammo Homerico*, Upsala, 1872 ff.— Hinrichs, *De Homericae Elocutionis Vestigiis Aeolicis*, Jena, 1875.— Cobet, *Homerica*, in his *Miscellanea Critica*, pp. 225—437, Leyden, 1876.—*Monro, *A Grammar of the Homeric Dialect*, Oxford, 1884.— *Seymour, *Introduction to the Language and Verse of Homer*, Boston, U. S. A., 1885.

IV. *Lexicons and Concordances.*

Lexicons.—Crusius, Leipsic, 1856. English transl. by H. Smith, ed. T. K. Arnold, London, new ed. 1871.—*Ebeling, *ib.*, 1871 ff.— *Autenrieth, *ib.*, 1877. English transl., with additions and corrections, by R. P. Keep, London, 1877.—Seiler, ed. Capelle, *ib.*, 1878.

Concordances.—Seber, *Index Homericus*, Oxford, 1780. [Still convenient, as containing both *Il.* and *Od.* in one vol. It gives only the number of the book and verse in which a word occurs, without quoting the passage.]—*Prendergast, *Iliad.* (Every verse in which a given word occurs is quoted in full under that word.) London (Longman), 1875.—*Dunbar, *Odyssey.* (On the same plan as the last.) Oxford, 1880.

V. *Works illustrating the Antiquities of the Homeric Poems.*

Bellum et excidium Troianum ex Antiqq. reliquiis, tabula praesertim quam Raph. Fabrettus edidit Iliaca, delin. et adi. in calce commentario illustr. ad. Laur. Begero. Berlin, 1699 (Leipsic, Rud. Weigel). 58 copper-plates, with text. [The *tabula Iliaca* is a marble relief, inscribed Τρωικὸς (πίναξ), now in the Capitoline Museum at Rome. The central

subject is the destruction of Troy, while on either side are numerous
scenes from the *Iliad* and from other epics of the Trojan cycle.—The
work is perhaps of the 1st cent. A.D.: see Bergk, *Grk. Lit.* I. 913.]—
*Iliados picturae antiquae ex Codice Mediolanensi Bibliothecae Ambrosi-
anae.* Rome, 1835. (Leipsic, Weigel.) This 'Codex Ambrosianus
pictus' was first published by Angelo Mai, Milan, 1819.—Inghirami,
Galleria Omerica. (A collection of ancient monuments illustrative of
Homer.) Florence, 1827 ff.—Völcker, *Ueber Homer. Geographie und
Weltkunde.* Hanover, 1830.—Gladstone, *Studies on Homer*, London,
1858: *Juventus Mundi*, 1869.—Nägelsbach, *Die Homerische Theologie*,
Nuremberg, 1861.—Brunn, *Die Kunst bei Homer*, Munich, 1868.—
*Buchholz, *Die homerische Realien*, Leipsic, 1871 ff.—*Harrison, Miss
J. E., *The Myths of the Odyssey*, London, 1882.—Bunbury, *History of
Ancient Geography*, vol. I. ch. 3 ('Homeric Geography'), London, 1883.
—*Helbig, *Das homerische Epos aus den Denkmälern erläutert.* Leipsic,
1884.

VI. *The Homeric Question.*

Robert Wood, *Essay on the Original Genius of Homer*, London,
1769.—Wolf's *Prolegomena.* Halle, 1795.—Volkmann, *Geschichte und
Kritik der Wolfschen Prolegomena zu Homer.* Leipsic, 1874.—Lachmann, *Betrachtungen über Homers Ilias.* Berlin, 3rd ed. 1874.—Her-
mann, *Dissertatio de Interpolationibus Homeri.* In *Opusc.* v. p. 52,
Leipsic, 1834. *Ueber Homer und Sappho*, ib. VI. pars 1. p. 70, 1835.
De Iteratis apud Homerum, ib. VIII. p. 11, 1840.—Köchly, *Iliadis
Carmina XVI. restituta.* Turin, 1861.—Nitzsch, *De Historia Homeri*,
etc. (See above, p. 121, n. 3.) Hanover, 1830 ff.—Welcker, *Der
epische Cyclus*, Bonn, 1835 ff.—Grote, *Hist. of Greece*, Part I., ch.
XXI. (Vol. II., p. 160.) London, 1st ed., 1848: new ed., 1870.—
Friedländer, *Die homerische Kritik von Wolf bis Grote.* Berlin, 1853.
—Lauer, *Geschichte der homerischen Poesie.* Berlin, 1851.—Sengebusch,
two *Dissertationes Homericae*, in Dindorf's Homer (Teubner). Leipsic,
1855 f.: new ed., 1873.—Paley, Introductions to *Iliad* (see under I.),
vol. I. pp. xi—li, 1866; vol. II. v—lviii, 1871. See also his tract,
*Homeri quae nunc exstant an reliqui cycli carminibus antiquiora iure
habita sint.* London, 1878.—Nutzhorn, *Die Entstehungsweise der
Homerischen Gedichte*, Leipsic, 1869. [Originally in Danish: Copen-
hagen, 1863.]—Kirchhoff, *Die Composition der Odyssee. Gesammelte
Aufsätze.* Berlin, 1869. [His *Odyssey*, 2nd ed. 1879, should also be
consulted.]—Geddes, *The Problem of the Homeric Poems.* London,
1878.—Fick's views are given in his *Odyssey*, 1883, and *Iliad* (1st
half, 1885): see under I.—W. Christ, *Prolegomena* to the *Iliad* (see
under I.): 1884.—Wilamowitz, *Homerische Untersuchungen.* Berlin,
1884.—Leaf, Introduction to *Iliad* I—XII (see under I.), pp. xi—xxvi,
1886.—Seeck, *Die Quellen der Odyssee.* Berlin, 1887.

Histories of Greek Literature.—In regard to the Homeric question, much that is valuable will be found in the work of Theodor Bergk, vol. I., Berlin, 1872 : also in Bernhardy's History, vol. II. part I. (3rd ed., Halle, 1877). The chapters on Homer in Mure's work are interesting as a defence, marked by much ability and freshness, of the old conservative view (vols. I. II., bk. ii., chaps. ii.—xvii., 2nd ed., London, 1854).

VII. *English Translations.*

Verse. — *Iliad.* Chapman. — Pope.—Cowper. — Lord Derby.— Cordery (with Greek text).—Way (I—XII, 1886).—*Odyssey.* Pope.— Worsley and Conington.—Schomberg (Gen. G. A., 1879).—Way.— Lord Carnarvon (I—XII, 1886).

Prose.—*Iliad.* Lang, Leaf, and Myers.—*Odyssey.* Butcher and Lang.—G. H. Palmer (I—XII, Boston, U. S. A., 1884).

THE END.

Catalogue of Books

Published by

James MacLehose & Sons

Publishers to the University of Glasgow

GLASGOW : 61 St. Vincent Street

1899

PUBLISHED BY

JAMES MACLEHOSE AND SONS, GLASGOW,

𝔓𝔲𝔟𝔩𝔦𝔰𝔥𝔢𝔯𝔰 𝔱𝔬 𝔱𝔥𝔢 𝔘𝔫𝔦𝔟𝔢𝔯𝔰𝔦𝔱𝔶.

———

MACMILLAN AND CO., LTD., LONDON.

New York,	*The Macmillan Co.*
London,	*Simpkin, Hamilton and Co*
Cambridge, -	*Macmillan and Bowes.*
Edinburgh, -	*Douglas and Foulis.*

———

MDCCCXCIX.

CLASSIFIED LIST OF BOOKS IN

THE FOLLOWING CATALOGUE

BIOGRAPHY

POETRY

GENERAL LITERATURE

PHILOSOPHICAL

THEOLOGICAL

MEDICAL

TOPOGRAPHICAL

UNIVERSITY AND OTHER TEXT-BOOKS

PUBLISHERS TO THE
UNIVERSITY OF GLASGOW

Messrs. MACLEHOSE'S

Publications

AGLEN—THE ODES OF HORACE. Translated into English Verse by the VENERABLE A. S. AGLEN, M.A., Archdeacon of St. Andrews. Crown 8vo. 4s. 6d. nett.

ANDERSON—LECTURES ON MEDICAL NURSING, delivered in the Royal Infirmary, Glasgow. By J. WALLACE ANDERSON, M.D. Sixth Edition. Fcap. 8vo. 2s. 6d.

"An admirable guide."—*Lancet.*

ANDERSON—ON AFFECTIONS OF THE NERVOUS SYSTEM. By T. M'CALL ANDERSON, M.D., Professor of Clinical Medicine in the University of Glasgow. Demy 8vo. 5s.

BARR—MANUAL OF DISEASES OF THE EAR, for the Use of Practitioners and Students of Medicine. By THOMAS BARR, M.D., Lecturer on Aural Surgery in the University of Glasgow. New Edition. Re-written and greatly enlarged. Medium 8vo. 12s. 6d. nett.

BATHGATE—PROGRESSIVE RELIGION. By the late REV. WILLIAM BATHGATE, D.D., Kilmarnock. Crown 8vo. 6s.

BIRRELL—Two Queens : a Dramatic Poem. By C. J. Ballingall Birrell. Crown 8vo. 3s. 6d.

BLACKBURN—Caw, Caw ; or, the Chronicle of the Crows ; a Tale of the Spring Time. Illustrated by J. B. (Mrs. Hugh Blackburn). 4to. 2s. 6d.

BROWN—The Authorship of the Kingis Quair. A New Criticism by J. T. T. Brown. Demy 8vo. 4s. nett.

BROWN—The Life of a Scottish Probationer. Being the Memoir of Thomas Davidson, with his Poems and Letters. By the late James Brown, D.D., Paisley. Third Edition. Crown 8vo. 5s.

"A very fresh and interesting little book."—*Saturday Review.*
"This life of an unknown Scotch probationer is equal in interest to any-thing of the kind we have seen since Carlyle's 'Life of Sterling' was written."—*Blackwood's Magazine.*
"It is an unspeakable pleasure to a reviewer weary of wading through
"A charming little biography."—*Spectator.*

BROWN—Life of William B. Robertson, D.D., of Irvine, with Extracts from his Letters and Poems. By the late James Brown, D.D. Fourth Edition. Crown 8vo, with two Portraits. 5s.

"This memoir is one to have, to study, and to go to frequently."—*Cambridge Express.*

BUCHANAN—Poems by the late David Buchanan, Kirkin-tilloch. Crown 8vo. 5s.

CAIRD, Principal—An Introduction to the Philosophy of Religion. By the Very Rev. John Caird, D.D., LL.D., late Principal and Vice-Chancellor of the University of Glasgow. Sixth Thousand. Crown 8vo. 6s.

" A book rich in the results of speculative study, broad in its intellectual grasp, and happy in its original suggestiveness. To Dr. Caird we are indebted for a subtle and masterly presentation of Hegel's philosophy in its solution of the problem of religion."—*Edinburgh Review.*

CAIRD, Principal—UNIVERSITY ADDRESSES on Subjects of Academic Study delivered to the University of Glasgow. By JOHN CAIRD, D.D., LL.D., late Principal and Vice-Chancellor of the University of Glasgow. Third Thousand. Crown 8vo. 6s. nett.

CONTENTS—The Unity of the Sciences—The Progressiveness of the Sciences—Erasmus—Galileo—The Scientific Character of Bacon—David Hume—Bishop Butler and his Theology—The Study of History—The Science of History—The Study of Art—The Progressiveness of Art—The Art of Public Speaking—The Personal Element in Teaching—General and Professional Education.

"The Master of Balliol lays us under great obligation by giving to the world this relic of his distinguished brother. It is a book, almost every page of which we have read with unflagging interest."—*The Guardian*.

" They give evidence at every turn of courage of conviction and luminous understanding of the trend of thought in the present age."—*Speaker*.

" The volume will be welcome to all readers who value the utterances of a mind of a very high and rare order on themes of perennial interest to all students of literature, science, art and religion."—*Spectator*.

" The subjects, it will be evident. are all of such a kind that an acute and original mind could not apply itself to their treatment without producing a distinctly happy result. These essays are full of attraction for a thoughtful and solid reader."—*Daily Chronicle*.

CAIRD, Principal—UNIVERSITY SERMONS. Preached before the University of Glasgow, 1873-1898. By PRINCIPAL CAIRD. Fourth Thousand. Crown 8vo. With Portrait. 6s. nett.

CONTENTS—What is Religion?—The Likeness and Unlikeness of God's Ways and Man's Ways—Evil Working through Good—The New Birth—The Christian Way of Reconciling Man with Himself—Can Righteousness be Imputed?—Is Repentance ever Impossible?—The Reversal of Nature's Law of Competition—Corporate Immortality—Truth and Freedom—The Guilt and Guiltlessness of Unbelief—The Relations of Love and Knowledge—The Measure of Greatness—The Profit of Godliness—The Spiritual Relations of Nature to Man—Art and Religion—Things New and Old—The Temporal and the Eternal—The Law of Heredity in the Spiritual Life.

" This is perhaps the finest volume of Sermons in modern English. The collection which most seriously challenges its pre-eminence is Dean Church's ' Human Life and its Conditions'; and we are inclined to rank the volume before us even higher than the splendid masterpieces of the Anglican divine."—*Record*.

CAIRD, Principal—SERMONS AND LECTURES.   In separate
    pamphlet form.   Demy 8vo.   Paper covers.   1s. each.

  1. CHRISTIAN MANLINESS.
  2. IN MEMORIAM.   Very Rev. Principal BARCLAY, D.D.
  3. MIND AND MATTER.
  4. THE UNIVERSAL RELIGION.
  5. THE PROGRESSIVENESS OF THE SCIENCES.

CAIRD, Edward—THE CRITICAL PHILOSOPHY OF IMMANUEL
    KANT.   By EDWARD CAIRD, M.A., LL.D., Master of Balliol
    College, Oxford, late Professor of Moral Philosophy in the
    University of Glasgow.   2 vols.   Demy 8vo.   32s.

" It is quite the most comprehensive and maturely considered contribution
that has yet been made by an English writer to the understanding of Kant's
whole philosophical achievement.   It is the result of a study of Kant such
as perhaps no Englishman will again undertake, and is in every way a
thorough and masterly performance."—*Mind*.

CAIRD, Edward — ESSAYS IN LITERATURE AND PHILO-
    SOPHY.   2 vols.   Crown 8vo.   8s. 6d. nett.

CAIRD, Edward—THE EVOLUTION OF RELIGION.   Third
    Edition.   2 vols.   Post 8vo.   12s. nett.

" Professor Caird's lectures will form an epoch-making book, which more
than any other since England was startled by the sweet reasonableness of
'Ecce Homo' has given a firm, consistent, and convincing exposition, both
of the infinitely various manifestations of the earlier religions and of that
Christian synthesis which cannot die out of the human mind."—*Daily
Chronicle*.

CAIRD, Edward—THE SOCIAL PHILOSOPHY AND RELIGION
    OF COMTE.   Second Edition.   Crown 8vo.   5s. nett.

CAIRD, Edward—INDIVIDUALISM AND SOCIALISM.   Demy
    8vo.   1s.

CLELAND and MACKAY—THE ANATOMY OF THE HUMAN
BODY, for the use of Students of Medicine and Science.
By JOHN CLELAND, M.D., LL.D., D.Sc., F.R.S., Professor
of Anatomy in the University of Glasgow, and JOHN YULE
MACKAY, M.D., C.M., Professor of Anatomy in University
College, Dundee. Profusely illustrated. Medium 8vo.
28s. nett.

CLELAND and MACKAY—A DIRECTORY FOR THE DISSEC-
TION OF THE HUMAN BODY. By JOHN CLELAND, M.D.,
and JOHN YULE MACKAY, M.D. Fcap. 8vo. 3s. 6d. nett.

CLELAND—EVOLUTION, EXPRESSION, AND SENSATION. By
JOHN CLELAND, M.D., D.Sc., F.R.S. Crown 8vo. 5s.

COATS—THE MASTER'S WATCHWORD : An Essay recalling
attention to some Fundamental Principles of the Christian
Religion. By the REV. JERVIS COATS, D.D. Crown 8vo. 5s.

DEAS—HISTORY OF THE CLYDE. With Maps and Diagrams.
By JAMES DEAS, Engineer of the Clyde Navigation. 8vo.
10s. 6d.

DICKSON—ST. PAUL'S USE OF THE TERMS FLESH AND
SPIRIT. Being the BAIRD LECTURE for 1883. By
WILLIAM P. DICKSON, D.D., LL.D., Emeritus Professor of
Divinity in the University of Glasgow. Crown 8vo. 8s. 6d.

DOUGLAS—CHEMICAL AND MICROSCOPICAL AIDS TO
CLINICAL DIAGNOSIS. By CARSTAIRS C. DOUGLAS,
M.D., B.Sc. Crown 8vo. Illustrated. 4s. 6d. nett.
[*This day.*

DOWNIE—CLINICAL MANUAL FOR THE STUDY OF DISEASES OF THE THROAT. By J. WALKER DOWNIE, M.B., Lecturer in the University of Glasgow on Diseases of the Throat and Nose. Crown 8vo. Illustrated. 6s. nett.

DUNCAN—MEMORIALS OF THE FACULTY OF PHYSICIANS AND SURGEONS AND OF THE MEDICAL PROFESSION OF GLASGOW. By ALEXANDER DUNCAN, B.A., LL.D., Librarian to the Faculty. Crown 4to. 10s. 6d. nett.

EGGS 4D. A DOZEN, AND CHICKENS 4D. A POUND ALL THE YEAR ROUND. Containing full information for profitable keeping of Poultry. Small 8vo. Twentieth Thousand. 1s.

FORSYTH—A GRADUATED COURSE OF INSTRUCTION IN LINEAR PERSPECTIVE. By DAVID FORSYTH, M.A., D.Sc., Headmaster of the Central Higher Grade School, Leeds. Third Edition. Royal 8vo. 2s.

FORSYTH—TEST PAPERS IN PERSPECTIVE. 26 papers. Full Government size. Third Edition. 1s. 6d. per set.

GAIRDNER—THE PHYSICIAN AS NATURALIST, Memoirs bearing on the Progress of Medicine. By SIR W. T. GAIRDNER, K.C.B., M.D., LL.D., F.R.S., Professor of Medicine in the University of Glasgow. Crown 8vo. 7s. 6d.

GLAISTER—DR. WILLIAM SMELLIE AND HIS CONTEMPORARIES. A Contribution to the History of Midwifery in the Eighteenth Century. By JOHN GLAISTER, M.D., Professor of Medical Jurisprudence in the University of Glasgow. With Illustrations. Demy 8vo. 10s. 6d. nett.

GLASGOW HOSPITAL REPORTS, 1898. Edited by
GEORGE S. MIDDLETON, M.A., M.D., and HENRY
RUTHERFURD, M.A., M.B., C.M. With many Illustrations.
8vo. 12s. 6d. nett.

GLASGOW UNIVERSITY CALENDAR FOR THE YEAR
1899-1900. *Published annually in Midsummer*, with full
official information. Crown 8vo, Cloth. 3s. nett.

GLASGOW—THE OLD COUNTRY HOUSES OF THE OLD
GLASGOW GENTRY. Royal 4to. [*Out of print.*

GLASGOW—MEMOIRS AND PORTRAITS OF ONE HUNDRED
GLASGOW MEN who did much to make the City what it
now is. Two vols. Royal 4to. Half Red Morocco, gilt
top. £7 7s. nett.

GLASGOW—THE UNIVERSITY OF GLASGOW OLD AND NEW
By WILLIAM STEWART, D.D., Professor of Biblical
Criticism in the University of Glasgow. With 107 Engravings. Imperial 4to, £5 5s. nett; Large Paper Copies,
£10 10s. nett.

GLASGOW—A ROLL OF GRADUATES OF THE UNIVERSITY
OF GLASGOW, from 31st December, 1727, to 31st December,
1897. With short Biographical Notes. Compiled by
W. INNES ADDISON, Assistant to the Clerk of Senate.
Demy 4to. 21s. nett.

GLASGOW—ITS MUNICIPAL ORGANIZATION AND ADMINIS-
TRATION, by SIR JAMES BELL, Bart., Lord Provost of
Glasgow, and JAMES PATON, F.L.S., President of the
Museums Associations of the United Kingdom. Crown
4to. 21s. nett.

GLASGOW ARCHÆOLOGICAL SOCIETY'S TRANS-
ACTIONS.
First Series. Demy 8vo.
Volume I.   Parts I. to V.   5s. each nett.
Volume II.   Parts I. to III.   5s. each nett.
New Series. Foolscap 4to.
Volume I.   Parts I. to IV.   6s. each nett.
Volume II.   Parts I. to IV.   6s. each nett.
Volume III.   Parts I. and II.   6s. each nett.

GRAHAM—THE CARVED STONES OF ISLAY, with descriptive
Text. By ROBERT C. GRAHAM, F.S.A.Scot., of Skipness.
Demy 4to. With 71 Engravings on Copper, Map, Plans, and
many other Illustrations. £1 11s. 6d. nett. *Sixty-five
Copies, with Proofs on Japanese, bound in Half-Morocco,
Gilt Top, £3 13s. 6d. nett.*

"This is a sumptuously printed and illustrated book, dealing in a most
thorough manner with the Christian sculptured monuments of one district
of the west coast of Scotland."—*Reliquary.*

"Mr. Graham is to be congratulated on the manner in which he has
mingled purely antiquarian lore with what is interesting historically or
picturesquely."—*Saturday Review.*

"The work, which has been a long labour of love, has been done with
patient thoroughness and complete success."—*Daily Chronicle.*

"An elaborate monograph, very handsomely printed and illustrated."—
Times.

HAMILTON, Janet—POEMS, ESSAYS, AND SKETCHES. By
JANET HAMILTON. New Edition, with portrait. Crown
8vo. 6s.

HASTIE—THEOLOGY AS SCIENCE, and its Present Position
and Prospects in the Reformed Church. By W. HASTIE,
D.D., Professor of Divinity in the University of Glasgow.
Crown 8vo. 2s. nett.

HASTIE—THE VISION OF GOD AS REPRESENTED IN
RÜCKERT'S FRAGMENTS. Rendered into English Rhyme
by W. HASTIE, D.D. Fcap. 4to. 2s. nett.

HENLEY—A Century of Artists : a Memorial of Loan Collection of the Glasgow International Exhibition, 1888. By W. E. Henley. Extra pott folio, £2 2s. nett. Large Paper, with plates on Japanese, £5 5s. nett.

HUNTER—Hymns of Faith and Life. Collected and Edited by the Rev. John Hunter, D.D., Trinity Church, Glasgow. New and Enlarged Edition. Fcap. 8vo. 3s. 6d. nett.

"No more catholic collection of hymns has ever been given to the world." —*The Christian World.*

"For private devotion it is above all price and praise. It should be on the same shelf as Thomas à Kempis."—*Sheffield Independent.*

HUNTER—Devotional Services for Public Worship, including additional Services for Baptism, the Lord's Supper, Marriage, and the Burial of the Dead. Prepared by the Rev. John Hunter, D.D. Sixth Edition, revised and enlarged. Crown 8vo. 3s. nett.

"It is striking for the comprehensive character of its prayers, the beauty of their expression, and the spirit of devotion which they breathe."—*N. B. Daily Mail.*

JACKS—The Life of Prince Bismarck. By William Jacks, LL.D. Demy 8vo. With many Illustrations. 10s. 6d. nett.

"The fullest and most carefully accurate biography of the Iron Chancellor yet written in English."—*Daily Mail.*

JACKS—Robert Burns in other Tongues, being a critical account of the translations of the principal poems of Robert Burns which have appeared in Foreign Languages, together with the Foreign Texts. With numerous Portraits. By William Jacks, LL.D. Extra post 8vo. 9s. nett.

JACKS — LESSING'S NATHAN THE WISE. Translated by
WILLIAM JACKS, LL.D. With an Introduction by Arch-
deacon FARRAR, and Eight Etchings by WILLIAM
STRANG. Fcap. 8vo. 5s. nett.

JEBB—HOMER : AN INTRODUCTION TO THE ILIAD AND
THE ODYSSEY. For the use of Schools and Colleges.
By R. C. JEBB, Litt.D., M.P., Professor of Greek in the
University of Cambridge. Sixth Edition. Crown 8vo. 3s. 6d.

"We heartily commend the handbook before us to the diligent study of
all beginners and many 'ripe scholars.'"—*Athenæum.*

"A trustworthy and indispensable guide."—*Classical Review.*

JEBB—THE ANABASIS OF XENOPHON.—Books III. and IV.,
with the *Modern Greek Version* of Professor Michael Constantinides. Edited by Professor JEBB. Fcap. 8vo. 4s. 6d.

JONES—BROWNING AS A PHILOSOPHICAL AND RELIGIOUS
TEACHER. By HENRY JONES, M.A., LL.D., Professor of
Moral Philosophy in the University of Glasgow. Crown
8vo. Third Edition. 6s. nett.

"Mr. Jones is a diligent and appreciative student of Browning, and he
handles the philosophical topics suggested by his subject with firm grasp
and clear insight."—*Times.*

"A most absorbing volume. It is fresh, thorough, and judicious without
dreariness."—*Christian Leader.*

JONES—A CRITICAL ACCOUNT OF THE PHILOSOPHY OF
LOTZE—THE DOCTRINE OF THOUGHT. By Professor
JONES. Crown 8vo. 6s. nett.

"This is a genuine contribution to philosophy. It amounts to a
destructive criticism of the half-hearted attitude adopted by Lotze towards
the problem of thought and reality."—Mr. BERNARD BOSANQUET in the
Pall Mall Gazette.

KANT. *See* CAIRD'S KANT.

KANT. *See* WATSON'S KANT AND HIS ENGLISH CRITICS.

KANT—THE PHILOSOPHY OF KANT, as contained in Extracts from his own Writings. Selected and Translated by JOHN WATSON, LL.D., Professor of Moral Philosophy in the University of Queen's College, Kingston. Crown 8vo. Fourth Edition. 7s. 6d.

LEISHMAN—A SYSTEM OF MIDWIFERY. By WILLIAM LEISHMAN, M.D. Fourth Edition. 2 vols. Demy 8vo. 24s.

LOTZE. *See* JONES' LOTZE.

LOVE and ADDISON—DEAF-MUTISM. A Treatise on Diseases of the Ear as shown in Deaf-Mutes, with Chapters on the Education and Training of Deaf-Mutes. By JAMES KERR LOVE, M.D., and W. H. ADDISON. Demy 8vo. Illustrated. 9s. nett.

MACCUNN—ETHICS OF CITIZENSHIP. By JOHN MACCUNN, M.A., Professor of Philosophy in University College, Liverpool. Crown 8vo. Third Edition. 2s. 6d.

"A little book which, for general usefulness, far exceeds the massive tomes in which sociological philosophers are accustomed to impound the darkness of their cogitations. Its chief value is not for professional thinkers, but for the ordinary sensible man who wants to understand his duty to his country and his neighbours."—*Pall Mall Gazette.*

"There are ideas, and the courage of them, in 'Ethics of Citizenship'; indeed, the scholarly little treatise is mixed with brains."—*Speaker.*

MACDONALD—CATALOGUE OF GREEK COINS IN THE HUNTERIAN COLLECTION—University of Glasgow. Volume I. Italy, Sicily, Macedon, Thrace, and Thessaly. By GEORGE MACDONALD, M.A., Lecturer in Greek in the University of Glasgow. Demy 4to. 560 pages. With Plates of over 600 Coins. 63s. nett.

MACEWEN—PYOGENIC INFECTIVE DISEASES OF THE BRAIN AND SPINAL CORD. By WILLIAM MACEWEN, M.D., LL.D., Regius Professor of Surgery in the University of Glasgow. Illustrated. Demy 8vo. 18s. nett.

MACEWEN—ATLAS OF HEAD SECTIONS. 53 Engraved Copper Plates of Frozen Sections of the Head, with 53 Key Plates with Detailed Descriptions and Illustrative Text. By Professor MACEWEN, M.D. Demy 4to. 70s. nett.

"These volumes are of extreme value and importance; both as a record of successful work and as written and pictorial instruction to other workers they have rarely been surpassed."—*The Lancet.*

"It is hardly possible to imagine a more admirable text-book, from cover to cover, or a more difficult and important field of surgery."—*Edinburgh Medical Journal.*

M'KECHNIE—THE STATE AND THE INDIVIDUAL : an Introduction to Political Science with Special Reference to Socialistic and Individualistic Theories. By WILLIAM SHARP M'KECHNIE, M.A., LL.B., D.Phil., Lecturer on Constitutional Law and History in the University of Glasgow. Demy 8vo. 10s. 6d. nett.

M'KENDRICK — TEXT-BOOK OF PHYSIOLOGY. By JOHN GRAY M'KENDRICK, M.D., LL.D., F.R.S., Professor of the Institutes of Medicine in the University of Glasgow; including HISTOLOGY, by PHILIPP STOHR, M.D., of the University of Würtzburg. 2 vols. Demy 8vo. 40s.

(*The volumes are sold separately, as follows*)—

Vol. I.—General Physiology, including the Chemistry and Histology of the Tissues and the Physiology of Muscle 542 Pages, 400 Illustrations. 16s.

Vol. II.—Special Physiology, including Nutrition, Innervation, and Reproduction. 830 Pages, 500 Illustrations. 24s

MACKENZIE—AN INTRODUCTION TO SOCIAL PHILOSOPHY. By JOHN S. MACKENZIE, M.A., Professor of Logic and Philosophy in the University College of South Wales, Fellow of Trinity College, Cambridge. Second Edition. Crown 8vo. 7s. 6d.

"We can heartily recommend this book to all who are interested in the great social and vital questions of the day."—*Westminster Review.*

MACKINTOSH—THE NATURAL HISTORY OF THE CHRISTIAN RELIGION, being a Study of the Doctrine of Jesus as developed from Judaism and converted into Dogma. By the late WILLIAM MACKINTOSH, M.A., D.D. Demy 8vo. 10s. 6d. nett.

MACLEHOSE — TALES FROM SPENSER, chosen from The Faerie Queene. By SOPHIA H. MACLEHOSE. Second Edition. Fcap. 8vo, ornamental cloth, gilt top, 3s. 6d. Also a Cheaper Edition in Paper Boards, 1s. 6d.

"The tales are charmingly and very dramatically told."—*Times.*

"This is a charming book of stories from the 'Faerie Queene.' It is just the sort of book for a good uncle to give to niece or nephew."—*Scots Observer.*

MITCHELL—BURNS AND HIS TIMES. As gathered from his Poems by JOHN OSWALD MITCHELL, LL.D. Post 8vo. 3s. 6d.

MONRO—RAYNAUD'S DISEASE (LOCAL SYNCOPE, LOCAL ASPHYXIA, SYMMETRICAL GANGRENE): its History, Causes, Symptoms, Morbid Relations, Pathology and Treatment. By T. K. MONRO, M.A., M.D., Physician to the Glasgow Royal Infirmary. Crown 8vo. [*In the press.*

MOYES—MEDICINE AND KINDRED ARTS IN THE PLAYS OF SHAKSPEARE by Dr. JOHN MOYES, Largs, with Introduction by Dr. JAMES FINLAYSON. Crown 8vo. 2s. 6d. nett.

MÜLLER—Outlines of Hebrew Syntax. By Dr. August Müller, Professor of Oriental Languages in the University of Königsberg. Translated and Edited by James Robertson, M.A., D.D., Professor of Oriental Languages in the University of Glasgow. Demy 8vo. Fourth Edition. 6s.

MURRAY—Attic Sentence Construction. By Gilbert Murray, M.A., Professor of Greek in the University of Glasgow. 8vo. 1s. nett.

MURRAY—The Property of Married Persons, with an Appendix of Statutes. By David Murray, M.A., LL.D. Medium 8vo. 9s.

NEILSON—Annals of the Solway, until A.D. 1307. By George Neilson, author of "Trial by Combat," etc. Fcap. 4to. With 5 Maps. 3s. 6d. nett.   [*This day.*

NEWTON—Sir Isaac Newton's Principia. Edited by Lord Kelvin, Professor of Natural Philosophy in the University of Glasgow, and Hugh Blackburn, M.A. Crown 4to. 31s. 6d.

NICHOL—Tables of European History, Literature, Science, and Art, A.D. 200 to 1888, and of American History, Literature and Art. By the late John Nichol, M.A., Professor of English Literature in the University of Glasgow. Fourth Edition. Royal 8vo, printed in Five Colours. 7s. 6d.

"About as convenient a book of reference as could be found."—*Spectator.*

OLRIG GRANGE. *See* Smith.

PATERSON—Nithsdale. A Series of Photogravures from Water-colour Drawings by James Paterson, R.S.W. With Letterpress. Folio, proofs on French and Japanese, £5 5s. nett; Ordinary impression, £2 2s. nett.

RAMSAY—ATLAS OF EXTERNAL DISEASES OF THE EYE. 48 full-page Plates in Colour and Photogravure, with full Descriptive Text. By A. MAITLAND RAMSAY, M.D., Ophthalmic Surgeon, Glasgow Royal Infirmary. Demy 4to. Buckram, gilt top. With 48 full-page Plates of the Eye in Colour and Photogravure and Descriptive Text. 63s. nett.

"A more beautiful and complete collection of coloured and uncoloured pictures of Eye Diseases does not exist."—Mr. G. A. BERRY in the *Edinburgh Medical Journal.*

RANKINE—SONGS AND FABLES. By W. J. MACQUORN RANKINE, late Professor of Engineering in the University of Glasgow. Illustrated by J. B. Second Edition. Extra fcap. 8vo. 6s.

RAWNSLEY—LITERARY ASSOCIATIONS OF THE ENGLISH LAKES. By the REV. H. D. RAWNSLEY, Vicar of Cros-thwaite, Honorary Canon of Carlisle. With Map. 2 vols. Crown 8vo. 10s. nett.

Vol. I.—Cumberland, Keswick, and Southey's Country.

Vol. II.—Westmoreland, Windermere, and the Haunts of Wordsworth.

" A tramp of intelligence, however exacting, who carries the book in one pocket, and a good ordnance map in the other, will find himself amply provided for an exhaustive tour in the Lake Country."—*Illustrated London News.*

RAWNSLEY—LIFE AND NATURE AT THE ENGLISH LAKES. By the Rev. H. D. RAWNSLEY, Honorary Canon of Carlisle. Crown 8vo. 5s. nett. [*This day.*

" This pleasant volume is made up of about a score of papers, any one of which must interest anybody who has either been to the Lake Country or means to go there."—*The Scotsman.*

"Every lover of lake-land should secure these essays, for they afford unique casements opening on to a world of beauty."—*Manchester Courier.*

RAWNSLEY—HENRY WHITEHEAD, 1828-1896. A Memorial Sketch. By the REV. CANON RAWNSLEY. Demy 8vo. 6s.

RAWNSLEY—VALETE : TENNYSON AND OTHER MEMORIAL POEMS. By REV. CANON RAWNSLEY. Crown 8vo. 5s.

ROBERTSON—LIFE AND LETTERS OF REV. WILLIAM B. ROBERTSON, D.D., of Irvine. *See* BROWN.

ROBERTSON—HEBREW SYNTAX. *See* MÜLLER.

SCHLOMKA — A GERMAN GRAMMAR. With Copious Exercises, Dialogues, and a Vocabulary. By CLEMENS SCHLOMKA, M.A., Ph.D. Fourth Edition. Crown 8vo. 4s. 6d.

" Wonderfully clear, consecutive, and simple. We have no hesitation in strongly recommending this grammar."—*School Board Chronicle.*

SCHLOMKA—GERMAN READER. Exercises for translating German into English and English into German. With Vocabularies for both. Third Edition. Crown 8vo. 3s.

SCOTTISH NATIONAL MEMORIALS. Extra pott folio, with 30 full-page Plates, and 287 Illustrations in the Text. £2 12s. 6d. nett.

" It will be enjoyed in equal measure by the Scotchman who is a student of archæology and history, and by the Englishman who has time to saunter through the sections into which it is divided, to sit down here and there, and drink in the significance of the pictures of Scotch life in the past that are presented to him in rich abundance and under the most fascinating guise."—*Spectator.*

SMITH, J. Guthrie—STRATHENDRICK, AND ITS INHABITANTS FROM EARLY TIMES : An account of the parishes of Fintry, Balfron, Killearn, Drymen, Buchanan, and Kilmaronock. By the late JOHN GUTHRIE SMITH, F.S.A.Scot., author of 'The Parish of Strathblane.' With Memoir and Portrait. Crown 4to. With numerous Engravings. 31s. 6d. nett.

𝔓𝔬𝔢𝔪𝔰 𝔟𝔶 𝔱𝔥𝔢 𝔄𝔲𝔱𝔥𝔬𝔯 𝔬𝔣 "𝔒𝔩𝔯𝔦𝔤 𝔊𝔯𝔞𝔫𝔤𝔢."

SMITH, WALTER C.

OLRIG GRANGE. Fourth Edition. Fcap. 8vo, cloth, gilt top. ' 5s.

KILDROSTAN. Fcap. 8vo, cloth, gilt top. 5s.

A HERETIC, AND OTHER POEMS. Extra fcap. 8vo. Blue cloth. Edges uncut. 7s. 6d.

THOUGHTS AND FANCIES for Sunday Evenings. Second Edition. Crown 8vo. 2s. 6d.

SELECTIONS from the Poems of Walter C. Smith. Second Edition. Crown 8vo. Cloth. 3s. 6d.

"A graceful anthology, and sure of a welcome from his many admirers."
—*The Times.*

SPENSER—Tales from Spenser, Chosen from The Faerie Queene. By Sophia H. MacLehose. Second Edition. Fcap. 8vo, ornamental cloth, gilt top, 3s. 6d.
Also a Cheaper Edition in Paper Boards. 1s. 6d.

"A delightful book for children. It could not have been better executed had it been the work of the Lambs."—*Saturday Review.*
"A dainty volume. It makes a charming introduction to a great poem."—*Guardian.*

STEVEN—Outlines of Practical Pathology. An Introduction to the Practical Study of Morbid Anatomy and Histology. By J. Lindsay Steven, M.D. Cr. 8vo. 7s. 6d.

WADDELL—The Parmenides of Plato. After the Paging of the Clarke Manuscript. Edited, with Introduction, Facsimiles, and Notes, by William Wardlaw Waddell, M.A., one of Her Majesty's Inspectors of Schools. Medium 4to. £1 11s. 6d. nett.

WADDELL—Verses and Imitations in Greek and Latin. By W. W. Waddell. Fcap. 8vo. 2s. 6d.

WATSON, Prof. John—SELECTIONS FROM KANT. *See* KANT.

WATSON—CHRISTIANITY AND IDEALISM. The Christian Ideal of Life in its relations to the Greek and Jewish Ideals and to Modern Philosophy. By JOHN WATSON, M.A. LL.D., Professor of Moral Philosophy in Queen's University, Kingston, Canada. Crown 8vo. 5s. nett.

WATSON—AN OUTLINE OF PHILOSOPHY. By Professor WATSON. Second Edition. Revised and greatly enlarged. Crown 8vo. 7s. 6d nett.

" It is a book which attests on every page the ability of the author to present his subject in a lucid and attractive way."—*International Journal of Ethics.*

WATSON—HEDONISTIC THEORIES, FROM ARISTIPPUS TO SPENCER. By Professor WATSON. Crown 8vo. 6s. nett.

WOTHERSPOON—THE DIVINE SERVICE. A Eucharistic Office according to Forms of the Primitive Church. Arranged by the REV. H. J. WOTHERSPOON, M.A., Minister of Burnbank. Fcap. 8vo, Paper Boards. 6d.

GLASGOW: PRINTED AT THE UNIVERSITY PRESS BY ROBERT MACLEHOSE AND CO

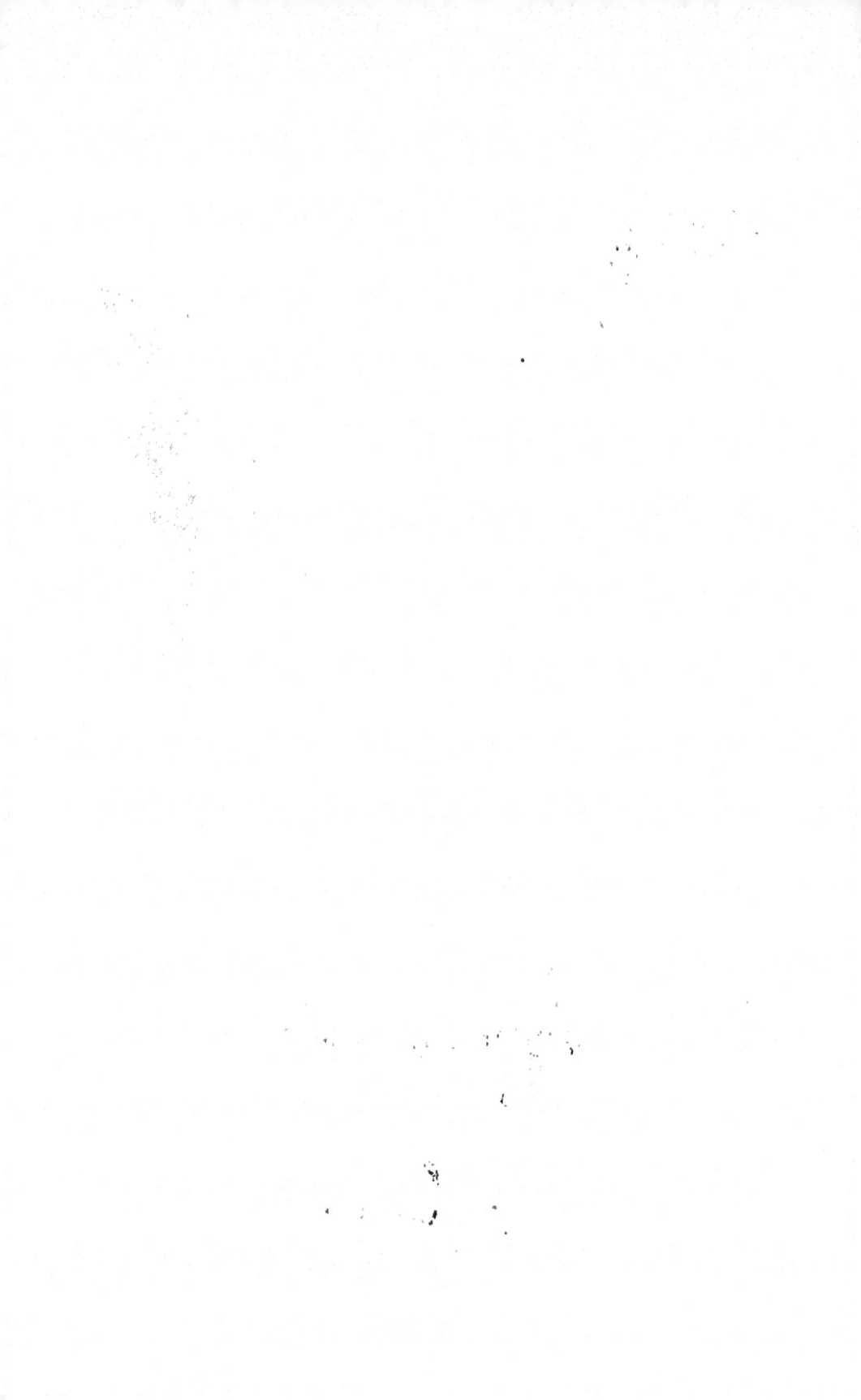

FRAGILE DOES NOT
CIRCULATE

PHASED
DETERIORATION

CONSERVATION 1994

Lightning Source UK Ltd.
Milton Keynes UK
UKOW06f1940100917
308944UK00009B/207/P